D1265417

WORLD IN TRANCE

From Versailles to Pearl Harbor

WORLD IN TRANCE

26658

From Versailles to Pearl Harbor

By Leopold Schwarzschild

L. B. FISCHER PUBLISHING CORP.

New York

Translated by

NORBERT GUTERMAN

PRINTED AND BOUND IN THE U. S. A. BY
KINGSPORT PRESS, INC., KINGSPORT, TENN.

Contents

WORLD IN TRANCE

From Versailles to Pearl Harbor

Part One: 1918-1923

1: The Spirit of the First Hour

TOWARD NOON, on October 7, 1918, the Swiss chargé d'affaires left the White House, having remitted the historic note from Berlin. It contained the words the world had been awaiting for two days: Germany wanted peace.

This was not the first time. There had been previous German peace offers. One after the other had been rejected. Wilson was opposed to any peace not "sincerely purposed." For the present, there is "but one response possible for us," he had proclaimed that Spring, "Force, Force to the utmost, Force without stint and limit." [1]

Had the circumstances changed?

The President had been thinking the matter over for two days. His mind was almost made up. Yes, this time the circumstances seemed different. The offer seemed "sincerely purposed."

This time the Imperial Army was no longer victorious. Since July it had been defeated in battle after battle, repeatedly compelled to yield ground. Accordingly Berlin was proposing not merely peace but "the immediate conclusion of an armistice." This was scarcely the attitude of a foe claiming equality. It was an entreaty, an acknowledgment of inferiority.

9

Moreover this time the Germans not only accepted peace pure and simple, but a peace of a special kind. They were accepting the "Wilson Peace" which they had hitherto scorned and ridiculed—and which unfortunately was still, openly or secretly, scorned and ridiculed by so many. "The German Government accepts, as a basis for the peace negotiations, the program laid down by the President of the United States in his message to Congress of January 8, 1918, and in his subsequent pronouncements." This message contained the famous 14 points. Subsequent pronouncements were his "4 principles" of February, his "4 ends" of July, his "5 particulars" of September. All this code embracing 27 rules was now recognized by the enemy. First among the warring governments, Germany pledged herself to accept reorganization of the world according to Wilson's most personal principles. Did it not look as though the enemy in the field wanted to be the first ally at the peace table?

It was not inconceivable! For this time other changes had occurred. Upheavals were taking place in Germany whose consequences were still incalculable. At last the victorious force of democracy seemed to be moving forward to triumph even in Germany.

Wilhelm II had issued an Imperial Rescript. According to the cable from the Hague which lay on Wilson's table, he had proclaimed: "I wish to have the German people cooperate more effectively than heretofore in determination of destiny of fatherland. It is therefore My will that men supported by confidence of people shall participate to large extent in rights and duties of government." [2] The terms "democracy" or "parliamentary system" were avoided. But the German press was unanimous in its comment: "The old autocracy has come to an end and parliamentarism has begun in Germany." [3]

A new Reich Chancellor was appointed: Prince Max, successor to the throne of the Grand Duchy of Baden. On October 5, while the plea for peace was still en route to Washington, he had introduced himself to the new Reichstag with a speech. Again the words democracy or parliamentary system were avoided. But he did say that "the German Empire has undergone a fundamental change." He did say that this was "the beginning of a new epoch in Germany's internal history." [4]

This might be a manoeuvre. But those who had ears heard the steps of history!

History, despite all its detours and interruptions, is the eternal progress of mankind from lower to higher stages. Progress has its tides and those who could hear and see knew that the time had long been ripe for this stage. President Wilson had clearly stated that one of the most sacred aims of this war was the destruction of the absolute monarchies. The most important of his "four ends" of July ran as follows: "The destruction of every arbitrary power anywhere that can separately, secretly and of its single choice disturb the peace of the world; or, if it cannot be presently destroyed, at least its reduction to virtual impotence."

It was not in the President's manner to express himself in practical or trivial terms. His style favored solemn, abstract circumlocutions. This often made his meaning vague to others and sometimes even to himself. But this time there was no obscurity: he meant the destruction of the absolute monarchies, and that was what he said. And wasn't the German monarchy being destroyed? Wasn't this one more reason to consider Germany's plea for peace with the greatest sympathy?

True, the reaction in America and in Europe was hostile. People were fed up with the Germans. They wanted victory not negotiations or compromise. They wanted to beat the Germans, they wanted the armistice to disarm them. They wanted to dictate *their* peace to the Germans without any show of "negotiations." These peace offers were just another of the countless enemy tricks. Hypocrisy calculated to obtain easy terms at the last moment. This was the opinion of most newspapers, most legislators in the Allied countries.

It was not the President's opinion. Though a democrat, he had the ability to draw strength, in an emergency, from the realization that the majority was against him. "A democrat with aristocratic taste," he had called himself. And he was extremely sensitive to his responsibility.

The note lay on the desk before him. Perhaps it was the dividing line between two epochs. Hitherto he had been forced to write in the book of war, the book of mankind as it was. Now, perhaps, the opportunity was at hand to make the first entries in the book of peace, the book of mankind as it was to be. Yes, this might be the opportunity to make entries in his own personal hand. The appeal was addressed to him, not to the Allies. He alone was asked "to take steps," "to bring about." Destiny had apparently chosen him to guide human affairs into new channels from which they would not easily be turned aside.

The President rose. He had finished with his reflections. He was in a position to act, and would act within a few hours. The next visitor was admitted: Eric Geddes, Winston Churchill's successor as First Lord of the Admiralty. The President spoke of conditions for an armistice.

The previous night, Wilson had telephoned Colonel House in New York. House was the only man whom Wilson wholly trusted, whom he believed to be of one heart and mind with himself. He asked House for his advice.

The Colonel was among those profoundly convinced that the President had a very special mission in history, who thought he should maintain a considerable distance from the heads of all other governments, acting as an "associate," not an "ally." He supported the President in his sentiment that the statesmen of the European democracies were far less noble and ethical than the present stage of human development required.

Yet, after House had thought the matter over, he wired to Wilson: "I would suggest making no direct reply to the German note. A statement from the White House saying 'The President will at once confer with the Allies . . .' should be sufficient. I would advise that you ask the Allies to confer with me in Paris at the earliest opportunity. . . ." [5] No private correspondence with the Germans! Only a consultation with the Allies!

But the President had made up his mind. He had conceived a plan, or, more exactly, he had conceived two plans: one with regard to the Germans, and another with regard to the Allies. His two plans required him to do the very opposite of what his friend House had recommended: no consultation with the Allies! Only private correspondence with the Germans!

That day he was ill with influenza. Nevertheless he remained at his desk until one in the morning, working at his answer to Berlin.

His plan with regard to the Germans was prescribed

by circumstances. He would have to be benevolent and hard at the same time. He must tell them, not in these words but by implication, that he was ready to satisfy their wish. Yes, I am prepared to bring about a Wilsonian Peace and an honorable armistice! Yes, I am prepared to use all my influence with the Allies to grant you both! But before I can undertake this, you must fulfil a severe condition: you must expel your Kaiser and proclaim the Republic. At the very least, you must convince me that you have really become an honestly democratic, constitutional monarchy. "If the United States must deal with the military masters and the monarchical autocrats of Germany, it must demand not peace negotiations, but surrender." [6]

This is what he would write them. And should the correspondence be protracted, he would repeat it with increasing violence. As far as the Germans were concerned, the Republic, in his mind, represented the essence of all present problems. At the very least, a constitutional monarchy! And he would say just that, without mincing words: "The President feels bound to say that the whole process of peace will, in his judgment, depend upon the definitiveness and the satisfactory character of the guarantees which can be given in this fundamental matter." [7]

This was to be the main point of his private correspondence with the Berlin government, embracing three notes to them and three replies over a period of sixteen days.

To the Allies he did not show a single line of his projected notes. He did not ask their opinion, let alone agreement, on a single point. They watched the proceedings from outside, not jealous and insulted, as Wilson later interpreted their feelings, but anxious and uneasy.

They feared a private agreement, even one conditional on their consent. One fine day they would have to decide whether to accept a German-American agreement. And at that point it would be impossible to reject details. The nations and armies of Europe would refuse to go on fighting if the United States judged the peace terms adequate. The Allied governments were eager to prevent even a conditional agreement between Wilson and the Germans. They guessed accurately what he was aiming at. This was in fact his second plan, his plan with regard to the Allies.

But they had no say in the matter. When he sent a note to Berlin, all they could do was to protest after the fact, or to make reservations on this or that point. He did not ask their collaboration.

On October 7th, having drafted his first answer, he showed it to Colonel House who had hurriedly returned to Washington. "He seemed much disturbed," noted the Colonel, "when I expressed a decided disapproval of it. I did not believe the country would approve of what he had written." [8]

2.

The country did not approve. The country showed a "nearly unanimous sentiment against anything but unconditional surrender." [9]

One point of the note aroused particular consternation. The President had indicated to the Germans what military conditions he had in mind for the armistice: the German army would have to withdraw from the invaded regions!

Was that all? Only that? The German army was to be let out of the iron vise which gripped it? To march back across Germany's frontiers unhindered? To be permitted to rest from its exhaustion? To influence the peace negotiations by its very existence? Possibly to resume war after a few months of fruitless negotiations? Was that what Wilson intended? What was he thinking of?

The struggle which now began concerned the temporary existence of the German army. Its ultimate fate was of course to be determined later, in the peace treaty. For the present, only the interval between the armistice and the treaty was in question. Should a German army in fighting condition survive the conclusion of the armistice? Should peace be made under the muzzles of its guns? Or should its elimination as a fighting force be one of the conditions of the armistice?

Many sentimental and romantic words were woven around this theme. There was talk of "hard" and "mild" conditions, "humiliation" and "magnanimity." The real question was not sentimental. Cannon are not a fit subject for sentimentality.

Wilson had apparently decided for himself. To Sir Eric Geddes he had said that the conditions must prevent the German army from becoming stronger, not that they must make it weaker. And: "Undue humiliation would be inexcusable." [10] Now he had sent his note. The only condition it mentioned was withdrawal behind the German frontiers. What was he aiming at?

In Paris, in the spectators' stand, sat three Allied chiefs: Clemenceau, Lloyd George and Sonnino. They read the text and were seized with dismay. Was this conceivable? They quickly summoned Generalissimo Marshal Foch. Then they sat down and drafted a cable to Wilson.

The Allied Governments read his reply to the Germans "with the greatest interest," they told him. "They recog-

nize the elevated sentiments which have inspired this reply." But they felt obligated to point out that the evacuation of all invaded territory, "while necessary, would not
be sufficient." They declared: "The conditions of an armistice cannot be fixed until after consultation with military experts." Marshal Foch, they went on, had worked
out a few "considerations," and "to these considerations
the Allied Governments draw the entire attention of
President Wilson." [11] The tone was unusual, particularly
toward a man who had always been treated with the
greatest courtesy.

Wilson's opinion remained unshakable. But he realized
that he must be more cautious where the army was concerned.

Even his own country could not be trifled with on the
subject. The country had become war conscious, "war
mad" as Colonel House expressed it. An electoral battle
began whose outcome was absolutely vital for the fate of
Wilson's ideas. Congressional elections were due in November, and the coming Congress would decide on the
peace! These elections had to be won at any cost. The
campaign had begun and the opposition limited itself almost entirely to one slogan: Wilson is too weak. He is
chasing rainbows. The Germans must be dealt with ruthlessly: "Put them behind the bars, put them in a padded
cell," [12] in Theodore Roosevelt's words. Wilson's opponents were convinced that this was the essence of the
American mood and they proved to be right! At any
rate, it was not the moment to give this opposition proof
of its contentions. Moreover, in army questions the opinion of Europeans had inevitably the greatest weight. It
was they who had borne the brunt of the German assault.
The French casualties up to this moment were over 1,-

300,000 dead and 4,000,000 wounded. The correspond-
ing English figures were 900,000 and 2,000,000. America's
tribute to Moloch was less than 2% of the total.

And would this proportion change if the struggle was
resumed after the collapse of negotiations? Not essentially. Even the eighty American divisions planned for
the following year's campaign would at most constitute
one third of the entire Allied force.

True, the contribution of the United States was not
limited to troops. In money, foodstuffs, raw materials,
shipping space and a few types of munitions, it had been
enormous and would increase. But the President knew
—he knew it better than the public—that even in this
respect America was still remiss on decisive points. He
knew of her failure in the matter of planes and tanks.

Protesting against "bombastic claims" in the press, General Pershing had cabled him in February: "As a matter
of fact there is not today a single American-made plane
in Europe." [13] At that time it had been hoped that the
first machines would be shipped in May and that before
October a monthly figure of 600 would be reached.[14] But
that too had remained on paper. Not only had America
been unable to deliver a single plane to her friends. Up
till that day, her own army had been using French-made
planes almost exclusively.

Things were even worse with regard to tanks, the new
weapon conceived by Winston Churchill in the first
months of the war. As late as April 1918, the tank was a
curiosity in America. An English model was put on exhibit in Washington. The President himself had gone to
see the rare machine, and in entering had burned his
hand on a hot pipe so that he had to keep it bandaged
for three weeks.[15] Toward the end of July, Marshal Foch

had for a second time pointed out the urgent need of tanks to Pershing. "But we were without tanks. . . . The proposal that we should develop our own tanks at home had come to naught." [16]

With all these deficiencies and gaps, America's war power had, to be sure, become an absolutely indispensable element of the common front. It was the surplus on one side of the balance. Nevertheless Wilson knew that in military matters he was not on the firmest ground. He realized that he must take into account the mood of his own country and the protests of the European spectators and that he must do so quickly, before they grew even worse. In his two subsequent notes to Germany, his indications as to the future of the German army were more severe. In the last note, on October 23rd, he adhered to the formula which had been created in the interval: the military conditions must be such as "to make a renewal of hostilities on the part of Germany impossible."

But he adhered to it without being entirely convinced. As we shall see, he hoped that even this formula would permit the maintenance of a considerable German army.

This same note of October 23rd ended the President's open correspondence with the Germans. He turned his face to the Allies and a secret tête-à-tête began.

It would be hard to say what he had gained from his dealings with the Germans.

The Kaiser was not driven out, the Republic was not proclaimed. The Germans were not to drive out Wilhelm II until November 9th.

Concerning the miraculously begun democratization under the Kaiser's rule, absolutely nothing new was brought to light. The German notes reiterated the solemn declaration that Germany was now democratic. For the third time, the words "democracy" or "parliamentary system" were avoided. The Germans merely said euphemistically that the new government was "supported by the approval of the overwhelming majority of the German people."

Wilson himself was not satisfied. "It does not appear," he replied, "that the principle of a Government responsible to the people has yet been fully worked out or that any guarantees either exist or are in contemplation that the alterations of principle and of practice now partially agreed upon will be permanent. The determinating initiative still remains with those who have hitherto been the masters of Germany." [17]

But the President was apparently possessed by an irresistible desire to believe in this democracy notwithstanding. For his actions immediately contradicted the words he had just spoken. He had called German democracy inadequate; he treated it as adequate.

The previous evening he and his advisers had still been assailed by doubts. Wearied by the incessant flow of opinions and counteropinions, he had admitted that afternoon that he was "unable to think longer." [18] The following morning his mind was made up. He began the struggle for Germany within the allied camp, the struggle for granting Germany the Wilsonian peace which, he had said, only an honest democracy could receive!

The scene changed to Paris. To begin with, Marshal Foch, chief of the military experts, was asked to propose his conditions for the German army.

On October 25 the generalissimo gathered around him the leaders of the national armies to hear their opinion as sub-experts. In reality he had his proposal ready in his pocket and took little part in the conversation.

What Sir Douglas Haig would tell him he knew in advance. All the Englishmen in Paris, with Lloyd George at their head, suddenly began to support the very policy which the cable of the three governments to Wilson had recently termed "not sufficient." Allow the German army, said Sir Douglas today, as Wilson had said before, to march back behind the frontiers of the Reich, and that will do. This is "sufficient to seal the victory. . . . If more is demanded, there is a risk of prolonging the war." [19]

The Marshal knew that the German fleet had something to do with this attitude. The English had tried of late to eliminate the entire German fleet in the armistice, and were ready in compensation to let the land army off more easily. "Lloyd George changes his mind as easily as he changes his shirt. More often if anything," Foch would say a few years later.[20] His judgment may have begun to be formed on that day.

The American generals were a surprise. Haig only reflected his government's opinion with military trimmings, but Pershing and Bliss differed from their President as heaven from earth. They said that the mere retirement of the German army behind the Reich borders was absolutely unsatisfactory, and that it was indispensable for the Allies to occupy parts of Germany. More than that, the German army, they said, must not retain any heavy armament and must hand over every cannon and machine gun. For good measure, they concluded, it must be demobilized at once.

This went much further than the plan which Foch had in his pocket. Foch's plan demanded the occupation of the German industrial regions up to the Rhine, but provided for the delivery of only one third of the German cannon, a little over half of the machine guns and approximately two thirds of the planes. The chief expert's proposal was thus half way between the proposals made by the American and English generals and the Americans remonstrated even against this middle course.

On October 28, General Bliss wrote a memorandum against Foch's "partial disarmament," demanding "complete disarmament." [21]

On October 30, Pershing went one step further. He sent in a document [22] in which he described even complete disarmament as a bad, makeshift, solution. The correct line, he said, was not to grant any armistice at all, but to continue the war until the destruction of the German army would appear plainly as a purely military event.

Among Wilson's intimates the maximalism of the American generals aroused "frank expressions of distress." "It is really tragic!" wrote a member of his Cabinet.[23] The consequences were to be foreseen. The very fact that Pershing and Bliss made Foch's proposals seem moderate was bound to make them almost unassailable.

Colonel House arrived in Paris as "Special Representative." On October 28, he received the President's instructions to weaken each of the generalissimo's conditions as much as he could. But in this House encountered a stone wall.

He fought according to his commission. On October 29, he wrestled with Clemenceau in a long stormy conference, from which the old Tiger emerged *"très énervé, exaspéré même."* The same night when he told his adjutant the main incidents of the conversation, he was still pale with emotion. The next day his adjutant asked the seventy-seven year old Clemenceau how he had slept. "I haven't shut an eye," he answered. "But I profited by my wakefulness to give the matter careful consideration and I resolved that come what may I shall not allow the victory to be sabotaged." [24]

The struggle was resumed that morning; the sleepless night had not weakened the old man. Colonel House came to see him at 10:00 A.M., and when he left the room he had given up! He had accepted Foch's conditions, acknowledging that he was unable to carry out the President's instructions. That day the military conditions of the armistice as laid down by the Marshal were accepted by the three principal powers. A German army of serious weight would not survive the armistice.

Most important in the entire episode is that Wilson's intentions were entirely different, and his motive is revealing. This motive is clearly expressed in his telegram instructing Colonel House to moderate Foch's conditions. What was his reason for trying to secure greater strength for the German armistice army? "Because it is certain," says the instruction, "that too much successs or security on the part of the Allies will make a genuine peace settlement exceedingly difficult, if not impossible." [25]

This announced metamorphoses which were to make history!

Not too much security for the Allies? Not too much security, lest the Allies be enabled to oppose his genuine peace? Insecurity guaranteed by the enemy army?

What a complicated "balance of power" calculation! How little compatible with Wilson's solemn ban on "the great game, now forever discredited, of the balance of power!" [26]

Above all how rapid the process of his inner detachment from all reality which had hitherto been present to his mind! We see all hitherto concrete factors of the com-

mon struggle gradually fading away: we see their place
taken by the abstract vision of the new world order.

In the concrete world, Germany remained for Wilson
what she had been: the instigator of the war. A few
weeks later, when the Frenchmen wanted to show him
the devastated regions, he replied: "I could not despise
the Germans more than I do already." [27]

But in the light of his abstraction, even before victory
had been consummated, the Allies began to appear as the
adversary and the enemy as an ally. The democracies of
yesterday changed into dangerous reactionaries and the
reactionaries of yesterday into a hopeful democracy.

Wilson's "balance-of-power" idea concealed a clearly
discernible calculation. To be sure, the German army
was to be made too weak to make another stand against
its combined adversaries. Yet he wanted it to remain
strong enough to threaten the Allies without the United
States. Conflicts between Wilson and the others would
arise in the process of realizing the new world order. The
Allies must be checked by the danger of America's withdrawal from the common cause, by fear of having to face
German arms alone.

When Wilson was engaged in these calculations, he
did not know what Hindenburg and Ludendorff were
calculating at the same moment. Yet their calculations
corresponded to Wilson's as the negative of a film to its
positive.

For during those days Hindenburg and Ludendorff
were preparing instructions for the presumptive German
negotiators. They assumed that a considerable German
army would survive the armistice. It was to be hoped, the
instructions said, that conflicts would arise between Wilson and the Allies on the subject of the new world order.

"The eventuality is not excluded that the United States would refrain from continuing the war. The struggle against the Franco-British armies alone would be far from hopeless, particularly if Belgium, too, refuses to carry on." [28]

This was the German version of Wilson's "not too much security for the Allies."

This paradox was to appear again and again! This was not the last time when the ideas of a high flying idealism had an exact counterpart in the most callous realism!

3.

The German armistice army was important only for a few months. But "the program laid down by the President of the United States" was important for all time to come. The Germans had accepted the fourteen points, or, more accurately, the twenty-seven points, bodily, as a general line. The problem was to obtain Allied acceptance of that program.

And this had to be obtained before the Armistice! Later, Wilson and America would no longer be needed and Allied support would no longer be obtainable. This was Wilson's second purpose in his private correspondence with Berlin: to couple the armistice and the program of the new world order so inseparably that one could not be accepted without the other.

In September, before anyone had expected the Germans to sue for an armistice, Colonel House had warned the President: "As the Allies succeed, your influence will diminish. This is inevitable. . . . Therefore I believe that you should commit the Allies now to as much of your program as possible. . . . Could not a plan be

thought out by which the Entente would be committed?
. . ."[29] Now Allied victory was about to be sealed. The
moment had arrived to commit them to this program.
The President was firmly resolved to impose it.

He did not doubt that it would be hard.

He had drafted all his points entirely on his own. He
had proclaimed the aims of a coalition war without consulting any of the allied powers. Under these circumstances complete agreement would have been strange.

But he had never harbored the illusion that his allies
would be in agreement with him. Quite the contrary!
He knew with certainty that he and they represented two
different worlds. Their ideas, their ethics were totally different from his.

True, he believed that the people, the inarticulate
masses, were inwardly in agreement with him. "I am satisfied that if necessary I can reach the peoples of Europe
over the heads of their rulers."[30]

But the statesmen, the politicians, the influential circles
everywhere, scarcely excluding those of his own country,
"have not the same views with regard to peace that we
have by any means."[31] He judged them all "cynical," "reactionary," "immoral," "selfish." "I know that Europe is
still governed by the same reactionary forces which controlled this country until a few years ago."[32] He told himself with noble grief but also with theological solemnity
that he could feel "associated" with such co-belligerents
only negatively, in their opposition to Germany. When
they wanted to speak of positive things, of war-aims, he
reacted with nervousness: "I must say I am afraid of any
expression of policy" by these allied powers, he said
shortly after America's entry in the war. "There has been

none yet that seemed to me even touched with wisdom." [33]

How, then, was he to induce these allies to accept his world program? And how was he to induce them to accept it quickly, on the spot, in the five remaining minutes before the armistice?

He had always been convinced that one day this would have to be done by coercion. As early as the middle of 1917 he had, in a written communication to Colonel House, developed the plan "to force them" [34] at a given moment. "They need to be coerced," [35] he said now. "We should play a strong hand," [36] echoed Colonel House from Paris.

By the middle of 1917, he even had a precise conception of the means of coercion to be applied. Considering his idealistic purpose, these means were fairly realistic. "When the war is over," he wrote to Colonel House, "we can force them to our way of thinking, because by that time they will, among other things, be financially in our hands; but we cannot force them now." [37]

And once again Colonel House, while beginning to apply coercion echoed: "I would suggest that you quietly diminish the transport of troops giving as an excuse the prevalance of influenza or any other reason but the real one. I would also suggest a little later that you begin to gently shut down upon money, food and raw material. I feel confident that we should play a strong hand. . . ." [38]

In the end it was not necessary to use these drastic means. But it is hard to disregard Wilson's idea of forcing them "to our way of thinking." Is there no difference between capitulation and changing one's way of thinking? Wilson's confusion in that respect, toward the Allies, to-

ward Germany, toward the entire world, was to become
the fundamental fallacy of the new age.

But Colonel House sat in Paris. He had been sent there
to exercise coercion, and he was determined to carry out
his assignment.

Outside battles were raging. The Germans—bleeding
and retiring, without hope—continued to fight as they
had done for four years. They fought the British on the
Schelde, the French on the Serre and Aisne, the Americans in the Argonne.

At the conference front, in a room at the Quai d'Orsay
where the coercion was to begin on this October 29, two
Frenchmen, two Englishmen and one Italian confronted
one American. Until then, they had been discussing the
ephemeral military clauses. Now Lloyd George attacked
the other, the eternal question. Was it true, he asked,
that granting the Germans an armistice at the present
time implied the obligation of concluding with them a
peace based on the fourteen points?

Yes, replied House, that was the case.

If so, Lloyd George declared, England could not be a
part of this. Many things in these fourteen points were
absolutely unacceptable for his country.

Clemenceau leaned toward him and compressed all his
thoughts into one question: "Have you ever been asked
by President Wilson whether you accept the Fourteen
Points? I have never been asked."

"I have not been asked either," replied the British
Prime Minister.

"Then I want to hear the Fourteen Points," said Clemenceau.

"Yes, and the five more and the others," added Sonnino.

Sonnino's desire to be clarified on the "five more and

the others" would never be satisfied. Later, at the peace conference and during twenty years of debates, these thirteen all told "subsequent pronouncements" were to be quoted no less frequently than the fourteen preceding ones. Nor were they any less important. On the contrary.

The fourteen points were devoted only to particular, concrete questions. The thirteen were a universal, all-embracing catechism. They contained Wilson's entire philosophy—or theology—or mythology—of peace. These thirteen subsequent rules went in reality far beyond the person of their author. They were a distillation of the entire perfectionist current which, at first as a sect, and later as a mass striving, gushed forth on all the corners of the earth.

Among them were postulates such as the following: "The impartial justice meted out must involve no discrimination between those to whom we wish to be just and those to whom we do not wish to be just. It must be a justice that plays no favorites and knows no standards but the equal rights of the several peoples concerned." [39]

What did this mean? President Wilson justly regarded Germany as the instigator of this war, as responsible for the devastations and miseries of this war. The time when it would be fashionable to deny even this premise had not yet come. But since the beginning of the world, justice had meant: unequal treatment for the perpetrator and for the victim of an evil deed. And since the beginning of the world, justice meant: discrimination between the injurer and the injured. That is justice in every code. That is justice in every religion. Was this millennial justice to be suddenly replaced by its untested opposite?

Or take that other postulate which demanded: "The settlement of every question, whether of territory, or sov-

ereignty, of economic arrangement, or of political rela-
tionship, upon the basis of the free acceptance of that settlement by the people immediately concerned, and not
upon the basis of the material interest or advantage of
any other nation." [40]

What did this mean? Would the peace fail to impose
on Germany any condition that was in the interest of any
other nation? Would the treaty stipulate only conditions
which Germany would find favorable to her own interests? Since the beginning of the world, victors had a certain influence on peace treaties. If the words had any
meaning, this time the vanquished was to dictate the conditions. When he and he alone is allowed to decide what
is convenient or inconvenient for him, the vanquished
dictates the peace. Once again the practice of thousands
of years was apparently to be replaced by the reverse, a
practice never tested or even imagined.

The idea that the method of saving the world ultimately consisted in proclaiming and applying the exact
opposite, reversal, negative of the most important norms
of all preceding history—the conviction that this was
quite possible and that norms stood on their heads would
function smoothly in accordance with a plan: such was
the essence of the entire perfectionist current. And the
essence of this essence was Wilson's thirteen all-embracing postulates.

But in the end the discussion never went beyond the
fourteen points, which Colonel House read to the assembled statesmen.

These began with the condemnation of secret diplomacy. From now on, only "open covenants, openly arrived
at." Obviously, two different things were involved here.
That all agreements be published—that was conceivable,

though those present did not approve even this part of the statement on account of its absoluteness. But what did the words "openly arrived at" mean? Were state affairs—in contrast to all other human affairs—to be conducted in a manner that would allow every neighbor and competitor to overhear every conversation?

It seemed unfeasible. In this complicated world it would even seem inevitably to create rifts rather than peace. At any rate, everything that had been normal for thousands of years was to be replaced by its completely incalculable opposite. Those present did not think that all the existing things were excellent. But they did not infer that for that reason the exact opposite of the existing would be possible and more excellent.

With this point Colonel House had less difficulty than with the others. In his pocket he had a number of typewritten pages. They were a commentary on the fourteen points recently written by two intelligent writers. Mr. Frank I. Cobb of the New York World and Mr. Walter Lippman, at that time employed by the government, had considerably softened that particular point. "The phrase 'openly arrived at' need not cause difficulty." [41] This postulate, House said reassuringly, can be regarded as non-existent.

All the stormier was the reception given to the second point: "Absolute freedom of navigation upon the seas, alike in peace and in war. . . ." Lloyd George declared curtly: No! at no price!

In this case, the meaning could not be softened by any skilful interpretation. In the future no fleet would have the right to exercise a blockade! What an idea—and at this moment! What concern—and at this moment! The war was still on. If England had not perished—England

and the rest—it was largely because of the blockade. And at that very moment, her own partner yearned to outlaw this deserving weapon! The blockade was half the value of the British fleet, the fleet was Britain's entire existence. And this inheritance of generations and generations was now to be given up in an instant just because a sect had taken it into its head that the existing world could only be saved by the opposite of the existing!

Lloyd George nearly lost his courtesy. No, he could not recognize that the weapon of blockade was particularly prominent among the causes of world miseries. The real world had often profited by the existence, latent or active, of this weapon. Some day the world might profit again from it! Be that as it may, he would not agree that on this point England and not Germany should be asked to subscribe to conditions. He would not give up the right of blockade, a foundation of British existence, any more than Wilson would give up the Monroe Doctrine, a foundation of American existence. If he did give it up, his action would be worthless anyhow: his parliament and his people would drive him out of office the following day.

Colonel House argued. The era of wars would be over. The League of Nations, about to be founded, would protect England even without the right of blockade.

If the League of Nations is so efficient, Lloyd George replied, that it will really do away with wars, no blockade will take place anyhow. Moreover, in that case, the League will be able and qualified to transform all the usages of war and all the weapons. Why then choose the blockade as the only weapon to be banned in advance?

Colonel House became threatening, unpleasant. If England does not renounce the blockade in wartime, he said, measures will have to be taken for the protection of neutral American shipping from interference by future blockades. The United States will be compelled to build a navy of unprecedented size and he could not advise England to engage in such a competition.

Such competition would be most painful, retorted Lloyd George, and in his opinion superfluous. But even before that England would not shy. The British Empire would rather sacrifice its last farthing to maintain its equality on the seas, than give up its strongest means of defense for the sake of a whim.

The talks were deadlocked.

Another point came up: what would the Germans have to pay?

According to the fourteen points, only a small fraction of the expenses and damages they had caused! They were expected only "to restore" the destroyed physical objects: the houses, machines, roads, trees, and that only in the regions they had occupied.

But why? What was the ethical difference between this kind of damage and others? Why was it just to hold the Germans responsible for a factory shot to pieces in Northern France and not for a ship sunk in the Atlantic? Why was it moral to demand that they rebuild a destroyed Polish peasant house, and not that they support a Polish peasant crippled by their bullets? How could a conceptual difference be established between the various items of war damage and war costs, when all derived from the same cause and all led to the same tax payer?

It might well be that the Germans would be unable to pay the entire astronomical bill. That was a purely practical problem which would have to be solved in a purely practical way.

It was an entirely different matter arbitrarily to single out some categories of damages as moral and others as immoral. Philosophically, the distinction was untenable, but its consequences would be real enough. For if it were admitted, the Germans would not only be protected against impossible demands, they would in fact receive a guarantee of not having to pay even what they could. Moreover, the peoples of the British Empire, whose territory had not been occupied, would be prevented in advance from recovering a single penny of their damages and expenses.

The conversation continued to progress from point to point. An overtone of impatience began to be felt. Colonel House was irritated by so much worldliness, the others by so much unworldliness. Sonnino, the Italian, exploded the bomb. He demanded that "the President be informed categorically that at this time the Allies could give him no assurance that his Points would be acceptable." [42]

Colonel House had been awaiting that moment. It was clear that the world of tomorrow could only be imposed on these obdurate remnants of the world of yesterday by coercion. He had long studied the most efficient means of coercion, and now he shot his bolt.

Very well, he said, if the gentlemen refused to accept the 27 points as the basis of peace, the negotiations with Germany which declared herself ready to negotiate only on that basis, were thereby cancelled. They "would have to be wiped off the slate." But then an entirely new question would arise. "The question would then arise whether America would not have to take these matters up directly with Germany and Austria." [43]

What was the meaning of this obviously well prepared phrase? What did he want to say? Was he threatening that America would stop fighting and conclude a separate peace with Germany unless his rules were accepted? Did he mean to go that far? Had the situation come to that?

Clemenceau asked the question without mincing words.

"That would amount to a separate peace between the United States and the Central Powers."

"It might," replied House.[44]

In his cabled report to Wilson, House observed: "My statement had a very exciting effect on those present." [45]

The conversation died away in the excitement. Everybody went home. In the whole war there had been nothing more difficult to ponder over than this extravagant threat, provided it was taken seriously.

Colonel House awoke at three in the morning. He could not fall asleep again. Had they taken him seriously enough? Had the excitement been violent enough, the effect crushing? He pondered until the early dawn of October 30, whether and how he should intensify the coercion. He reached a decision which he communicated to Wilson by cable before that morning's session.

At this session he repeated his threats of a separate peace more distinctly and with great detail, adding the threat of a historic scandal. If the Allies refused to accept the Principles, "it would be doubtless necessary for the President to go to Congress and place before that body exactly what Italy, France and Great Britain were fighting for." The Congress would then have to decide whether it was fitting for America to continue the war "in behalf of the aims of the Allies."

"As soon as I had said this," his cable ran, "Lloyd George and Clemenceau looked at each other significantly." [46]

On the same day Colonel House suggested to the President that he strengthen his "strong hand" by restricting troop transports and "to gently cut down upon money, food and raw material."

On the same day, Wilson replied to him: "I am proud of the way you are handling things." [47]

But it was unnecessary to promote the cause of the new world order with stronger coercive means. The threat of the separate peace had a magical effect. "Everything is changing for the better since yesterday," [48] House was to cable the following day. The Allies had apparently decided to submit to at least 25 out of the 27 principles. There was no more talk of these 25 principles.

They spoke only of the remaining two. The English resistance against the ban on blockades remained rigid. Colonel House felt that he, too, had to make concessions. He declared that he agreed to leave this question open, and to discuss it at some later time. Fortunately that later time never arrived.

Nor did the opposition to the point on the reparations abate. Colonel House conceded that German responsibility should not be limited to damages inflicted on objects, nor to damages caused in occupied regions. Instead, Germany was declared responsible for all "civil damages" as distinguished from military and state damages. The new formula, the bud of the future reparations problem, ran: "Compensation by Germany for all damage done to the civilian population of the Allies and their property."

That ended the conversations. The Allies ceased to make objections. Let us get it over with, they urged.

On November 4, everything was settled. The armistice document had been drawn up, and the Germans were invited to sign it. This document gave them the guarantee

that after the armistice a peace would be concluded and
a new world order founded on the basis of Wilson's 27
rules with one reservation and one change. This document legally pledged the Germans, the Americans and
the Allies to a new spirit and a new morality which guaranteed a new humanity.

"I consider," House cabled the President, "that we have
won a great diplomatic victory in getting the Allies to accept the principles. . . ."

Indeed, the victory of the new world order seemed to
him greater than the representatives of the old imagined.
"I doubt whether any other heads of the governments
with whom we have been dealing realize how far they
are now committed to the American peace program." [49]
In reality it was not the American peace program, as was
revealed that same day—for on that day Wilson lost both
houses of the Congress in the mid-term elections. But
aside from that, House must have imagined that the representatives of the old order had fallen into a kind of vir-
tuous trap, and that they would only later realize how
firmly they were caught. Their entrapment was embodied
in their signatures.

This was a surprising compliment to the Allied signatures. What they had signed was a conversion to extreme
virtue made under extreme duress. The champions of the
world of tomorrow regarded these converts as hardened
cynics. It was something to ascribe permanence to their
signatures—yet for a period of a few months they actually did remain in force. For, regardless of what the critics
said later, the peace treaty actually was drafted in accordance with the 27 points! This loyalty to the pledged
word was kept up amid fits of resistance, crises, compro-
mises, less because of the signatures than of the continued

coercion. But in the main, the signatories remained loyal
to their word.

But the main thing was to maintain this loyalty to the
principles for more than a few months! The powers
pledged themselves to abide by ethical principles—"a
way of thinking." It was not enough to follow these principles now, while the peace treaty was being drafted. It
was in the years and decades to come that the philosophy
and the institutions provided for in the treaty would have
to prove their real worth. This was the crucial point. It
was futile to write the peace treaty in the spirit of unprecedented new principles unless there was some likelihood that they would be accepted with some degree of
conviction.

Now, the Allies had not concealed the fact that they
had absolutely no faith in the ethics of the 27 points.

Contrary to what has been said later, they were not
hypocritical. They had made it sufficiently clear that in
their view this was an ethics for a world which actually
did not exist either in their own countries, in Germany, in
America, or anywhere else—a chimera as long as it remained on paper, ruinous if any attempt were made to
carry it out. The reason for their attitude may have lain
in their incurable wickedness, or in their better knowledge. At any rate, such it was. The spirit expressed in
these points was not theirs—let alone that of the Germans. What was gained by coercing them to submit to it
for a short time? The happenings of a few months cannot
determine the course of history, nor can a text of a peace
treaty determine the character of a peace. Both are a perpetual creation, with new situations arising daily and the
need of constantly new decisions. At what moment would
the enforced color fade, and the natural one reappear?

In the painfully laborious career of the messianic enterprise of 1918, this from the very beginning was the
flaw: the idea of coercion. Whatever may have been the
value of the 27 points, Wilson, who was a historian,
closed his eyes to the primary obstacle to the realization
of his plans: the truth that compulsory vows were worthless. They can never last longer than the compulsion. If
one is able to exert this compulsion only for what, in history, amounts to a fraction of a second, the enterprise is
not worthwhile.

And where was Germany in the whole scheme? After
all, Germany was not a negligible quantity of the new
world order, not an incidental signatory of the new ethics.

Germany had been told that she would be granted the
Wilsonian peace only if she reduced her masters and autocrats to the point of "virtual impotence." On October 23,
she had been told that her very sudden imperial autumn-
democracy did not satisfy these conditions. "The determining initiative still remains with those who have hitherto been the masters of Germany." Yet the next day
Wilson had begun to secure the 27-point peace for her,
and by November 4th, it was actually granted.

In the interval, nothing had changed in Germany! She
was still under the same imperial autumn-democracy! On
November 8, in Foch's parlor car, the document granting
her the 27-point peace would still be handed for signature to a delegation of the old-masters-democracy. For
this, nor for any other Germany, had the President fought,
for her he won the peace which he had explicitly reserved
for another Germany. The document guaranteeing this
peace was pressed into the hands of the delegates of Wilhelm II and Prince Max von Baden.

But before they had time to sign it, overnight they

changed into the delegates of a certain Mr. Ebert and a certain Mr. Haase. On November 9, the Kaiser and the Crown Prince left for Holland, and the Republic was proclaimed in Berlin; on November 11, the public learned the contents of the document signed on that day. It learned that the German Republic had received the guarantee of the Wilson peace; and the republic was after all indisputably a democracy. The fact that this peace had been granted six days earlier, to an entirely different Germany, was to remain unnoticed and without practical consequences. Nevertheless, the fact is not unimportant. It shows to what extent the President would close his eyes to obstacles facing his great enterprise, to facts of history and reality—even to facts which he himself had only a few days earlier described as being of prime importance.

The emergence of the German Republic threw everyone off the track. At eleven o'clock that morning the guns which for fifty-one months had been rending the body of the earth suddenly ceased their thunder. From the underworld of the trenches men mounted into the light. The man in the White House was deeply moved. He took his pencil, and with tears in his eyes, wrote this beautiful, humble, proud announcement to his people: "The armistice was signed this morning. Everything for which America fought has been accomplished. It will now be our fortunate duty to assist by example, by sober, friendly counsel and by material aid in the establishment of a just democracy throughout the world."

A cable from Paris was brought him. It was from his friend House:

"Autocracy is dead. Long live democracy and its immortal leader." [50]

2: *The Code of the New World*

IN THOSE days, the cry "Long Live Democracy" echoed also in the chaos that was Germany.

But in Germany it was not a cry of triumph, the realization of a long-cherished aim. It was rather a fervent appeal to cherish from then on the aim that had been realized. It was only an attempt to give the *fait accompli* a democratic content.

The actual events had had little in common with democracy. Those who believed otherwise—and there were even a few Germans who did—were profoundly mistaken.

The revolution had gone through three stages in the space of six weeks. First, the regime had been "democratized"; then the Kaiser had been expelled; and finally the monarchy as a system had been abolished. How had all this taken place?

Toward the end of September, Hindenburg and Ludendorff finally found the courage to admit that the war was lost. On September 28, in a state of panic, they revealed that an armistice was necessary at once, without delay.

Under normal circumstances, this would have been the end. But wasn't there that incredible saint named Wilson in America? And didn't he live in the clouds? Perhaps it was still possible to get something out of him. As late as September 24, Chancellor Count Hertling had

been running down Saint Wilson, as usual. He had re-
ferred to him as "the former ideologist and pacifist Wilson," now "metamorphosed into the chief of the American imperialists." [1] Four days later, the generals urged him
to cordially and respectfully address the announcement
of their collapse to this "imperialist."

Very well, replied the chief of the Foreign Office, a
naval man, a certain Admiral von Hintze. But we can't
approach this man as an absolute monarchy by the grace
of God. Any government that does not wear a democratic
wig has not a chance with him.

Then get yourselves the necessary wig, the generals
answered. But get it quickly. Within 24 hours, or at the
most, 48.

The Foreign Office worked fast. With a nimble hand it
wrote a memorandum dated the same September 28. This
document was the blueprint of what was now to happen:
"The most important prerequisite for the institution of
peace is the formation, upon the free initiative of His
Majesty the Emperor, of a new Government on a broad
national basis. For this purpose it would be desirable that
there should arrive at Berlin as early as tomorrow evening
a telegram announcing the acceptance of Count Hertling's resignation as requested by him. . . . The new
Cabinet should unite all the forces of the people. . . .
The new Government thus formed will approach President Wilson. . . ." [2]

The prescribed events took place promptly. The next
evening, the telegram that had been agreed upon arrived
in Berlin from General Headquarters, announcing the
Kaiser's acceptance of Count Hertling's resignation. It
further announced his desire "to have the German people
participate more effectively than heretofore in the deter-

mination of the destinies of the Fatherland." It proclaimed
the formation of a new Cabinet "supported by the confidence of the people." And the new Cabinet promptly
approached President Wilson.

Prince Max von Baden, the new Reich Chancellor
chosen to personify the alleged democratization, was a
distinguished and cultivated gentleman. Only no one had
ever known that he was a democrat. He had recently attracted attention by a speech in the Baden House of
Peers, which, while containing many caustic remarks
against Wilson, had been in essence a sort of sermon
about the Sermon on the Mount. This made him seem an
appropriate representative of the new line, at least until
a few days after his appointment, when a Swiss newspaper destroyed the pretty picture by publishing a private letter he had sent during that very year to a cousin
in Switzerland. This letter contained remarks hostile not
only to pacifism and the idea of a "negotiated peace,"
but also to democracy and parliamentarism.[3] Prince Max
was unable to deny its authenticity.

The new democracy's Reich Chancellor, who was no
democrat, was supported by a parliamentary majority
half of which was not democratic either. Of the four
parties which had formed a coalition to represent the
"support" of the Government "by the confidence of the
people," two had been strictly opposed to democracy and
parliamentarism throughout their entire history. Both the
Catholic "Center" party and the National Liberals had
never renounced their allegiance to the principle of absolute authority. Suddenly they appeared on the stage of
German politics as proponents and supporters of democratization.

Such was the first stage of the transformation of Ger-

many. Obviously, this democratization was purely for-
malistic, inspired "from above," and introduced as "the
cardinal prerequisite" for approaching President Wilson.
No government acts in a petty fashion when faced with
an extreme emergency. The Berlin regime had twice before played the comedy of democracy in emergencies.
The first time was in 1806, after Napoleon's triumph at
Jena. The second was in March, 1848, when the wave of
liberal revolution engulfed all Europe. The Hohenzollern
kings of those days had proclaimed every conceivable reform. When the pendulum swung back again—nine years
later in the first case, nine months later in the second—
they nullified all the concessions they had granted.

What led to the second stage, the dismissal of the
Kaiser and the Crown Prince?

Wilson's replies had clearly demonstrated that the September democratization did not satisfy him. His last note
admitted of only one interpretation: he still regarded the
Kaiser as the master of Germany, and to such a Germany
he would show no mercy.

The Kaiser stood in the way: and the Germans began
to say that as a practical expedient the Kaiser must abdicate.

There was no passion in this, no particular animosity;
nor any democracy either. It was all very matter-of-fact.
If the collapse would be less overwhelming without the
Kaiser, then of course, farewell, Kaiser! Let him abdicate,
and the matter settled! People had talked about and expected a settlement; when it failed to materialize they
grew annoyed. On October 25, two days after Wilson's
last note, an article appeared in the "Frankfurter Zeitung,"
which for the first time publicly stated what most people
were thinking.

The "Frankfurter Zeitung" was the most influential newspaper not only in Germany but on the entire European continent; what is more, it was really democratic. It had always treated the theatrical Wilhelm II, the imitator of Lohengrin and Siegfried, without any sympathy —and this was a rarity among German newspapers. In 1915, when the censors asked for too many alterations in their articles, the editors announced that they would cease to print editorials altogether. They continued this demonstration for months.

Now no one knew how they had managed to get that foolhardy abdication article past the censor. In reality, the censor, who was of the same opinion as the editors, was perhaps even more foolhardy than they. He had allowed the column to slip through. No matter whose fault it was, the cat was out of the bag. The article passed from hand to hand. It swept the country like wildfire. Everyone wondered what would happen next.

Nothing happened. The Kaiser refused to budge! Was such a thing conceivable? Was it fair? Was it not enough that he had lost the war? Was he now going to prevent the people from getting off cheaply, thanks to Wilson? The mood of the masses grew tense—and on October 29, Herr Philipp Scheidemann felt obliged to write a letter to Prince Max about it.

Philipp Scheidemann himself was a member of the Prince's Cabinet. He was its most Left member, and in a sense its strongest. He represented the largest and most organized party in the government: the "majority Socialists." The larger part of the workers marched behind this party. The dominant personalities in it were a small, corpulent man with a brown goatee, an ex-saddler and innkeeper, Friedrich Ebert; and, next to him, a tall, slender man, with a white goatee, an ex-typesetter, Philipp Scheidemann. It would have been impossible to "sell" the democratization to Wilson or to the Germans if this party and its leaders had shown themselves dissatisfied and failed to collaborate with the Government. For that reason, Herr Scheidemann was actually the strongest element in the Cabinet. When he demanded something, it was hard to resist.

Now, Scheidemann demanded that the Cabinet decide "to ask the Imperial Chancellor to advise His Majesty to retire of his own free will." And why? The letter cited one reason only: all the world, it said, was "convinced that the prospects of getting tolerable terms for the Armistice and the Peace were being ruined by the Emperor's remaining in his exalted office." [4]

On October 31, six days after the article in the "Frankfurter Zeitung," the point was reached where the Socialist Party as such, was forced to take a public stand. In an article entitled: "What will the Kaiser do?" the leading Socialist newspaper, the "Vorwaerts," did not state in plain terms what the Kaiser should do now. But it said that the monarch, "who did not wish this war," could perform an important service to insure a more favorable ending of the present conflict.

The same day, the discussion requested by Scheidemann took place in the Cabinet. The second-most important leader of the German workers once again explained why the Kaiser must retire. The party had nothing against him personally: "We have always tried to read into Wilson's notes our view that the President is not demanding the Kaiser's abdication. But the Foreign Office will corroborate me when I say that all foreign countries interpret them otherwise." [5] The country, too, including, gradually, more and more workers, interpreted them otherwise. "Let us make no mistake, this demand did not originate among workers but in middle-class circles." But now, he went on, practically all classes agree on this one point, including even many officers of all ranks, "up to and including that of Colonel." Public opinion was convinced that unless the Kaiser withdrew, "Germany would not get any peace such as would allow our people the chance of further development." [6]

Thus spoke the more radical, the more Leftist of the two leaders of the German Socialist Party. Once again, he raised the question of Wilhelm's abdication only from the point of view of Wilson and the peace terms. And even from this point of view he did not put forth his thesis as the opinion of the Socialist leaders, but as the opinion of the general public, "which cannot now be kept in hand any longer."

He was obviously in the right. At a galloping tempo the people had grown ever more bitter and rebellious. Since Wilson's rejection of the so-called democratization, nothing more had been heard from him. What was taking place in Paris was completely unknown in Germany. It seemed to the German public that everything was off, the armistice, the Wilson peace, and all hope of the slaughter's ever ending. This lost war, then, must continue only because of the Kaiser? And no cheap peace was to be obtained only because that man on top wanted to remain where he was? A tidal wave of anger arose.

This wave broke through all the dams in the first days of November, when sailors from the naval bases of Kiel and Wilhelmshaven appeared all over the country and related what had taken place there. The admiralty had

ordered the fleet to sail out and give battle to the British
Navy. No one knew with certainty—and no one knows
today—whether Wilhelm II, the supreme warlord, had
approved of this order. At any rate, the sailors had not. If
there was any prospect of armistice and peace, thanks to
Wilson, it would be ruined by the action in that moment.
If the prospect really existed, it was a criminal thing to
send the men to their death. The war was lost in any
case. This hopeless naval engagement, which had been
avoided for years, could not possibly change the outcome. The sailors could not understand why they should
sacrifice their lives at this moment. Most of the officers
could not understand it either, because, with a few exceptions, they reacted with complete passivity to what
was happening.

What happened? First, the crew of the warship Markgraf refused to obey sailing orders and extinguished the
fires; then the strike spread to the entire fleet; finally,
thousands of sailors had become mutineers, boarded
trains and carried in all directions the gospel of violently
enforcing the end to the war.

Wherever they appeared with their tale, popular indignation soared. So that's what the Kaiser was? Not only
could he not be induced to leave in order to open the
way for the Wilson peace, but he was also determined to
sabotage deliberately and perfidiously any possibility of
peace or armistice!

From that moment on, the temper of the masses was
ripe for a revolt against the Kaiser. An outbreak was only
a question of days. Those who were closest to the throne
now had only one thought: how could the Kaiser be
safely removed from the stage, before the volcano
erupted.

General Groener, who had replaced Ludendorff, suggested that the Kaiser seek a soldier's death in the trenches. His suggestion was rejected.

The Ministers and the Chancellor, first through deputations, then in increasingly frequent telephone conversations, demanded his voluntary abdication. But the Kaiser refused to budge.

At his General Headquarters in Belgium, he twisted and squirmed. Lamentable scenes followed one another at the Villa Fraineuse in Spa. To his military retinue the Kaiser aired a plan to leave the war to fate and march on the homeland. Seventy-seven-year-old General-Adjutant von Plessen had discovered that the army would readily agree to this scheme. All that was necessary was to tell the soldiers that "the Navy and Jewish war profiteers and traitors wanted to cut off supplies from the army." But Groener and Hindenburg declared that these schemes had no prospect of success. "The army," said Groener, "will march home in peace and order under its leaders and commanding generals, but not under the command of Your Majesty, for it no longer stands behind Your Majesty." [7] The Kaiser wavered from one theatrical pose to another, but could not reach a decision. To escape the pressing appeals from Berlin, which, on the fateful day of November 9, came to him almost every fifteen minutes, he finally cut his wires.

Then the news burst upon him that Prince Max von Baden had announced his abdication in Berlin. Fearing the outbreak of a revolt any minute, the Chancellor had published a report that the Kaiser had abdicated and the Crown Prince renounced his rights; in reality neither had done anything of the sort.

This was the end. For a few hours the Kaiser contin-

ued to reel giddily back and forth, rushing from his villa
to the Imperial train, from the train to the villa, and then
again from the villa to the train. At daybreak on November 10 he appeared with a small group of the faithful at
the Dutch-Belgian frontier and, after having been forced
to wait for a few hours in the autumn fog, was finally permitted by Queen Wilhelmina's Ministers to enter Holland.

This event, too, was entirely determined by Wilson and
the hoped for armistice and peace; it was the famous
"cardinal prerequisite." Republican and democratic convictions played not the slightest part in it. Even the most
radical party, the majority Social-Democrats, had explicitly desired to preserve the monarchy. Their idea was
to transfer the crown from the Kaiser to one of his grand-
sons; nothing more.

This was surprising in a group which, since its foundation, had advocated a Republic. But it is a fact that the
leaders of this Republican party made a strenuous effort
to avoid the Republic when it came.

On November 6, General Groener summoned the seven
most important leaders of the party, headed by Ebert and
Scheidemann, to a conference. Several years later, as a
witness in a trial, he was to state: "I found the Social-
Democratic representatives completely reasonable. They
did not voice a single thought which might lead one to
infer that they were struggling for a revolution. On the
contrary, from the first to the last word, the whole conversation turned on the means of preserving the monarchy." [8]

On the following day, November 7, Ebert concluded a
very special kind of pact with Prince Max. Ebert was the
head of a party whose program was not only republican,

but also socialistic. But on that day he allied himself with the Prince against the possibility that the revolt should degenerate into both republicanism and socialism.

"If I succeed in convincing the Kaiser," the Chancellor asked him, "can I count on your support in fighting the Social Revolution?" Obviously reeling under the impact of the Bolshevik uprising in Russia, the Socialist leader gave the "unhesitating and unequivocal" reply: "Unless the Kaiser abdicates, the social revolution is inevitable. But I will have none of it; I hate it like sin."

The Chancellor then asked Ebert whether his party would agree to the coronation of the Kaiser's eldest grandson, and to the regency of one of his sons until the monarch should come of age. "On behalf of himself and his party," Ebert expressed his agreement. "On these constitutional points no difficulties would be put in the Government's way." [9]

Yes, even when in the confusion of November 9, as a result of a slip Scheidemann had made in hot haste, the Republic was proclaimed in spite of everything, the future President of the Republic still tried for hours to preserve the monarchy by a ruse. He called upon Prince Max to remain as "Reichverweser" or "Reich-Regent." In monarchist terminology, a regent is the representative of a ruler under age; a "Reichverweser" is a monarchist transition from a dynasty which has died out to a new one. Even at that moment Ebert tried to hand over the Crown of Germany from the Hohenzollerns to some other dynasty, through the intermediary of a "Reichverweser." He proposed this solution to Prince Max, and wanted him to accept the post. He failed because the prince rejected his proposal.

All this took place after the slip. What slip? How was

the Republic born? Neither the first nor the second stage of the November events had had much in common with democracy. Had the third stage anything to do with it?

At that point a strange event took place.

The Kaiser's abdication had been proclaimed. In front of the building where the Social-Democratic leaders were gathered, a crowd assembled. They were hungry for news, and demanded a speaker. Scheidemann was sent to address them from a window.

But on his way someone stopped him and told him that in front of another window at the other end of the street another crowd had gathered. In a few minutes they were to be addressed by Herr Karl Liebknecht, Scheidemann's ex-colleague who had become a Bolshevik. And Liebknecht was going to proclaim the German Soviet Republic!

At that, Scheidemann threw all his ballast overboard. Now he felt only the urgent need to lure the crowd from the other end of the street to his end, and to do it in a few short minutes which might shake the world. He knew that this could be accomplished only by the magnetic attraction of a sensational announcement as revolutionary as the one Liebknecht was about to make. So he went to his window, and on his own initiative, instead of announcing the end of the monarch, announced the end of the monarchy. "The monarchy has broken down. Long live the new! Long live the German Republic!"

He turned from the window to his colleagues, and "Ebert's face turned livid with wrath when he heard what I had done. He banged his fist on the table and yelled at me, 'Is this true?' . . . He made a scene which passed my understanding. 'You have no right to proclaim the Republic. . . .'" [10] For many hours Ebert tried to ig-

nore the fait accompli. He hit upon the idea of a Reichverweser. Only when this proved impracticable, and
when the news of the proclamation of the Republic appeared in the German and foreign newspapers did he
give up his attempts to preserve the monarchy. The German Republic came into being against the will of the most
powerful person in the only party which called itself republican. It came into being not as a result of democratic
travail, but as a product of momentary panic, the momentary tactic and the formula improvised on the spot by one
man addressing a street rally.

On November 11, when the Armistice was concluded
with the "German Republic," the victors knew little of
these events. And even if they had known what had taken
place, they might still have believed that these steps had
been fumbling only in appearance and represented the
fundamental desires and instincts of the people. It might
have been said, and since then often has been said, that
all the actors in this drama had really been impelled by
the forces of democracy.

Today it would be hard to maintain this. During the
fourteen years of the Republic the German people
showed no democratic enthusiasm. Actually in 1918 the
idea that they felt strong democratic yearnings was
merely wishful thinking.

In America the group of perfectionists around Wilson
were only too inclined to believe that the whole world
was modelled after their own soul. They imagined that
Germany had experienced her 1776, and assumed that
every nation on earth yearned for a 1776. Only monarchist
oppression, they believed, had prevented Germany from
realizing her revolution before now, but at last her democratic instincts had triumphed. "We are not enemies of

the German people and they are not our enemies," Wilson had previously said. "They did not originate or desire this hideous war, and we are vaguely conscious that we are fighting their cause, as they will some day see it themselves." [11] The belief in the inherent equality and goodness of all nations, in their inherent longing for democracy, was a fundamental dogma of the perfectionist religion.

For those who knew the German people, their longing for democracy was always extremely doubtful. It was always a question whether the newspapers and parties that spoke of this longing were not misleading their readers and adherents. Not only were there millions of convinced anti-democrats in every stratum of the German population, but even among the others the interest in democracy was very weak.

The average German in the days of the Empire did not feel that he lived under an oppressive autocracy. He knew that certain features of the German constitution were often criticized: that the Reich Chancellor could act without the support of the majority in the Reichstag; and that war could be declared by the confederated princes. Many were inclined to agree with this criticism. But all that was far removed from concrete, everyday life in Germany, which was no different from that of the western democracies. It was the age of liberalism. The German enjoyed the same protection under the law, the same inviolability of person, the same freedom as the Frenchman or the Englishman. Autocracy existed only in the invisible, remote, abstract background. The need for reform was not a burning one. Democracy for the Germans of 1918 had not the fascination it had for the Americans of 1776, or the French of 1789.

Those who felt a burning need for a change were
mostly Socialists. In their eyes the main problem was the
overthrow of capitalism. It is true that the most powerful
group within the Socialist movement called itself "social-
democratic." But the theory animating the whole movement was that democracy would be a by-product of the
abolition of capitalism, and that under capitalism democracy was worthless anyhow. At that time, the Socialists
of all countries shared this view. Only gradually and re-
luctantly did they abandon it in the course of the tragic
decades that followed the war. In short, the majority of
Germans believed that they lacked no essential element
of democracy, and the minority believed that they lacked
something much more important.

That the Germans were imbued with a strong passion
for democracy was at best an assumption. It proved to be
rash and false. When the Republic was ushered in, it
quickly became apparent that no burning need had been
satisfied. The real democrats were dismayed at the popular apathy. The calvary of the Republic began with its
attempt to convince the people that democracy was really
desirable.

And besides, what had this whole question to do with
the actual situation? In 1918 the world wanted security
and peace. It wanted lasting freedom from German attacks. How would the birth of the German Republic affect world peace?

All the nations are fundamentally good, the idealists
answered. As soon as a nation adopts a democratic form
of government it can follow its own will in foreign affairs.
Thus it will refuse to tolerate war any longer. The war
was started by the German autocrats. The German nation—so ran the theory—had nothing to do with it. If

Germany had been a democracy, the German people would have prevented it.

But would they? If a republican Chancellor had asked the Reichstag to declare war, would it have behaved differently from the Imperial Reichstag of 1914? Would the government officials, army officers, politicians, newspapers and the nation at large have behaved differently? Would they behave differently the next time?

Obviously, the best that can be hoped from a democracy is that it will more accurately express the true instincts and ideas of the people than an autocracy. But have all nations the same instincts and ideas, in spite of their different history, education and tradition? What instincts and ideas had the German people revealed in regard to war since 1914, and particularly now, in 1918, at the end of the war?

The test was the so-called "war-guilt" question.

In 1914, the German people were told that the war had been perfidiously brought upon them by the enemy, that it was a sacred defensive war. Very well, millions could believe that.

And as long as the issue of the war remained undecided, others could regard it as their duty to close their eyes and mouths and act on the principle: "my country, right or wrong." This is of course a questionable attitude. There were better models to follow. The last one in sight of German politicians had been that of the eminent French historian, Thiers. After the outbreak of the Franco-German war of 1870, this leader of the opposition to Napoleon III rose in the French Chamber and declared: we shall help defend the country, but we condemn the share of our Imperial government in scheming to bring this war about, and one day we shall call them to account for it. Two months later he was the President of the French Republic, and his record was clear. His attitude could have been imitated in Germany during the World War.

Now the war was nearing its end, and the principle of "right or wrong" could no longer be invoked. On the contrary, German democracy had now appeared on the scene and had declared itself willing to do its utmost for the cause of world peace. The crime of unleashing a war was never to be committed again! What must be done in one's own country to prevent the crime of unleashing a war?

The revulsion against it must be intensified. All minds must be mobilized against it. The people must be made to understand that war has been and always will be a crime, because wars do not "break out" or "arise," but are deliberately unleashed. The tricks used to unleash wars must be unmasked, especially the trick of "self-defense." And how could all this be done effectively without citing the burning example of the war that had just been experienced? Hic Rhodos, hic salta! The best way to produce the necessary moral revulsion against war was to analyze the crime which had just been committed and from whose consequences the people were still suffering, rather than hypothetical future crimes. It is a bad sermon which thunders against the sin of tomorrow, but conceals or glosses over the sin of yesterday and today. All that could be done for the future peace depended on the manner in which the war of 1914–1918 was to be indicted and condemned by the new Republic.

The bare fact is that the new democracy refused to indict the war of 1914, and, what is more, that it was far from condemning the autocracy. It failed to do what the Utopians had assumed it would do as a matter of course.

The leaders of nine-tenths of the German people paid

very little attention to the theory that the moral attitude of a democracy toward war is different from that of an autocracy. They consistently expressed their complete respect for the war which had allegedly been the work of the autocracy. They continued to acquit both the nation and the Kaiser of any guilt in the crime of causing that war.

Their interpretation of the war wavered between two myths both of which had been current since 1914, and both were of bad omen.

Sometimes they alleged that the crime had been committed by the Allies; that the Allies had planned and staged the war and misled the world by their hypocritical accusations against Germany. This implied that the Germans were victims of a shameless injustice and that they could expect only further oppression from their deceitful conquerors.

At other times they said that no one had committed the crime; that the war had "arisen" or "broken out," as a result of the action of "historic forces" or the "capitalist system," or other objective realities. This interpretation implied that the Germans themselves were guiltless; that wars were the work of blind fate; and that all the talk about the coming Reign of Law and Order would lead to nothing.

Both explanations made the Germans think that all their actions had been justified, that they had nothing with which to reproach themselves, that they could remain as they had always been.

Such were the instincts and ideas with which even the leaders of German democracy had emerged from the so-called autocratic war. These were the ideas they spread among the people, and on which they nourished their followers. All one needed to discover this fact was one's two ears.

One had only to listen to the party which, among the exponents of the new regime, was supposed to be the most progressive, the most pacifistic, the most international-minded.

Oh, to be sure, the leaders of the Social-Democratic Party were sincere lovers of peace. Most of them were honest and well-intentioned men. They dreamed of an orderly world. They even promoted it in their fashion.

But at the same time the leaders among them were without realizing it normal products of the traditional German education. They were average patriots. We must not befoul our own nest, they said. We must not dishonor our own dead! We must not impose sackcloth and ashes on the German people! Why should we? Germany will always be just as good as any other country, if not better. Even now, they could not bring themselves to give up the myth of German innocence. They remained patriotically wedded to the war of 1914.

The very article of their newspaper which demanded the abdication of the Kaiser contained the following words: "The Kaiser did not wish this war!" [12]

At a workers' meeting in Berlin, Scheidemann stressed his "deathless pride" in his comrades' share in the war. "The people, and particularly the Socialist section of the people, gave a good account of themselves in this war. And if the victory for which they had bled and suffered had not materialized, the reason was that their voice had not been heeded." [13]

Ebert, in the most dramatic moment of his life, revealed the same patriotic pride. The Empire was at an end; Chancellor Prince Max came to bid him good-bye. At the door, overwhelmed by emotion, he turned to Ebert: "Herr Ebert, I commit the German Reich to your keeping!"— "I have lost two sons for this Reich!" replied the Socialist leader.[14] In his mind, the war had been and still was a war "for the Reich." Those who had died, had died in a good cause. Soon he would reach the point where he would even refuse to admit that Germany had been defeated on the field of battle. On December 11, when President Wilson's ship was approaching the coasts of Europe, the Guard regiment returned to Berlin, and Ebert made a speech celebrating the return of our "undefeated army."

The Socialist leaders of Bavaria were relatively strong. They demanded "the establishment of courts to indict and punish all the responsible persons . . ." Responsible for what? "All those who had contributed to the failure of previous attempts to make peace and who are thereby responsible for the unhappy outcome of the war." [15] Responsible for the unhappy outcome of the war, not for the war itself!

Subsequently this position with regard to the war became the essential tenet of the radical party. When they spoke of "guilt," they meant not the guilt of initiating the war, but of bringing it to an unsuccessful conclusion. In 1919, a parliamentary committee was appointed to throw light on two questions: the responsibility for the war, and the responsibility for the collapse. This Committee was active for several years. Concerning the responsibility for the collapse, thick volumes of expert opinion were printed, witnesses were examined and cross-examined, stenographic records of innumerable hearings were published. But the committee never found time to study the other responsibility, the responsibility for unleashing the war. Concerning that question, no hearings were held, no wit-

nesses called, no records published. In the beginning, a
few learned specialists were asked to prepare reports on
specific aspects of the question. But the committee never
found an opportunity to discuss their findings. They never
had enough money to print them. After having waited
for a long time, two prominent authors of such reports
asked me to print their investigations in one of my pe-
riodicals, if only to save them from complete oblivion. I
still recall the hurried efforts that were made to prevent
their publication. The Investigating Committee threatened to prosecute me, claiming that these reports were
their property, and that they had the right to do or not
do with them what they pleased.

The fact that the old Reich—"not a country with an
army but an army with a country," in Mirabeau's immortal definition—should still have partisans and enthusiastic
defenders was normal. What was tragic, however, was
that every difference between them and the leaders of the
new Reich disappeared as soon as the question of war
guilt was brought up.

No, the leaders of this democracy were not willing to
repudiate their support of the war. They clearly showed
this unwillingness from the very beginning. And if a democratic government reflects the will of the people, it
should have been clear that the people behind the Weimar
Republic were unwilling, too. Aside from a few isolated
individuals, no one desired a real reckoning. No one cared
about enlightening the people, the people did not desire
to learn the truth, nor to cleanse and purify their minds of
the old chauvinistic myths. The German nation was indifferent to the question of war guilt. The war was lost,
and that was bad. If it had been won, it would have been
good.

Who could believe that this people and this "democracy" were animated by instincts and ideals which would some day form a dependable dam against the flood of a new war?

In January, 1919, the delegations of the 27 nations which had finally mastered their four opponents, gathered in Paris. President Wilson disembarked in Europe on Friday, the 13th of December—a bad omen for those who were superstitious. At royal receptions tendered him in Paris, London and Rome, he had re-affirmed his hopes and his faith.

Upon his return to the Hotel Crillon on the Place de la Concorde, assigned for his residence by the French government, he received a long memorandum from Marshal Foch. Among other things, the generalissimo developed some thoughts upon a subject which could scarcely be called military. He spoke of the advantages for perpetual peace which could be expected to flow from the republicanization of Germany.

"The crisis may break again," said the memorandum dated January 10, 1919. "The change in form of the German government will undoubtedly not be sufficient to prevent it. A Republic based on the same principles of centralization and militarism as the old Empire will still present great dangers and will still be a redoubtable menace to peace. Such a Republic is easy to achieve, it seems to me, in a country imbued with Prussian spirit, Prussian methods and military doctrines, where the principle of authority still rules undisputed, because of the temperament and tradition of the people."

Yes, the Marshal's imagination carried him a step further. He became somewhat fanciful. He spoke of the possibility that at some future date the Republic might give

birth to a worse absolutism than the previous regime.
"More than that, Republican Germany, freed once and
for all from the fetters placed on the Empire by the existence of the little principalities, might increase in
strength . . . Institutions republican in appearance might
evolve endowed with all the strength of an absolutist government. We shall not witness such an evolution before
some time elapses, no doubt much time. But what
then? . . ." [16]

What strange ideas about republicanism and democracy! As a strategist, the Marshal had been brilliant, a
heaven-sent saviour. But politics was obviously not his
field . . .

2.

Three and a half months later, the prevailing mood in
the Hotel Crillon was one of depression. On that March
29, 1919, the President spoke in a weary voice: "Gentlemen, I am in trouble and I have sent for you to help me
out . . . I do not know whether I shall see Mr. Clemenceau again. I do not know whether he will return to the
meeting this afternoon. In fact, I do not know whether
the peace conference will continue. M. Clemenceau called
me a pro-German and abruptly left the room." [17]

Clemenceau did not appear at the afternoon session.
House tried to bring the two men together again. Through
a mutual friend he suggested to old "Father Victory" that
he talk things over with Wilson. "Talk to Wilson!" the
old man exploded. "How can I talk to a fellow who thinks
himself the first man in two thousand years to know anything about peace on earth?" [18]

But the old man knew that sooner or later he would

again speak to Wilson. He did not want to let the peace conference go up in smoke. Even in his outbursts of anger, he always remembered one thing: he was the champion of true reason, not only of French reason, but of Universal Reason. But may the Goddess of Reason, the ancient goddess of the Jacobins, forgive him! He was not fated to serve her well. He was ready to push his struggle for reason almost to the point of a break. But he realized that a real break would probably be worse than to yield.

This must have been his axiom, his guiding principle. He had drawn up the balance sheet of the war, and the end result was that it was necessary for France to preserve her friends. Preserve them at almost any cost!

This war had revealed a terrifying fact. It had shown that Germany was many times stronger than anyone had dreamed. For decades the Germans had been all too diligently giving birth to children. The significance of this fact was now clear. It had required half of mankind to subdue Germany. The task would have been hopeless if France had had to tackle it alone.

And from now on the outlook for France alone must inevitably be more and more hopeless. The number of her inhabitants remained constant, while across the border the population increased by approximately half a million each year. The comparative strength of the two countries which was already unfavorable enough with France's 39 to Germany's 66 millions, would every year grow less favorable. Weakness was the only outlook—eternal weakness in terrifying proximity to the most dangerous of all possible neighbors! If these Germans should once again develop military power, what then?

The fateful contradiction between the present and the future relentlessly pursued the old man.

The present had temporarily made France the strongest land power on earth. But she faced a future in which, if left alone, she would perhaps not even be able to hold for a few months. The imbeciles of the globe were fascinated by France's present. But Clemenceau groaned under the appalling burden of her future.

How could he meet this threat? France's current advantage could be exploited to its extreme limits. Germany could now be crushed to a pulp, for today no one could prevent this by military means. But considering the prevailing mentality, this would mean a break with official America at least, and what forces would sooner or later follow official America no one could say. In the end, France might be morally outlawed, with the entire world irrevocably turned against her.

Some of the men in his entourage were ready to risk this possibility rather than accept a peace which left too many loopholes open for a renewal of the horror. President Poincaré and Marshal Foch seemed more and more disposed to take the plunge and achieve an end by terror rather than a terror without end.

Clemenceau resisted this temptation, sometimes warily, sometimes angrily. He also struggled with himself. But for a potentially weakened nation even this solution was too risky. It would be a flight into immediate catastrophe at the hands of one's friends, to avoid future catastrophe at the hands of one's enemies.

The cup of fate had to be emptied! One must suffer the consequences of one's own weakness, grit one's teeth and at least avoid wrecking France's friendships on the shoals of this tormented conference, above all her friendship with America.

To fight for the most important points was possible to a

certain extent. All realized, though they did not completely understand the danger, that the crushing of the French spearhead by a Germany trying once again to break through to world domination would entail incalculable consequences. On this basis one could wrest this or that concession from them. One could eliminate the most absurd features of the proposed settlement and smooth it out so that it was imperfect rather than impossible. But it was better to accept an imperfect settlement with Germany and retain the reserve capital of old friendships, than to achieve a thoroughgoing settlement with Germany and change old friends into enemies. Whenever this question brought the conference near the breaking point, Clemenceau had to yield, against his knowledge, his judgment, his conviction.

He did it. He did it again and again. But it was a torture. "It made me suffer cruelly." [19]

Lloyd George was bad enough to cope with. This man had really experienced what Germany was. He knew how bitterly England and France needed each other. He realized full well that France's future was alarming and that her present security was illusory. Nevertheless, even this transitory French strength sufficed to Lloyd George in critical moments as a pretext for starting the famous pendulum swinging again, the Balance of Power. "From the very day after the Armistice," Clemenceau was to tell him a few years later, "I found you an enemy of France." "Well," Lloyd George replied frankly, "was it not always our traditional policy?" [20] At times the situation would become unbearable: "Never have two men in critical debates looked more like going down on one another's throat," [21] Clemenceau said.

But Lloyd George—one must almost say: fortunately —did not stick to principles. Neither to Wilson's nor to Clemenceau's nor even to the principle of the Balance of Power. He played politics. In his politician's trade, if in nothing else, he was certainly a virtuoso. But virtuosity can be met with virtuosity.

Wilson, that was the really difficult case. He deserved greater respect. "A man with excellent intentions," Clemenceau admitted; and even though he was "a doctrinaire," he was a doctrinaire "in the finest sense of the word." [22] But what a tragedy! "There are probably few examples of such a misreading and disregarding of political experience in the maelstrom of abstract thought," [23] was Clemenceau's well considered judgment of him.

To him, to this abstract man, "with rigidly fixed and crystallized emotions," [24] Clemenceau was compelled to surrender his reason: in spite of his firmly being convinced that only misfortune could come of all this.

According to the President's—and mankind's—desires, this was to have been the war to end war. According to Clemenceau's skeptical conviction, it could at least have been a war to eliminate the possibility of war with Germany for a very long time. But what was being prepared here, was rather a peace to end peace. Every time Clemenceau capitulated before one of the 27 points, whether he capitulated completely or three-quarters of the way or half-way—he was sure that the next war became more certain.

The core of the tragedy was that this whole sect of idealists, including Wilson, had no idea of the nature of man and of peoples; no understanding of the real forces moving the machine of history.

They wanted to improve the world—very well, why not? Why should it be impossible to improve the world? There was plenty of room for improvement, enormous room.

The gray old man was far from satisfied with the world. The best he had to say about our existence here on earth was caustic: "The glory of our civilization is that it enables us occasionally to live an almost normal life." [25] It was desirable to make the "occasionally" longer and the "almost" more complete!

Sometimes he had apocalyptic visions: "I pondered this night over that curious story which ends in slime. . . . There is no parallelism between the development of science and the development of the mind. Human beings are like apes who have stolen Jupiter's thunder. It's easy to foresee what will happen one of these days: they will kill one another to the last man. At most a dozen will escape, some negroes in the Congo. Then they'll begin the whole story again. The same old story." [26] Yes, there was room, there was need to improve the world.

But if one wanted to improve the world, one had to be exact, more exact than in any other undertaking. Clemenceau had been a physician, a scientist. One had to be a physician and a scientist. The properties of the object determine what can be done with it. One must start with the properties of the existing material, not with imaginary properties. One must construct according to the laws of nature, not according to an imaginary physics.

To Clemenceau's way of thinking, Wilson and his group were doing just that: they were not constructing a better machine for propelling the existing forces; they were constructing a machine for propelling forces better than the existing ones. They were planning improvements not according to eternal human nature, but according to an allegedly changed human nature.

The old man knew well that there was no task more thankless than that of confronting enthusiasts with reality, or inventors with the principles of physics. Enthusiasts resist reality in a fashion of their own. Ten out of a dozen of them become fanatics, and then all hope is lost. In newspaper clippings from all over the world Clemenceau found more and more frequent traces of fanaticism. The salvation of the world, one had to admit, had begun with a promising dose of hatred and lies—and ignorance.

He read descriptions of himself as one who despised and hated democracy, probably because he had stood on its most advanced bastions for fifty years, and certainly not only in fine weather when all the frogs croak in tune.

He saw himself pilloried as a "militarist," as though he had never strangled that "beau général," Boulanger's, dictatorial attempt; as though he had never waged his famous fight for that little Captain Dreyfus against the General Staff and brought it after nine desolate years of slander and intrigue to a brilliant victory; as though he had not always been the bogey of all the gold-laced képis; and as though he were not capable, even today, of ordering the only one among them whom he recognized and whom he himself had made great, the laureled Marshal of the victory, Foch himself, to keep still before the representatives of the world powers and of sending him out of the room as if he were a little secretary.

He saw himself portrayed as an imperialist, after a past in which he had furiously opposed every colonial acquisition of his own country, especially that of Indo-China: "Wanting colonies without colonists! The French don't want to leave Paris, Bordeaux, Marseille. The French don't want to have children. What's this fuss about colonies then?" [27]

A fine new world it will be when the menu begins with such caviar! It will be nicely safe for democracy and will do away with militarism and imperialism very successfully, if Clemenceau was to be held up as its antithesis!

But in all seriousness, what did they all reproach him with? Where was the nub of the whole matter? John Maynard Keynes, the most intelligent representative of the idealists, and a staff member of the British delegation, later summed it up in a book which was read all over the world. Everything that millions of men thought about the peace of Versailles for many years after actually came out of this best-seller with its dry title "The Economic Consequences of the Peace." Whole libraries of later books and mountains of newspaper articles written in the next decades were only variations on Keynes' conclusions.

Well, the indictment was to be that an old man named Clemenceau had lacked faith in the coming, perfect, new world, and that he took advantage of his intellectual superiority over a mediocre and helpless Wilson to sabotage it when it was manifestly close at hand.

Thus there was a certain amount of respect even in the accusation. "Clemenceau was by far the most eminent member of the Council of the Four, and he had taken the measure of his colleagues. He alone both had an idea and had considered it in all its consequences. His age, his character, his wit and his appearance joined to give him objectivity and a defined outline in an environment of confusion. One could not despise Clemenceau or dislike him. . . ."

But! But what? ". . . but only take a different view as
to the nature of civilized man, or indulge, at least, a different hope." [28]

. This summarized in one sentence the whole struggle
which took place in Paris, the whole problem of the peace.
Can the nature of civilized man be any different than he
has shown it to be in every aspect of his history? And if
there is nothing more reliable than "to indulge, at least, a
different hope," are we entitled to mould the fate of mankind exclusively according to this vague hope?

The perfectionists—even the most intelligent among
them—fanatically maintained that this hope was an absolutely secure foundation for the new order. Yet is there not
something to be said for the caution of those who refused
to entrust the fate of the world to the hazard of a mere
hope? According to Keynes: No! They had a "heart of
stone." Old man Clemenceau with his "cynical and almost
impish air" [29] refused to recognize "that we are at the
threshold of a new age." He stuck to his opinion "that
there is nothing very new to learn about this war." [30] He
could not be shaken in his conviction "that essentially the
old order does not change, being based on human nature
which is always the same." [31] What a reprehensible idea!
"The Old World was tough in wickedness."

Wickedness or wisdom, that was the question.

The problem of human nature came up again and again
from the first day of the conference. The 27 points had
been imposed, but when it came to the practical application of any one of them, it was impossible to prevent the
question from arising whether or not they were consistent
with human nature. And though norms, rules and concepts
had been accepted which were the reversal of everything

that had existed before, it still remained to be shown that a similar reversal had also taken place in the character of nations.

What about the nature of the German man? Old man Clemenceau, it must be admitted, was so far gone in cynicism that he refused to believe a syllable of all the promises of a change in the German character. Clemenceau had quite definite opinions about this character.

To him, the Germans remained the nation of which, when he was asked whether it would henceforth leave the world in peace, he answered: "No. I do not believe so." [32]

To him it remained the nation of which he said: "Mark well what I'm telling you: in six months, in a year, five years, ten years, when they like, as they like, the Boches will again invade us." [33]

To him it was still the nation of which he would write: "I was forced to realize that the German revolution was mere window dressing, and that, with the aggressor of 1914 not a whit cured of his insane folly, we should continue without respite to be subjected, in a new setting, to the same attack from the same enemy." [34]

It was still the nation that "joins to its wealth of intellectual culture a fundamental lack of moral culture." [35]

It was still the nation which he would characterize in almost Dantesque terms: "*Cher ami*, the nature of man is to love life. Germany has not this cult. In the German soul, in the art, the philosophy and the literature of her people, there is a lack of understanding of what life really is, of what really constitutes its charm and greatness; and there is a sort of morbid and satanic attraction for death. These people love death. The divinity which they contemplate with fear, but a fear mixed with ecstasy and intoxication,

is death. Where do they get this divinity. I have no idea.
. . . Re-read their poets: death everywhere, death on foot,
death mounted . . . always death! in every pose! in every
costume! They are guided, haunted by this idea. . . . Ponder well what I am telling you about the Boche. The
Boche loves war for its own sake and because at the end
of war, there is slaughter. War is a pact with death. There
the Boche encounters his best friend." [36]

It was the nation to which, in his view, the same thing
applied as to all other nations: "Each of us lives encased
in his own past. Auguste Comte said that we live dead
men's lives, and it is true. We are encased by the past
which holds us in its grip, and spurs us forward to new efforts." [37] Such was the conception of the German character
held by this representative of "wicked cynicism."

But this problem of human nature was perhaps even
more fundamental in its universal application than in its
application to Germany. A League of Nations was to be
founded. How was it to be adapted to the nature of civilized man, so that it could really function?

Shortly after the outbreak of the war, when the idea
emerged that this time peace should be concluded not only
for the contemporary present but forever, it had met with
little opposition.

Humanity had long dreamed of perpetual peace. The
Jews and the Greeks had dreamed of it. Three hundred
years before, "the good King," Henry IV—the same one
who had expressed the wish that on Sunday every Frenchman should have a chicken in his pot—with his Minister,
Cardinal Sully, had outlined a complete plan for a League
of Nations which was to be called the "République Chré-
tienne," and whose principal institution was to be a "Sénat
Européen." In 1795, at the beginning of the Napoleonic

wars, the philosopher Kant wrote a treatise on "Perpetual Peace" based on similar ideas. Napoleon himself had spoken almost lyrically on St. Helena of the future League of Nations. It was an eternal yearning of mankind.

There was a fairly unanimous desire to give it a real try this time. Societies had been formed in all countries to study the question: in America, under Wilson's predecessor, ex-President Taft; in England, under Sir Walter Phillimore; in France under the former Premier, Léon Bourgeois. On June 5, 1917, the French Chamber, by 467 to 52 votes demanded that a League of Nations be constituted after the war. On January 18, 1919, at the opening of the peace conference, there was in fact only one substantial group opposing the principle of a League of Nations: the isolationists in the United States. The majority were now concerned only with the method of realizing it.

But the difficulty lay precisely in the question, how? As is so often the case in great perfectionist movements, the idea in itself was the simplest, and so to speak, the least important part of the program. The real problem was how to carry it out. Anyone who pondered this question for even five minutes found himself confronted by a veritable mountain of difficulties. How much of their sovereignty and their independent power would the different states be willing to surrender to the League? What degree of independent power was needed by the League in order to enforce its decisions against the will of the individual states? There was a disquieting contradiction between what was essential to the independent existence of the states and the powers needed by the League in order to function.

Oddly enough, President Wilson did everything he

could to prevent an early and objective exploration of this whole problem, and particularly a discussion across the borders.

On July 20, 1917, the French government had written to him that France was "particularly impressed with the desire manifested by Mr. Wilson that a society of nations be constituted." It had proposed the creation of a joint committee for the study of the problem.[40] The President rejected this proposal, as "premature," explaining that it was advisable to avoid "new subjects of discussion and perhaps of difference of views."[41]

On September 3, the British government had made the same proposal.[42] Once again the President's attitude was negative. During all the long months when there had been time thoroughly to discuss this subject, nothing had been done.

But Wilson had not only rejected all attempts of the governments to study the problem; he had also used his influence to prevent serious private investigations, particularly international ones.

He had induced Mr. Taft's "League to Enforce Peace" to limit itself to general propaganda, and to refrain from attacking the real question of the organization of the League. On March 20, 1918, he had expressed his pleasure to Colonel House at having "prevented the particular thing I feared, that they would insist upon a discussion now of the constitution of the league of nations."[43] On July 11, 1918, Mr. Taft was surprised and vexed at being told that the President hoped "very sincerely that the League to Enforce Peace will not study the League-Problem in connection with committees abroad and not establish international connections."[44] More than that, when the English Phillimore Committee drew up a plan in writing, Wilson put pressure on the London government to induce the Committee not to publish it.

But if the President was against working out the League of Nations plan through a process of normal, democratic discussion, did he at least think it through in his own, somewhat autocratic mind?

Hardly. In July, 1918, when he received the Phillimore outline from England, he asked Colonel House to work out a better structure. One week later, Colonel House handed him the results of his efforts. These did not satisfy Wilson, either. In August, he worked for two days at putting his own ideas down on a few sheets of paper. They failed to satisfy House, who subjected several of his points to sharp criticism and even used the expression: "an idealistic dream that could not be made practical." [45] The President put his manuscript away in a drawer—and this was the end of his scientific exploration of the problem.

Upon his arrival in Paris, he said that the League of Nations was "the center of the whole program." But when serious discussions began it appeared that he himself had no plan of organization prepared. It became evident that he was "hazy" about the most important part of the whole scheme.

The power that should be given to the League, the amount of physical compulsion it should be able to exert, was obviously the most important point of the program.

All his lifetime the President had a violent aversion for everything that even remotely suggested force and compulsion. Shortly before the war, on June 5, 1914, he had proclaimed his faith that "the new things in the world are the things that are divorced from Force." [46]

The outbreak of the war in Europe had made him less

secure in this faith. In the draft of a speech which he was to make on May 16th, 1916, before Mr. Taft's League, he voiced for the first time the thought that violence was required to combat violence. But at the last moment this idea seemed so repugnant to all his instincts that he crossed it out.

After America's entry into the war, his changed ideas on this subject became more firmly fixed, and later, speaking of the idea of a League of Nations, he went so far as to use the following expression: "Force must be created, force so superior that no nation or combination of nations can challenge or resist it." The new things were no longer to be divorced from Force, but wedded to Force.

But although he spoke these words, his soul was in reality still divided. It was impossible to think through a plan for an effective League without realizing that compulsion would be required not only with regard to the evil-doers, but also with regard to the good. And that was the crux of the matter.

The Utopians contented themselves with vividly picturing the threats with which the evil-doers would be confronted each time they transgressed the law. The entire world would break off relations with them. No one would buy from them or sell to them. Everything would be unleashed against them, armies, navies, swarms of airplanes. Very good. That would suffice. No single state could resist a united world. One need not enlarge on the fate of the evil-doers, provided that the forces for good prepared that fate in common.

The forces for good, that was the Achilles heel. Would they really mete out the deserved punishment to violators of the Covenant? Could we rely on their doing it? How could we make sure that they would?

Murderers are to a certain extent restrained by the existence of the police. Decent citizens are not murderers.

But suppose a decent citizen is walking along a highway and sees murderers armed with knives and revolvers attacking a stranger. What would the ordinary citizen do? Would he plunge into the fight to prevent the murder from being committed? This happens, but not often. The ordinary citizen has responsibilities to his wife and children. In most cases he would rather take to his heels than intervene. We are told that even police have sometimes taken to their heels in such cases. Without a strong authority that would punish them if they deserted a victim, many policemen would run away.

Such is our experience with plain citizens. This is the human nature of decent people. They do not do evil. But they often fail to do good. There is an enormous difference between doing evil and failing to do good!

What is the human nature of ordinary decent nations, those who for the time being and in a given case are ordinary decent nations? History teaches us that their consistent instinct is to take to their heels. The simple fact that almost all the wars of the past were duels proves this. Even in the case of the great conquerors, from Darius and Xerxes to Napoleon, who obviously threatened everyone, it took a long time and many laborious efforts to create coalitions against them. The coalitions were always preceded by wars of the conqueror against one single victim after another, in which those who were not attacked had always shunned participation. Whenever they were free to choose, nations have avoided wars more often than they have waged them.

The League of Nations was a problem of the good nations. As a rule, human nature desires to stay out of trouble, to let well enough alone. The great question was how to prevent this instinct from asserting itself.

There was only one possible solution: the League of Nations must be endowed with coercive powers, it must be constituted an effective supreme authority over its individual members. To a certain, probably a considerable, extent, the free will and the military power of the individual states must be surrendered to the League.

But for this very thing Wilson was not ready!

He did not believe that it would be possible. No country in the world, least of all the United States, would accept it.

He did not even believe that it was desirable. Such a super-state would really be a directorate of the great powers. Just as in a business combine the firm with the greatest capital has the dominating position, so in such a super-state the nation with the greatest capital of power would exert a decisive influence. To Wilson such a directorate was terrifying and sinful.

He had never ceased to be a split personality with regard to this question. He had never ceased to waver in an insoluble dilemma. The League of Nations needed effective power over its members—yet the League of Nations must not have effective power over them.

Wilson escaped into the assumption that morality could be an effective power. The personal morality of the different rulers of the future, the public morality of their diverse nations, the universal morality of civilized mankind,—this must be the force which could, without physical means, compel the good not to fail to do good.

Human nature has never been like that? Perhaps, but now it had changed! Wilson clung to this belief. In April, 1918, he gave it a characteristic formulation.

Mr. Strachey, the editor of the London "Spectator," had warned him in a letter against the idea that a League of Nations based on nothing but promises could stand the test of reality. The good nations and governments, he pointed out, would make themselves scarce at the critical moment. Particularly after this terrible war, they would exploit every loophole and pretext to avoid the obligation of taking up arms in other people's interests.

Wilson replied: "I feel the full weight of your fear. . . . But it seems to me that the effects of this war may just as reasonably be expected to operate in the other direction." [47]

President Wilson's very first experiences in Paris should have shaken him in this expectation. Before taking up the subject of the League of Nations, the Peace Conference discussed the position of Germany's former colonies. And what Wilson had to hear on this occasion from the Australian Prime Minister Hughes would have bruised less weather-proof dreams.

Mr. Hughes was not a representative of cynical Europe, but of the new, the newest world. But even in London, his hostility to Wilson and all his ideas had been almost savage. "I hear that you are a cannibal!" Clemenceau smilingly said when he was introduced to him at the opening of the conference. "The report is grossly exaggerated," the representative of the youngest continent replied modestly.[48]

But it is not exaggeration to say that in the quarrel over the colonies he treated Wilson as a sort of querulous grumbler. According to Lloyd George, Wilson's reaction was "dictatorial and somewhat arrogant." At one point he threw into the Australian's face a heated speech culminating in the sentence: "Mr. Hughes, am I to understand that if the whole civilized world asks Australia to agree . . . Australia is prepared to defy the appeal of the whole civilized world?" The Australian's reply was calm and cutting: "That's about the size of it, President Wilson." [49]

This should have been a good opportunity to reflect on the degree of coercive power possessed by what the President regarded as the morality of civilized mankind.

But he had nothing else to offer, and now the time had come to work out detailed plans.

On January 25th, 1919, the Peace Conference appointed a committee to give concrete form to the idea of a League of Nations. The five great powers and five small ones were represented on it, with President Wilson as chairman. The first session of the committee was fixed for February 3d.

At that moment, a fever of League of Nations projects broke out in Paris. Within the space of three weeks Wilson put no less than three on paper. The South African Smuts, the Englishman Lord Robert Cecil, the British government, the Italian Orlando, all produced schemes.

Then it came out that Lloyd George did not attach any particular importance to expressing his personal opinion on the subject. He suggested that the English and American projects be somehow combined and sent to the committee.

Thereupon the best jurists of both delegations were put to work preparing various combinations of projects. One of them was baptized the Hurst-Miller draft. On February 3d, when Wilson opened the sessions of the committee, he submitted this draft for consideration.

In it, the League of Nations assumed the form of a club constitution, a set of rules governing a club of states.

Each state was to take two sets of vows: one about its behavior within the club, and one about its behavior outside the club.

As a League member, sitting in the Council or in the Assembly, each would vow to help conscientiously in determining whether an act of aggression had been threatened or had taken place anywhere, and to help just as conscientiously in determining the measures to be taken.

Outside the League, in its quality as a state pure and simple, each member would vow conscientiously to comply with the decisions of the League.

Thus, the members were asked only to take vows, little enough. But even these vows were considerably qualified.

The measures decided upon by the Council or the Assembly could not provide for armed intervention. If the good nations could impose their will on the bad only through war, the League was not legally empowered to decide that this be done. The Council or the Assembly could only "recommend" war and each state would be fully free to follow or reject the recommendation. Many errors concerning this point would, in the course of the following decades, arise in the mind of the man in the street. But these were the facts. Each separate "good" nation was entitled to refuse to go to war in order to stop an aggressor. The really binding pledge was limited to measures short of war.

But even the adoption of measures short of war was qualified. In most cases only unanimous decisions were to be binding. One single vote could prevent a decision. Any state which as an independent state wanted to avoid fulfilling its obligation, in most cases needed only to vote against it as a League member.

In brief: to fail to do the right thing, not even a technical breach of the club regulations was in most cases necessary, according to this draft. To fail would be a violation of the spirit of the Covenant, but certainly not of the letter. It is questionable whether, in the futile and undistinguished career of the League, the letter has ever been violated.

Such was the Hurst-Miller draft. It embodied a sincere attempt to achieve two incompatible objectives: to subject the states to a higher will, and to avoid restricting their individual will. No one should be able to say that any "sovereignty" was impaired. Morally everything should be absolute; but materially and legally everything should be almost absolute voluntarism. It was a profession of altruism through thick and thin, of a spirit of eternal cooperation but without any realistic insurance that its promises would be kept.

Mr. Lansing, Wilson's unfortunate Secretary of State, never really informed as to what was going on and whose super-idealistic sensitivity gradually reached a point where he considered both a strong and a weak League of Nations impossible had expressed the following ideas in a memorandum shortly before the conclusion of the armistice: "From the little I know of the President's plan I am sure that it is impracticable. There is in it too much altruistic cooperation. . . . It may be noble thinking, but it is not true thinking. . . . I can see lots of trouble ahead unless impractical enthusiasts and fanatics are suppressed. This is a time when sober thought, caution and common sense should control." [50] Soon he, too, would be branded with the stigma of wickedness, just as Clemenceau, and, in the end, even Colonel House, were stigmatized.

President Wilson handed the committee the draft he

had approved. He moved that it be considered the basis for discussion.

Léon Bourgeois, Clemenceau's representative in the Committee, and his League of Nations specialists asked for the floor. Bourgeois drew his own project out of his briefcase, distributed copies of it, and requested that nothing be decided for twenty-four hours. He explained that he had not studied Wilson's project, that Wilson had not studied his, that the other committee members had not studied either; and that each required some time for reading.

The chairman displayed a certain irritation. With a "bad diplomatic beginning," [51] he opposed adjournment and requested that the committee decide to proceed on the basis of the Hurst-Miller draft. For the first time he set the voting machinery in motion, and with the weight of British-American collaboration behind it, it proved a steam-roller. The Clemenceau-Bourgeois project was filed.

It goes without saying that M. Bourgeois did not give up advocating the ideas of his government.

He moved to modify almost every separate article of the Hurst-Miller draft—and his motions were based on his own project. He was a monotonous, pedantic and verbose speaker, and his continued lectures during the ten days' debate were all the more boring because this conference marked something new in the annals of diplomacy: the leaders of the world no longer understood one another! Among the "big four" and many of the smaller fry, Clemenceau was the only one so international and old-fashioned as to have mastered the two languages of the conference: he had lived for five years in the United States and his wife came from Springfield, Massachusetts.

For the others, interpreters had to translate everything that was said, sentence by sentence, and this was a tiresome procedure. As it was apparent to everyone that M. Bourgeois would be outvoted in the end, his insistence was considered unreasonable.

In retaliation, the other delegates began to treat him more rudely every day. On February 11th, Lord Cecil, a fiery League enthusiast, let himself be carried away by his impatience and suddenly declared "very frankly" that M. Bourgeois should not forget that the whole League of Nations was "practically a present to France." If the French were not satisfied "because more was not offered," he wanted "to warn very frankly" that the alternative was no more and no less than "an alliance between Great Britain and the United States. He asked them, the French, to consider this before they made any final conclusion." [52]

This did not convince Clemenceau that the League of Nations as it was being planned here would have any force. If, even today, right after the war, the League was not based on the serious conviction that peace was indivisible and the need for it universal, if even today, in the minds of the fiery enthusiasts, a difference could be made between the security of one particular state and the security of all, then the bacilli of decay were not just a future danger, they were already there.

What were Clemenceau's own proposals? What did the so-called Bourgeois project contain?

Naturally it embodied a principle which was the exact opposite of Wilson's. Clemenceau's proposal was based on the principle that the morality of the governments and nations, however much they might be esteemed, was not a sufficient guarantee that evil-doers would always be opposed and the necessary good action never be omitted.

It was based on the conviction that the League must either be nothing or endowed with actual power.

Clemenceau was not ashamed of believing in all conscience that in human relations power is indispensable. The police, the courts and the prisons insure the reign of law among the citizens. Ages ago, the establishment of the royal power replaced the thousand endless quarrels between counts, princes, cities and provinces by the reign of law within the national states. It would be impossible to achieve a similar result in the international field without creating a super-power. This power, once created, could be made as invisible as possible. It could grant a large measure of freedom, of voluntarism, tolerance, democracy. But the power had to be there.

The dreamers and visionaries began to invoke Heaven and Hell against this wicked reactionary conviction that, as later expressed by Keynes, "the politics of power are inevitable." [53] But they could not change the *fact* that the politics of power are inevitable. The question was not: power or no power? It was: power in whose hands and for what purpose?

Such was Clemenceau's project. It was far from perfect. It had been accepted as an axiom that the various states should not be merged into one single state with one government. In view of this axiom, there could be no complete solution of the problem of coercing the League members.

But Clemenceau wanted the League to have at least its own power. If the power of the states was not to be abolished, then the League must be given power, too. If such a power were present, strong and ever ready to act, its members would be much more willing to vote for really energetic measures in an emergency.

The tendency to omit doing the required good deed would then be much weaker.

The most striking feature of the Clemenceau-Bourgeois project was that it provided for a separate League executive: a separate League army distributed over all the countries.

It also provided for a separate General Staff, which was to be an essential organ of the League.

This General Staff was to be granted extraordinary powers. It would not only determine the size, training, equipment and recruitment of the League's own army, but would also supervise the existing national armies. And more than that! The League Council, the project proposed, "shall be entitled at any time to require that the member States introduce any alteration into their national system of recruiting which the Staff may report to be necessary." [54]

No one could fail to see that this enabled the League to demand for instance that England or the U.S.A. preserve conscription to a certain extent, so that they, like France, would dispose of an active army, plus trained reserves and officers, plus well equipped arsenals. This in fact was one of the main purposes of the project. One of the most intense French aims was obviously the preservation of strong British and American military forces.

For Clemenceau, the whole problem always inescapably led to the combination: England plus America plus France. This was the center of everything. Whether the form it would take was a League of Nations, or an alliance, or whether it was not formally organized at all did not really matter.

To prevent war was, according to Clemenceau, a matter of superior force, under any circumstances. A German attack could be prevented only by the combined powers of England, France and America. Nothing less would suffice; and nothing could replace any one of them. The essence of the matter was the same, whatever the angle from which it was considered: individual French security, or world peace, or peace through the League of Nations. Everything depended on the rapid and unfailing cooperation of an English and American army with the French.

This was the lesson of the last war. While the fanatics gloated over having exposed Clemenceau's alleged desire for a world dominated by French military power, Clemenceau himself concentrated his efforts on preserving England's and America's military strength. What else could the League be but the united power of the three great democracies? To call it a "directorate of the great powers," or to declare that it was immoral, was just a cliché, pure hypocrisy. Clemenceau believed that the world must be either a directorate of the great powers or anarchy.

But the prospect of a large standing army or the continuation of conscription even in this year 1919, when both countries already had them, did not appeal to the British or American mentality. Equally terrifying to the perfectionist soul was the idea that the League of Nations, the instrument of peace and democracy, should be at bottom a military instrument. President Wilson absolutely refused even to discuss anything of the sort.

He justified his position with practical arguments. Months before, he had labelled as "unfeasible" even the modest idea that the League members should put armies at its disposal in case of need: "The United States would never ratify any treaty which put the force of the U.S.A.

at the disposal of such group or body." [55] To the less modest idea that League members should permanently put
troops at the League's disposal and submit to its military
control even in peacetime, Wilson's opposition was even
stronger. "We must distinguish," he said in the Committee, "between what is possible and what is not. No nation
will consent to control, . . . no nation would accept . . ." [56]

Aside from practical obstacles, he would not have
wished to establish the League on such a basis: "The only
method lies in our having confidence in the good faith of
the nations who belong to the League. . . ." [57] Moreover,
one should not try to get everything at once! Step by step
the things that were lacking today could be added later.
"The Constitution of the League must grow and not be
made." [58]

Thus was the Clemenceau-Bourgeois project crushed
to pieces by the steam-roller.

One cannot help noting that this project was the only
opposition Wilson encountered at the time of the found-
ing of the League. During all the previous years the idealistic prophets had voiced gloomy predictions of certain
sabotage. Toward the end of the war, Lord Cecil, in a
letter to the President, had foreseen the wildest intrigues
and obstructions.[59] Someone else came to see Wilson and
told him how Lloyd George made fun of the League and
how Clemenceau "sneered at it." "Yes," Wilson replied
seriously, "I know that Europe is still governed by the
same reactionary forces which controlled this country until a few years ago. But I am satisfied that if necessary I
can reach the peoples of Europe over the head of their
rulers." [60]

And now his League draft had come up for discussion

and there was not a trace of hostility or sabotage! Everything was accepted without the slightest difficulty, exactly as he had proposed it. There was only one opposition group; and their aim was not to make the League
less efficient, but more efficient.

There was no doubt about that. In September, 1919, a
young journalist named William C. Bullitt who had
played a certain role in Paris and who was far from sym-
pathizing with the "reactionary forces," was called to
testify at a hearing of the Senate Foreign Affairs Committee in Washington. He was questioned about the other
nations' attitude toward the League project—at that time
there were as yet not many published documents. He
answered: "The French were not only anxious for it,
but I believe were anxious greatly to strengthen it.
They desired a League Army to be established immediately. . . ." [61]

What a strange world! The President had believed that
only by the prestige of his presence in Paris and by stak-
ing all his authority would he be able to put through the
League plan against the opposition of the reactionaries.
And now it was apparent that this very plan had encountered only applause from every source but one.

The President was all the more elated when the Committee approved his project and when, on February 14th,
he could submit it to the Peace Conference for final approval. "A definite guarantee of peace," he called it in his
address. "It is a definite guarantee by word against aggression." The plenary session of the Conference voted
the adoption of the project. The President was so convinced that the most important features of the new world
order were now secured that on the same day he left

Paris for a short stay in America. He was to return one
month later.

On hearing the phrase "a definite guarantee by word,"
Clemenceau, the chairman of the conference, could not
suppress a momentary gesture. He pressed his eyes with
his fingertips, encased as ever in his famous gray gloves.
He had correctly performed his duties as chairman. But
he felt as a sensitive actor might feel having to perform
in a bad play. It was an "unsolvable problem" to make a
human code "a living thing without investing it with any
executive power. . . . A parliament of super-parliamentarians without any instrument of authority, that is the
talisman we received." [62] If ever a League of Nations had
been or was possible, this one would surely lead to nothing.

But this alone was not yet a misfortune. It was legitimate to try. But it was important to realize that all this
was only a try.

As far as Germany was concerned, everything must be
done, according to Clemenceau, as though no League of
Nations existed. Guarantees must be created which
would remain in force even if the League collapsed from
sheer powerlessness. These guarantees could not be abandoned or decreased merely because a few persons maintained that a new-born baby of dubious vitality would
grow up into a giant who could protect the world.

The League of Nations was to be superimposed on a
world which was the product of a thousand highly old-
fashioned peace settlements. No one thought of destroying the network of the thousand older settlements
stretched over the five continents. The enthusiasts did not
doubt for a moment that even in a world which was the

product of all these sinful agreements the League would
be a source of blessings.

Well, then, why should it not be such a source if only
one further agreement were added to this world? Why
should the League's blessings come to fruition only if it
were established not after a normal peace settlement, but
instead of it? The whole attempt would not be justified,
if one acted now as though it had already proved itself
successful!

The old man whom these enthusiasts called frivolous
could discover only one frivolity in the Peace Conference,
and it was an unconscious frivolity: the general readiness
to take the haziest uncertainty as a substitute for the most
absolute certainty. What a mad gamble! The result of
four infernal years lay on the table before mankind—and
this whole sum of horror and suffering was to be staked
again on the roulette of fate in one throw of the dice. It
was to be staked on one unreliable number, named
"League of Nations."

"That will even multiply our winnings!" said the gam-
blers. And what if your number does not win? Then you
lose everything! Had anyone ever heard of such a thing?
The old Roman saying that absolute justice could become
absolute oppression came to one's mind. *Summum ius,
summa iniuria.* The maximum of idealism can become the
maximum of frivolity.

Clemenceau made every possible effort to prevent this.
After Wilson's departure he became more insistent every
day. The League of Nations was nothing but a question
mark. Even his modest attempts to make its structure
stronger and more reliable had come to nought. The alternative was: normal "guarantees of another nature" despite the League, "Guarantees on the frontiers." The

struggle around the conditions to be imposed on Germany, for the destruction of German military might, not for a few years but for a long time, not by formulae and unreal institutions but effectively, had begun.

Suddenly the problem of the League came up again. On March 14th President Wilson returned from America. He revealed that he must request two other small changes in the constitution that had been adopted.

Technically, this meant that the entire project had to be re-discussed. The Committee once again began with Article I; M. Bourgeois again presented his motions and again was outvoted. Then Wilson expressed his new requirements.

First, he requested that the voluntary nature of the whole organization should be emphasized by giving to each state the right to resign or secede from the League.

M. Bourgeois objected that such a clause would make the League even less a reality than it already was. Each state would leave whenever it did not like whatever happened, and some day the League would have no members at all.

The President absolutely disagreed. This clause, he explained, would obviously have only academic significance. It was designed to facilitate his task of having the League approved by the United States Senate. No state in the world, he said, would dare or desire actually to resign from the League. The stenographic record noted: "President Wilson said that he did not entertain the smallest fear that any State would take advantage of the proposed clause. Any State which did so would become an outlaw. . . ." [63]

The new clause was adopted.

Secondly, the President moved for the adoption of the

following addition to the original text: "Nothing in this Covenant shall be deemed to affect the validity of . . . regional understandings like the Monroe doctrine."

The French objection to this change was even sharper. The Monroe doctrine, M. Bourgeois pointed out, contained two different principles. First, that European states had no right to intervene in matters concerning the Americas. Second, that the United States should not intervene "in the wars" or in "matters" concerning European powers. What would be the meaning of the new clause then? the French asked. That the League would not have the right to intervene in American problems? That the U.S.A. would not assume any obligation to collaborate in the solution of European problems?

President Wilson declared that the clause really meant nothing at all, that it, too, was designed to make the whole thing more acceptable to the Senate. But how could something without meaning or content win over the Senate? And even if President Wilson attached no meaning to the clause, what meanings might one of his successors discover in it?

Clemenceau's interest in this legalistic discussion was not very great. Any child could see that the two new clauses were further weakening a structure altogether too weak. From Wilson's admission that without these clauses he was "afraid that the Senate would not agree to come in," [64] a beginner could understand that Wilson regarded the chances of having the League accepted in his own country as doubtful.

This was an additional reason for Clemenceau to regard the whole matter with indifference. The real question was no longer the League. Let them make it as they want! The real question now was the "guarantees of another nature."

Since Wilson's return, during the month of March, the discussion of this problem had reached an acute stage. Clashes multiplied. Irritability reached a high pitch. A storm was gathering. On March 29th it suddenly broke. Wilson tried to nullify certain concessions previously granted by his representative, House. Clemenceau "became very much excited." [65] He called the President a pro-German.

"Then if France does not get what she wishes," said Wilson, "she will refuse to act with us? In that event do you wish me to return home?"

He did not say it threateningly, but anxiously. He did not want to return home without achieving success.

"I do not wish you to go home," Clemenceau replied, "but I intend to do so myself." [66]

And the old man walked out.

3: *Watch on the Rhine*

FOR CLEMENCEAU, the destruction of German military power must begin with the amputation of German territory.

These were not Biblical times. To solve the problem of Germany by exterminating part of her population and enslaving the rest was out of the question. What was possible, however, was to deprive the Reich of as much territory as could safely be handed over to other nations. This is one of the most realistic methods of destroying a military power. Loss of territory means a decrease in the very source of power, in the war "potential" of a given nation. It brings about a lasting, irrevocable decrease in manpower and economic capacity.

Methods that decrease the temporary utilization of this potential rather than the potential itself are poor substitutes. Any kind of disarmament, above all, is an "ersatz." No disarmament can be lasting and irrevocable. Disarmament restricts existing weapons and armies, but not the capacity to produce weapons and armies. If the artificial brake is weakened for any reason, the disarmed power can use its still intact potential once again. Napoleon who disarmed Prussia in 1806, learned this lesson in 1813. The French government at the end of World War I did not believe in the possibility of really effective disarmament. Even during the war, as soon as they began to believe in their own eventual victory, they put the diminution of Germany foremost among their war aims.

This implied the support of every demand made by any state for a part of German territory. Clemenceau was ready to grant every claim put forward by Poland, Belgium and Denmark. He rather regretted that no one else wanted a piece of Germany.

But in the West, at the very gates of France, there was a particularly well developed and valuable German region. Alsace-Lorraine, with about two million inhabitants, was part of it. That the Reich would lose these two provinces was a foregone conclusion: the return of Alsace-Lorraine to France was one of Wilson's fourteen points. But the loss of this territory would not in itself seriously diminish the Reich. There was an even larger area which

Clemenceau wanted, not in order to incorporate it into France, but to take it away from Germany. He wanted to amputate from the Reich all the territory on the left bank of the Rhine together with large bridgeheads on the right bank. This would have meant the loss of five and one-half million inhabitants in addition to the six and one-half million that the Reich would lose elsewhere. This territory included a considerable part of German industrial capacity: for instance, about 30% of her metallurgical industries alone. From the Duesseldorf bridgehead, the entire German "armament foundry"—the Ruhr region with Essen, Dortmund and Duisburg—would be within the range of medium artillery. God himself had seen to it that all these plants were situated not in the interior of the Reich, but at its frontiers.

Since 1916 the French had made determined efforts to obtain support for this plan which was their principal war aim. In 1917, Premier Aristide Briand had commissioned his ambassador in London to sound out the British government on this subject. The Secretary of the Foreign Office had not said yes, but he had not said no, either. This lack of opposition was interpreted in Paris as a half-assent.

Two days later an unqualified written assent arrived from Russia. The Petrograd Foreign Minister confirmed that "the Government of the Republic could rely on the support of the Imperial Government." He agreed to the return of Alsace-Lorraine to France. He also agreed to the following: "The rest of the territories situated on the left bank of the Rhine which now form part of the German Empire are to be entirely separated from Germany and freed from all political and economic dependence upon her."[1]

One month later, the Imperial Russian Government was overthrown by the February Revolution. The democratic government that came to power stood by its predecessor's promise. But the Bolsheviks, who seized power in November, 1917, tore up this agreement along with all the other treaties of the preceding governments. They went further. They blasted the criminality of bourgeois diplomacy with fanfares of denunciation and immediately published the agreement concerning the proposed diminution of Germany. It was a bad omen that a number of so-called progressives in all countries at once joined the chorus of indignation from Moscow, and that the British Foreign Secretary felt called upon to declare the innocence of his government before the House of Commons on December 17, 1917: "We have never expressed our approval of it. . . . Never did we desire nor encourage the idea."

But the French did not give up their plan. One year later, as soon as the guns were silent, Clemenceau laid his cards on the table. A few days after the armistice, he and Foch, the two fathers of the Allied victory, the two greatest Frenchmen of their time, indeed, the last two great Frenchmen, arrived in London for a state visit. They were received with an enthusiasm which seemed to belie the British character. Twenty years later Lloyd George would look back with distaste upon this incident. In his Memoirs he calls their reception one such "as I have never seen accorded to any foreign visitor. . . . The intensity of the enthusiasm displayed was beyond anything I ever witnessed." [2] It embarrassed him. He was already preparing to resume the "traditional" British policy of working for the balance of powers. This time it would be a false balance.

Marshal Foch was commissioned to present the first official proposals for the amputation of the Rhineland from the Reich. His main argument in favor of it was that the Rhine was the only safe strategic frontier for France and he submitted a memorandum supporting this thesis. Lloyd George's attitude was rather antipathetic. But the atmosphere of those festive days was such that once again he could not afford to reject the French demand outright.

Before the opening of the peace conference, Foch had prepared a second memorandum. "Henceforth," its main argument ran, "the Rhine must be the Western frontier of the German peoples. Germany must be deprived of all access to it or all military utilization of it, that is to say, of all territorial sovereignty on the left bank of the river." [3]

But what was to be the fate of the amputated region?

The French wanted a small part of it, the Saar Basin, for themselves. They argued that there was no difference between the Saar and Alsace-Lorraine, that the Saar, too, had formerly belonged to France and had been artificially Germanized.

But the Saar Basin was only a small corner of the Rhine zone. All the rest was to be taken away from Germany, but not given to France. One or more republics could be formed from it. The Rhenish state or states would be permitted to adopt any form of government they liked. Only they must no longer form a part of the Reich. In addition, and this was the heart of the plan, they would have to maintain for all time an Anglo-French-American garrison. These Allied regiments would symbolize the durability and the solidity of the separation and of the peace.

The idealistic world saviors who, as Clemenceau had previously noted, began their careers with a generous dose of hatred and lies, did not fail—and were not to fail for the next twenty years—to distort completely the meaning of the Rhineland project. They said at the time of the peace conference and continued to say that the French, greedy for spoils, wanted to swallow up the Rhineland, to bring the poor Rhinelanders under foreign domination and to establish their own military hegemony over the continent.

In his Memoirs, Lloyd George who claimed to belong to these world saviors à posteriori, managed to put forth this interpretation as well as its opposite. In fact, only 27 pages separate one interpretation from the other. On page 264 he says that the French proposals "were not due to a greed of possession. They were prompted by the obsession of France with the fact that in spite of the victory Germany would have a population nearly twice as large as that of France." On page 281, he says that the same proposals were intended to exploit "the best opportunity ever afforded to France of satisfying her age-long ambition for the establishment of French control, not only on the left but on both sides of the Rhine." Among the great figures of our time, Lloyd George will be remembered as one of the most changeable. On almost every subject he has professed almost every opinion.

In this case, what the French really wanted was expressed by Lloyd George No. 1, not Lloyd George No. 2. Marshal Foch's memorandum of January 10th, 1919, had clearly stated the French thesis: "The Rhine, military frontier, without which cannot be maintained the peace aimed at by the coalition, shall not be a territorial benefit for any nation. It is not a question, in fact, of annexing the left bank of the Rhine, of increasing France or Belgium's territory . . . but to hold securely on the Rhine, the common barrier of security necessary to the League of Demo-

cratic Nations. It is not a question of confiding to a single
power the guarding of this common barrier, but to ensure by the moral and material cooperation of all democratic powers, the defense of their existence and of their
future." [4]

André Tardieu, Clemenceau's assistant, had expressed
it even more clearly. In his extensive exposition of France's
aims which remains the most memorable document of the
entire peace conference he wrote, on February 26th, 1919:
"France does not demand the left bank of the Rhine for
herself; she would not know what to do with it. . . ." On
the contrary, she demands a permanent "inter-Allied occupation," as the only adequate "protection, both national
and international." [5]

This French thesis was stated over and over. The nature of the demand was sufficiently eloquent in itself. A
country which wants to annex and dominate a territory
does not insist upon having it occupied, aside from its
own troops, by the troops of two other great powers. On
this point, as on all others, Clemenceau pursued a policy
not of strength, but of weakness. The ultimate purpose
of the Rhineland project was precisely to establish not a
French, but a collective military power. Thus, every German shot across the Rhine would be a shot directed at all
three powers, every German attack upon France would
ipso facto be an attack upon America and England, as
well. Such a situation would insure the maximum security for France.

Clemenceau was the very personification of anti-
isolationism. But his plan for collective security dispensed
with all romanticism and reduced the problem to its
prosaic core: when you say mutual assistance, do you
mean England, plus America, plus France? Do you mean

the unquestioning perpetual readiness of English, plus American, plus French regiments to act? Yes or no?

The disposition of a few regiments of three countries which had countless regiments stationed all over the world: this was the real problem.

After the armistice, the Rhineland, including the bridge-heads on the right bank, had in fact been occupied by Allied troops, but remained a political and administrative unit of the Reich. All that needed to be done was to sever these political and administrative ties and to make the Allied occupation permanent. What were the prospects of carrying out this plan?

No sooner had Clemenceau and Foch left London than Lloyd George showed his hand. As early as December, 1918, he waged war against the idea of occupying the Rhineland, which with his usual unscrupulous exaggeration, he represented as the terroristic occupation of the entire German Reich by hundreds of thousands of English soldiers. "There must not be an army of occupation," he had said, "a large army of occupation, kept in Germany indefinitely in order to hold the country down. That simply means keeping hundreds of thousands of young men from this country occupying Germany, maybe for a generation, maybe for more, withdrawing them from industry. . . . That would be bad business. Besides, it would simply provoke fresh conflicts, and instead of coming to an end of war we should be simply manufacturing fresh wars. . . ." [6]

The argument presented here was to be advanced over and over again for twenty years. Again and again the world was confronted with the choice between good and bad business—whereas in fact the choice was unfortunately that between bad business and worse business. And above all, for twenty years the world was to be obsessed with an axiomatic certainty about what would "simply" provoke fresh wars and what would insure lasting peace, a certainty so axiomatic that arguments to support it were considered superfluous.

No, Lloyd George never bothered to prove his two equations: Germany minus the Rhineland equals war, and Germany plus the Rhineland equals peace. He only asserted them, pulled them out of thin air, and that was all there was to it. But the fact remained that he asserted them. As soon as the peace conference opened, the British delegation showed its completely negative attitude. Under no circumstances must Germany lose more than Alsace-Lorraine in the West. Even the armistice occupation must cease after the signing of the peace treaty, and all the Allied troops must return to their homelands.

Indeed, Lloyd George even invoked the Fourteen Points and the right of self-determination. The "Watch on the Rhine," if maintained by the Allies, he said, would be "a definite and dishonorable betrayal of one of the fundamental principles for which the Allies have professed to fight." [7] It goes without saying that he continued to declare that "any attempt to divide Germany . . . would cause endless frictions and might provoke another war." [8]

In addition to these arguments, there was another insurmountable obstacle to the continued occupation of the Rhineland. It was invoked by Lloyd George's private secretary, Philip Kerr, later to become well-known under the name of Lord Lothian, in his bitter duels with Tardieu. The English nation, said Kerr, would not understand this amputation of German territory and this collective watch on the Rhine. "It is the duty of the British Government," Tardieu growled at him, "to make them understand.

Neither did the British understand the necessity of conscription in 1914." [9] For the next twenty years the different governments would repeatedly take refuge behind
their peoples' alleged inability to understand.

No, there was no way of coming to terms with Lloyd
George's delegation. But what about the Americans?

During the month of Wilson's visit to America Colonel
House served as his representative. Clemenceau dealt
chiefly with him and it must be admitted that House's
ideas did not have the inflexibility of a logarithmic table.
Contact with reality, rather than with abstractions, caused
him to change his mind. Clemenceau was one of these
realities.

A friendship developed between the two men during
those months. The old friendship between Wilson and
Clemenceau was later to die. After the signing of the
Versailles treaty in June, the President, without a word
of explanation, dropped his *alter ego* of so many years'
standing. He was never again to speak to him or see him.
But the new friendship between the sixty-three-year old
Texan and the seventy-eight-year old Vendéen would last
until the older man died ten years later. The Colonel's
obituary essay in honor of Clemenceau begins with the
following words: "In all my experience I have never met
a man who made upon me a more lasting impression." [10]
House's biographer says that his "feelings toward Clemenceau were a mixture of affection and admiration, into
which no suggestion of misunderstanding ever intruded." [11]

The truth is that House began to see the whole situation in a new light. His cables to Wilson on the course of
the Paris conversations soon filled the President with uneasiness: ("Am made a little uneasy.") The President requested that the Rhineland question not be settled in his

absence. "I hope you will not even provisionally consent
to the separation of the Rhenish provinces from Germany
under any arrangement, but will reserve decision on the
whole matter until my arrival." [12]

House followed these instructions. But before receiving
them he had already envisaged ideas which were at least
a partial concession to Clemenceau's conception. On
March 14th, when Wilson disembarked in France, House
reported to him aboard ship. And this was the President's
reaction: "House had compromised on every side, and so
I shall have to start all over again and this time it will be
harder, as he has given the impression that my delegates
are not in sympathy with me. . . ." [13]

2.

Who *was* in sympathy with him? He came before the
world with two declarations which corresponded to two
different meanings of the term "peace." For peace can
either prevail, or it can be concluded; in the first case, it
is a state, in the second an undertaking. Wilson had declarations concerning both the universal, eternal preservation of peace, and the specific conclusion of the present
peace. But in his mind, these two different declarations merged into one, as well as the reactions of the public to them. He thought that the general enthusiasm over
his promise of eternal and universal peace was also an
enthusiasm for his outline of the specific peace with Germany. He regarded himself as the representative of the
wishes of the "peoples" against the "reactionary forces,
which do not represent their own peoples," [14] with refer-
ence to both meanings of the term "peace." He saw himself as embodying the "will of the people, rather than

that of their leaders." [15] He was firmly convinced that he represented "the opinion of mankind," which demanded "an entirely new course of action." [16]

What mankind did he have in mind? How could he believe that "the people" wanted his kind of settlement with Germany? He was the victim of a hallucination.

Even if the peoples had shared his ideas, it is questionable whether that fact would have been a valid argument in their favor. Those who ascribe a mystic clarity of vision to the people are becoming increasingly rare. More than ever before have we reason to think that democracy is relatively the most desirable form of social organization. But less than ever before have we reason to think that democracy is desirable because it is an automatic expression of collective wisdom. Democracy is desirable for entirely different reasons: because it alone tends to secure the indispensable minimum of freedom, rights and dignity for the individual. But as far as wisdom is concerned, the will of the people is as confused and questionable a basis for decision as any other. The best democrat is not the man who denies this, but the man who knows it and remains a democrat notwithstanding.

It was obviously false to assume that in the matter of settlements with Germany, Wilson had the peoples behind him. In 1918 and 1919, the peoples' feelings were still quite normal.

Peoples manifest their opinions in parliamentary elections. Conversely, to a certain extent, parliaments manifest the opinion of the people. A democrat cannot dispute this.

Before the opening of the peace conference, Clemenceau submitted his program to the Chamber of Deputies, which gave him a vote of confidence by a majority of four-fifths. One year later, in November, 1919, there were new general elections in France. These "horison bleu" elections inflicted a crushing defeat on all parties and groups that were suspected of even the smallest amount of tenderness toward Germany.

In England, the elections had taken place one year earlier, in December, 1918, soon after the armistice: the "khaki elections." Every time the question of the settlement with Germany was brought up in the campaign, the Lloyd George government proclaimed anti-Wilsonian principles: "Hang the Kaiser!" or "Squeeze the orange until the pips squeak!" were its slogans. As a result, the Wilson-tinged opposition barely managed to win one sixth of the seats. Even its leaders failed of re-election: the Germanophile Liberals, Sir John Simon and Walter Runciman, and the labor leaders Ramsay MacDonald, Philip Snowden and Arthur Henderson.

One day they would all return to Parliament. But in 1919 it was not they who represented the will of the people. The English people, like the French, failed to reveal any mood in their democratic elections which could have justified Wilson in regarding his ideas as "the opinion of mankind." At a later date, Lloyd George wrote correctly: "It is worthy of note that all vocal criticism of the Peace Delegations in France, as well as in England . . . were anxious to make the terms harsher and more stern than those which the Peace Council ultimately presented to Germany. During the progress of the Peace Conference there was not a voice raised in favor of moderation . . ." [17]

But was Wilson perhaps entitled to identify the opinion of America with his own? A few years later, Clemenceau wrote: "President Wilson did not understand Europe . . . and his knowledge even of America was insufficient."

It is possible that all sorts of factors contributed to the President's defeat in the congressional election of 1918. But the fact remains that both he and his opponents had emphasized the problems of the peace in their campaigns. He himself had interpreted the elections as a mandate upon the question: would he be able to conclude the peace according to his principles? In violation of all American traditions, he, the chief of state, had issued a proclamation in which he represented a Republican victory as almost a national catastrophe.

The opposition took up the fight on the same grounds. Its most prominent leader was Senator Henry Cabot Lodge, the powerful chairman of the Senate Committee on Foreign Relations. Mr. Lodge concentrated his fire on the forthcoming settlement with Germany. He formulated his point of view as follows: "No peace that satisfies Germany in any degree can ever satisfy us!" [18]

The least we can say is that the majority of the American people had shown no enthusiasm for Wilson's ideas of the peace. Some commentators recognized no bounds in expressing this fact. For instance, a Boston newspaper addressing itself directly to Europe voiced the hope that the European statesmen had "learned what the majority in the United States think . . . and preferred to be in harmony with the majority than with a repudiated President." [19]

After the elections and after the armistice, Mr. Lodge, the spokesman of the new majority, became more and more articulate. His misfortune, and perhaps the misfortune of the world, was the complexity of his mind. His

contemporaries were unable—and even future generations will long be unable—to understand its disparate
elements.

With horror and aversion Wilson saw in him above all
the adversary of the League of Nations. He was that. He
was against universal obligations of a compulsory nature.
He was an isolationist when confronted with the word
"must." Thus, he would ultimately be the cause of America's not joining a League of Nations containing even as
few "musts" as Wilson's. In so far as it can be maintained
that this structure, decadent in its very essence, could
have been made more vital by America's adherence to it
—which is questionable, extremely questionable!—the
chief responsibility for its failure will rest upon Mr. Lodge.
He will be regarded for decades as having played the part
of chief opponent of the League.

But Mr. Lodge had a complicated mind. Though he was
against universal, compulsory obligations, he was by no
means against obligations freely agreed to and independ-
ently assumed. He did not advocate the kind of isolationism that developed later and that entailed much more
serious consequences than America's failure to join the
League. He did not advocate the undifferentiated, color-
less passepartout isolationism which tries to escape not
only juridical, but also factual ties, which tries to eliminate not only every "I must," but also every "I will." He
even advocated the very opposite of such isolationism.
With regard, for instance, to the definite, contemporary
task of making a settlement with Germany, he was against
every kind of isolationism, even purely moral isolationism.
The liquidation of the war, he asserted, must be carried
out in unbreakable union with the Allies.

On December 21st, 1918, even before the opening of

the peace conference, he developed all these ideas in a Senate speech which today, after a quarter of a century, is still convincing. Like Clemenceau, he insisted that a harsh settlement with Germany was an inescapable necessity, if the peace of mankind was to be preserved. "The attempt to form now a league of nations—and I mean an effective league, with power to enforce its decrees, no other is worth discussing!—can tend in this moment only to embarrass the peace that we ought to make at once with Germany." [20] He demanded that practical conditions be imposed upon Germany, "which will make it impossible for her to break out again upon the world with a war of conquest." He demanded "heavy indemnities for the ruin she has wrought." He warned against illusions about the new Reich: "It is well to remember that Germany did not change her nature when her Kaiser ran away to Holland." [21]

He particularly stressed the relations between the Allies. The armistice had barely been concluded, the guns had barely ceased firing, when the Senator spoke of attempts to split America away from her Allies: "Do not forget that German propaganda with this object in view is as active and poisonous today as it has ever been. The people here and in the allied countries who were favorable to Germany are again busy in the effort to part the allies and the United States from each other, and their efforts find expression . . . in the thousand and one forms with which we have been painfully familiar in the years just past." [22]

The man who was later to be condemned as an arch-reactionary, as the negator of brotherhood among nations, emphatically advocated brotherhood among the Allies: "To encourage or even to permit any serious dif-

ferences to arise between the United States and Great
Britain, or France, or Italy, or Belgium, would be a world
calamity of the worst kind." It would be "deplorable in
the highest degree" "abominable" "inconceivable" "un-
thinkable." [23] What he meant was clear. The President's
camp-followers were manifesting a rapidly growing tendency to give the most ardent support to the idea of a
strong world-union for all time to come, while splitting
and disrupting with equal ardor on the most important
practical questions of the moment. Promises of marriage
were freely given but the future idyll was being inaugurated with the school-master's rod. For twenty years all
sorts of dreamers, zealots and self-appointed moral tutors
of the universe were to devote themselves, in an unholy
alliance with German propagandists, to creating sharpening and exasperating these very differences between the
Allies, which the Senator had in advance called a "world
calamity."

But despite all the evidence to the contrary, the President remained firm in his belief that he alone had been
anointed with the oil of knowledge about the peoples'
deepest desires.

On March 14th, when upon his return from America
he declared: "I shall have to start all over again," the
"dark period" began. The peace conference degenerated
into conflicts, scenes, insults, crises and bitter public quarrels among the allies of yesterday. That March 28th when
Clemenceau called the President a pro-German and
walked out of the conference room, was one of the quieter
days. There were worse days before May 7th, when the
text of the treaty was finally presented to the Germans.
And even worse days were to follow before June 28th,
when the Germans signed it in the Hall of Mirrors.

The end of the conference was marked by successive or simultaneous convulsive scenes between Wilson and each of the Allies. The President was wounded and tormented, filled with sorrow and anger. But he never gave up his conviction that he expressed the peoples' will. On the contrary, during that very last phase of the conference he erected the most peculiar monument to his faith in his own popularity. On the memorable day of April 24th, he barked into the face of Orlando, the Italian Premier: "I know the Italian people better than you do!" [24]

And this, "on the strength of a three-day visit to Italy," [25] Winston Churchill commented later in "The Aftermath."

He uttered these words during the tragic and scurrilous quarrel over the little town of Fiume which had formerly belonged to the Austro-Hungarian empire. The town was indisputably Italian; but the country all around it was indisputably Slavonic. To whom should it belong? To Italy? Or to the newly born state of Yugoslavia?

The Italians demanded Fiume with energy, with bitterness, and finally, in the words of State Secretary Lansing, with "desperation" and "in fever heat." But the attitude of the perfectionists toward Italy, democratic, Allied Italy, was one of irreconcilable hostility. In 1915, by the secret treaty of London, she had obtained the guarantees of certain territorial gains in the event of an Allied victory. In the eyes of the idealists, she had thereby perpetrated several mortal sins. It was a mortal sin to conclude a secret treaty. It was a mortal sin to seek advantages from a victorious war. It was a mortal sin to covet territory containing a part of the strategic Tyrolian highlands with 150,000 German-speaking inhabitants. 150,000 Germans under the cruel yoke of a democratic

foreign power! What was even more horrifying was that
the treaty was valid, that it had to be carried out.

The very fact that it had to be carried out aroused a
kind of vendetta among the zealots. If they had to respect
the secret treaty of London, so much the worse. But that
treaty had not promised Fiume to the Italians. Therefore
they must not get it no matter what happened. We'll show
them! said the idealists, we'll teach them a lesson! The
progressives were possessed by a fanatical desire to hu-
miliate Italy on the issue of Fiume. The "nationality principle" demanded the handing over of the little Italian
town to Yugoslavia. The "right to self-determination"
made it possible to make a caricature of a sovereign state
out of it. And the latter was actually done. Anything
rather than give it to Italy.

Even the American delegation was divided on this
question. House and half the experts ended up by rejecting the complex implications of Wilson's hair-splitting
theoretical justice. They began to support the Italian
claims all but openly. But to their despair, Fiume, as one
of the dissident experts said, was a fetish for Wilson. No,
no! Never would he hand it over to the Italians!

What was the result of this stubborn refusal? In less
than four years this fetishistic "no" would contribute deci-
sively to spreading a plague over the earth, and would be
flouted in spite of everything.

The plague was to be Fascism in search of its first adherents. Nothing would bring as much publicity, fun,
glory, emotion and patriotic prestige to the d'Annunzio-
Mussolini gang as their various adventures in Fiume.
Nothing would compromise Italian democracy more than
the sad part it was condemned to play in this affair. One

might say that, just as Romulus and Remus grew strong
on the milk of the wolf, so d'Annunzio and Mussolini grew
strong on the milk of Fiume.

Fascism destroyed Italian democracy in October, 1922.
The calendar moved forward to January, 1924. And then,
vanity of vanities, Fiume came under Italian domination
after all. The Yugoslavs themselves ceded it to her by
direct agreement. They themselves impiously gave up the
prize that the Holy War had won for the Slavs. During the
same week, on the other side of the Atlantic, a broken
man named Woodrow Wilson died.

During those critical days of the Paris conference, Signor Orlando was, of course, unable to foretell the exact
course of coming events. All he could say was that the
Italian people would regard the loss of Fiume as a spite-
ful provocation and that incalculable resentment would
result.

But Wilson had countered these observations with his:
"I know the Italian people better than you do." And he
actually meant what he said.

The Italian Premier "went straight to the railway station and departed in voluble indignation to Rome." [26] His
Foreign Minister followed him. Italy, the fourth of the
Big Four, had now left the peace conference. She would
return only to sign the treaty in the creation of which she
took no further part. But all this could be explained by the
President's firm conviction that he was the representative
of the peoples. He called upon the "reserve capital" of his
heart which during the entire war had given him a mystic
confidence in himself: "Yes, I know that Europe is still
governed by the same reactionary forces. . . . But I am
satisfied that if necessary I can reach the people of Europe over the heads of their rulers." [27]

This time he thought it was necessary. The moment had come. Signor Orlando left the conference a few hours after Wilson had carried out his cherished idea and done something which, even in Lansing's reserved language, was "most unusual." He had published "a statement on Fiume and Italy's unjustifiable claim to the city, which was in fact if not in purpose an appeal to the Italian people over the head of their government. The statement . . . issued at a time when feeling in Italy was at fever heat, caused a tremendous sensation. Doubtless President Wilson . . . believed that his popularity was sufficient to change the tide of public sentiment and that the Italian people would perceive the injustice of the claim because he declared that it was unjust. . . ." [28]

Signor Orlando, from the train which carried him to Rome, replied just as publicly with a bitter counter-manifesto. He said: "The step of making a direct appeal to the different peoples certainly is an innovation in international intercourse. . . . However, if such appeals are to be considered as being addressed to the peoples outside of the Governments that represent them, I should say almost in opposition to their Governments, it is a great source of regret for me to remember that this procedure, which, up to now, has been used only against enemy Governments, is today for the first time being used against a Government which has been, and has tried to be always a loyal friend . . ." [29] It was just such a spectacle as Senator Lodge had, months in advance, called "deplorable," and, in very truth, a "world calamity."

But what about the Italian people? They were the only guinea pigs upon whom Wilson had ever tested his theory that he was the divinely ordained representative of humanity. And the results cruelly refuted him. The Italian people revealed their complete agreement with their own government and their complete hostility to Wilson. "From one end of Italy to the other the statement was received with a storm of abuse and insult." That, Lansing thought, "must have opened the President's eyes to the fact which had not been hidden from others, that his popularity with the peoples of Europe was rapidly receding, and that they were no longer willing to accept his declarations as the utterances of the inspired leader of international thought, the apostle of the new gospel." [30]

But can any man see through an illusion which is the very essence of his spiritual life? The President was never to have any doubts about his own role.

During the struggles and crises aroused by the French Rhineland project, his inspiration told him not only that the separation of these provinces from the Reich contravened the will of mankind as a whole, but also that it violated the will of the Rhinelanders themselves. This conviction was so unshakable that he never felt impelled to learn their wishes by consulting them. Tardieu's proposals and House's informal ideas on the subject implied that the Rhinelanders should be consulted. But the President did not need to let the Rhinelanders determine their own fate in order to know in advance what the principle of self-determination required in this case. The Rhinelanders, he had decided, wished to remain with the Reich.

Did they really wish it? Would an independent Rhenish republic have been contrary to their desires? To assume this was consistent with a stereotyped interpretation of the principle of nationality. But the will of a people is far from being constant and rigid; it is not determined by mechanical applications of abstract principles. The will of a people is more flexible, more opportunistic than the dogmatists think.

After the armistice, the Rhinelanders assumed that their provinces would be separated from the Reich almost as a matter of course. The writer of these lines can testify to this fact, because at that time he lived there. The only group who really opposed the separation plan were the extreme "Reds"—and not for reasons of patriotism. They refused to be separated from a country which they thought was only one small step away from the triumph of socialism. Among the other strata of the population, feelings about the project ranged from stolid indifference to joyful approval. Why not seize this opportunity to pass from the camp of the defeated to that of the conquerors? *Ubi bene, ibi patria.* That the project would be carried out, no one doubted. The shrewdest of the leaders had begun to prepare for it, in particular the Catholic Party; the "Center," which was socially and politically dominant in the Rhineland.

On December 4th, 1918, two official "Center" mass meetings took place in Cologne: most respectable assemblies. The most important speakers were the old party leader Trimborn and a supreme court justice named Wilhelm Marx, who was soon to achieve the highest distinctions in the new Reich. He was to be Reich Chancellor twice, and would just miss winning the Presidency. In 1925 he lost the election to Fieldmarshal Hindenburg by only a small margin. Yes, these meetings in Cologne, one month after the armistice, were respectable meetings. And both of them passed resolutions to proclaim an "independent Rhenish-Westphalian Republic," because they believed that "the Rhine provinces and Westphalia possessed sufficient political, cultural and economic power to form a state." [31]

These resolutions were carefully draped in a declaration that the "independent Rhenish-Westphalian Republic" should form a part of the "German Reich." When the most substantial leaders of an important province take a step which technically borders on high treason, they do not forget formally to insure themselves against any eventuality. But their meaning was clear. The leading party of the Rhineland had taken an official stand for separation.

Their move was thus interpreted by the Workers' Council of Cologne which angrily exposed this "clerical-capitalistic manoeuvre to bring the Western German provinces under the protection of the occupying powers at the danger of their severance from the Reich." [32] It was interpreted in the same sense by the Berlin government which put everything in motion to counteract it, and by the general public in the Rhineland, which expected an imminent separation from the Reich any moment.

Soon afterwards this trend underwent a change. After the peace conference in Paris began its sessions, the bewildering news trickled through that separation was far from certain. It became known that the Americans and the English were against it. From that moment on, people naturally readjusted themselves to the new situation. The leaders beat a retreat. Suddenly they ceased to speak even of a Rhenish Republic which would "form a part of the Reich." The "people" who had so obviously been preparing themselves for separation from the Reich, began to prepare themselves for staying within it. The respectable period of Rhenish separatism came to an end.

During the subsequent months and years, the commanders of the French army of occupation made new attempts to induce the Rhinelanders to engineer a separatist revolution in spite of everything and everybody, a revolution which would have had to be carried through against the decision of the peace conference, against the will of London and Washington, against the authority of Berlin, against the power of the American and English troops of occupation. Needless to say the leaders and the majority of the people refused to engage in these adventures. To make a revolution in favorable circumstances is one thing; to undertake a completely hopeless revolution is another. Only obscure dupes and a small mob could now be recruited for the cause of separation.

But this does not mean that the Rhinelanders would not have been perfectly satisfied with a respectable, legal separation. If the Allied Powers had wanted to carry it through, the Rhinelanders would have wanted it also. It is not true that Wilson respected the will of the Rhinelanders; in actual fact, the Rhinelanders accepted his will.

We must harbor no illusions on this score. The will of a people is only too often as flexible as putty, particularly in periods of great change, the only periods when questions of this kind arise. The very assumption that a people or a section of a people always have a definite will is one of the many questionable aspects of the principle of self-determination. It is not, however, the most important objection to it. This is the fact that the merger or separation of nations often involves interests too universal to be decided by the will or whim of one people, one region, one province, town or street. Where shall we place the limit upon the principle of self-determination? Some day the world will understand that the principle of self-determination can be invoked both for devilish and heavenly undertakings, and that there is no principle so strong, infallible and universal that it can be applied in every case everywhere.

The statesman may steer his course toward some philosophical goal and in that case we must desire that his goal be freedom, dignity and justice for the individual. But there are no maps upon which the paths toward that goal are exactly charted. There are no universally applicable principles. Statecraft is not an exact science; it is an art.

It was not textbooks on counterpoint and harmony that enabled Beethoven to write his symphonies. On the contrary, he broke at will the few poor technical principles the contemporary textbooks set forth; observance of rules has not the slightest part in the immortality of a single bar of his music.

The same is true of statecraft. No principle has the same effect when applied under different conditions, and the difference in its effect under different circumstances can be as great as the difference between virtue and vice. The principle of nationalities applied mechanically would destroy the oldest and most successful state on earth, Switzerland. With the principle of self-determination one can bury Lincoln and the whole U.S.A. True statecraft is compounded of imagination, historical instinct and savoir-faire, of sensitivity, flexibility and vision. The notion that a few rigid principles can regulate our immensely complicated multinational world with its tremendous range of customs and economic conditions, is one of the fundamental errors of perfectionism.

While the French saw the Rhineland project in the light of a lofty and universal aim, that of the preservation of a practical peace, President Wilson saw it in the light of his precious principles. Thus, it was totally unacceptable to him. He rejected the idea that an independent Rhenish state should be established. He rejected the idea of an occupation, collective or individual, permanent or temporary, under any name or title. For the sake of his ideals, he took the same position that Lloyd George supported for entirely different reasons: a falsely conceived balance of power, in the name of which he wanted to strengthen Germany, and weaken France.

But Wilson was not content to reject the project himself. In the last analysis, the French could act alone. They could obtain the security they craved by the exercise of brute force, and no one could stop them. The problem was to induce them to give up the Rhineland project of their own free will. Lloyd George's tactical genius gave birth to the idea of offering them an English-American alliance in its place: the famous "pact of guarantee," which solemnly promised America's and England's intervention with all their armed might, if Germany committed an unprovoked attack against her Western neighbors.

This seemed like an enormous concession. When Lloyd George made his proposal, and Wilson seconded it, Clemenceau was stunned for a moment. World history seemed to be suddenly reversing itself. For more than a hundred years, America, behind the rampart of her seas, had eschewed all "entangling alliances." From across the channel, the English had always considered it the essence of wisdom never to pledge themselves in advance to participate in any war. Only a short time ago, during the conversations about the League of Nations, both England and America had categorically affirmed these policies. They had insisted that the Covenant be drafted in such a manner that no member be compelled to take military action against an aggressor. And now, were these two

great powers suddenly ready to throw overboard the tradition of centuries? Did they believe that they could win
approval of their parliaments for such a guarantee? Was
France now to obtain by a separate treaty what England
and America had insisted upon leaving out of the Covenant?

During Wilson's trip to America, Clemenceau had become the last casualty of the war, or the first of the new
world; a zealot had shot him in the chest. He was not yet
completely recovered. Every time he spoke he was seized
with an agonizing fit of coughing. Now he asked: "For
how long do you offer this guarantee?"

"For three years," answered Lloyd George.

The spell was broken. Lloyd George was still Lloyd
George.

3.

Clemenceau went home. For two days he consulted
with his Ministers.

The answer to the offer of a three-year guarantee was
obvious: "It is not within the next few months that Germany will again become dangerous, it is later." [33] But the
problem was not limited to the question of the duration
of the guarantee. Even if the guarantee were to be extended, it would still be inadequate.

A promise is not the same thing as a fact. The museums
of history are filled from cellar to attic with unfulfilled
promises. Promises given by one nation to another, and
nations cannot be sued for breach of promise in any court,
are broken not only because of bad faith, but also because
of the wonderful gift humans have for considering right
and just whatever satisfies their needs of the moment. A

government and a people who do not wish to abide by a treaty will always find convincing reasons for saying: It was not meant that way. When, for instance, is an attack "unprovoked?" There are always loopholes even in the most solemn pledges.

A promise to send troops cannot be compared with the actual presence of troops. It is a bad bargain to exchange an actual advantage or one that can become actual in the immediate future for a promise. For twenty years the history of the Allied peace with Germany was to consist in the exchange of one *fait accompli* after another for one unkept promise after another. Lloyd George's offer of a guarantee was only the first of a long line. But it was not hard to grasp its meaning.

And that was not all. There were more important considerations. An army of occupation can fight at once, on the spot. The promise of help under certain conditions can materialize in the form of troops only after a considerable time has elapsed. The French were tormented by their awareness of their future weakness. They doubted whether in a future war they would be able to resist until the promised help arrived. Behind closed doors they made no secret of their dark apprehensions. At every opportunity they insisted on the fact that the speed with which England and America would materially intervene was a question of "the utmost gravity." It was impossible to rely on a repetition of the miracle of the Marne in 1914.

From year to year it was less and less probable that this miracle would be repeated. There was a real possibility that the next time France would be crushed by the first blow. All collective security, says Tardieu in his book, must begin with collective measures which will prevent "French territory being overrun in a few days." [34]

Overrun in a few days! During the catastrophic days of 1940, no one had any right to say that warnings had been lacking. When the post-war world was being molded, the Frenchmen of 1919 strove to convince the world that in the future they would inevitably be relatively weaker than Germany, that they would be unable, all by themselves, or almost by themselves, to act once again as the breakwater of democracy against a Germany twice as large as themselves. They even went further: they described exactly what the conquences would be if France were overrun in a few days. Thus, in his book, Tardieu explains clearly that these consequences would not be limited to the loss of France's fighting power. In addition to that, America and England would scarcely have a base left from which their own forces could operate: "Should there not remain enough French ports for the overseas armies to debark their troops and war supplies, should there not remain enough French territory for them to concentrate and operate from their bases, the overseas democracies would be debarred from waging a continental war against any power seeking to dominate the Continent. They would be deprived of their nearest and most natural battleground. Nothing would be left to them but naval and economic warfare. . . ." [35]

The moment would come, a difficult moment, when there would be a demand in America and England for the creation of their own front against Germany, and when battlegrounds from which to operate could not be found. All this was foretold in 1919.

Decidedly, the pact of guarantee could not be considered equivalent to the collective watch on "the frontier of freedom," [36] as Wilson himself had called the Rhine.

Clemenceau declared that such a guarantee, naturally

for a longer period than three years, could take the place of the separation of the Rhine provinces from the Reich, but not of an army of occupation. He accepted it as a substitute for the further amputation of territory from the Reich and for all the opportunities that an independent Rhenish state would have presented. He refused it as a substitute for the common Allied occupation of the Rhine provinces. For that he refused any substitute. And he detailed the "minimum guarantees" which, according to him, were "indispensable," [37] in addition to the pact.

He demanded thirty years of collective occupation, until 1950, when the generation which had passed through the mill of Imperial conscription and through the war would be dead or gray-headed or useless.

He demanded that the occupation be extended or resumed if the Reich ever at any time violated the stipulations of the peace treaty.

He demanded the demilitarization of a zone 50 kilometres wide on the right bank of the Rhine, and an absolute promise that any military activity in that no-man's-land would be dealt with as with an act of war.

He demanded that a collective control commission see to it not only that Germany disarmed now but also that she did not rearm later. For Lloyd George had insisted with ominous stubbornness that the disarmament control be only temporary. Once Germany had reduced her army according to the provisions of the treaty—it had been proposed that she do this within three months after its ratification—she should be trusted. Later, the only recourse against her rearmament would be a complaint before the League of Nations. The burden of proof would rest on the plaintiff who, lacking any organs of control, would not be able to supply any proof.

Clemenceau's program unleashed a Homeric struggle which lasted six weeks. Other problems were utilized as weapons in it: the amount of reparations to be paid which was finally left out of the treaty and decided on later; the French claim to the Saar, settled in a similar manner by postponing the final decision for fifteen years and leaving it to a plebiscite. And innumerable other factors played their part. But they were all secondary. The peace settlement was in essence the prevention of a new German outbreak. The main issue was the means of prevention which the French leaders of 1919 considered necessary.

In this struggle both parties displayed all their powers and brands of persuasion, used all the means of pressure available. The relations between Clemenceau and Lloyd George were sometimes reduced to a mutual bombardment of memoranda written in a tone of brutal mockery. Throughout, there sat across from a rigid, grippe-ridden Wilson a still wounded Clemenceau, shaken by recurring coughing fits, who declared upon one occasion that he had enough of this hopeless situation and would resign, which implied that he would be followed by an ultra-intransigent successor. A few days later Wilson provoked a sensation by requesting his ship, the "George Washington," to come to Cherbourg, which implied that he was going home.

At one point Foch, the general of their victory, came to the three chiefs of state, adjured them "with all his strength"[38] to accept Clemenceau's proposals. A little later he refused to obey them. The conference had decided to extend a temporary invitation to the German peace delegation to come to Paris. According to the protocol, the invitation was to be transmitted by the chief of the armistice commission. Foch refused to transmit the order to General Nudant.

During this struggle, Wilson gave in to some extent. His only purpose, his only obsession, was to do the right thing. When an argument convinced him—which was rare—he was capable of yielding; he discovered that the old, seemingly cynical maxim: *"Paris vaut bien une messe!"* (Paris is well worth a mass) was as valid for him as for all other politicians and statesmen. He wanted to establish the League of Nations, and to prevent a desperate individual action by the French. To a certain extent, he had to compromise. Even a statesman who is 100% idealist—whether his idealism is glorious or absurd—cannot follow his ideals 100%.

But every inch he conceded had to be wrested from him by dint of the utmost eloquence, fanaticism and diplomacy. Every nuance of each new formulation was a new battle. And there came a moment when the limit of his concessions was reached.

On that day, he accepted to a limited degree the idea of a collective military occupation of the frontier of freedom. The Rhineland was divided into three zones. The collective occupation was to last five, ten and fifteen years, until 1925, 1930 and 1935, in each of the three zones respectively.

And after that? What about the really dangerous years?

The occupation might be extended in the two following situations:

If something went wrong on the side of the Allies—if, for instance, the "pact of guarantee" was not ratified—which actually came to pass. Then the collective occupation might be extended. But this was only a weak "might." [39] Or, if Germany violated the peace treaty. And in that case, not only would the extension of the occupation be permissible but any other measure considered necessary. None of the three signatory powers would be obliged to intervene, but each confirmed the right of the others to do what they considered necessary. That was something.

It was not the most important thing by far. The most important thing to the French in 1919 was the continuance of collective military action. Wilson was not ready to guarantee this beyond five to fifteen years. But at least France was to receive the solemn consent of her Allies to the extension of the watch on the Rhine against a treaty-breaking Germany. In addition she was to receive their consent to take "in general such other measures" as she herself "might determine to be necessary in the circumstance." [40]

In addition, Wilson accepted the demilitarization of a fifty kilometer zone along the right bank of the Rhine. But he rejected the permanent control of German armaments. There was to be a standing inspection committee only until disarmament was completed; no standing committee was to prevent rearmament. Only the League of Nations, acting on a complaint, would have the right to institute a solemn "inquiry." [41]

And this was Journey's end. The President could not be brought to concede anything beyond this maximum. Lloyd George, ill-humored even at these concessions, said: "I accept." The French had to declare themselves for acceptance,—or what was the alternative?

The commander-in-chief, with bitterness and eloquence, declared himself against the treaty. The President of the Republic silently opposed it.

Clemenceau resolved to accept it. The alternative was no better.

He did not deceive himself. At the very time when Germany might again be dangerous, the collective watch on the Rhine would cease. France would be alone. Through the mist of questionable institutions and equivocal or conditional promises, he clearly discerned a future in which almost the entire military burden of resistance against Germany would again be borne by all-too-weak France. It was impossible to embellish that picture. The main pillar of the entire peace structure had collapsed. Clemenceau was bitter, too. He knew that Wilson and Lloyd George had made a mess of things.

They had freely acknowledged that in her relations with Germany France must not be regarded as a separate entity, but as an advanced bastion of world civilization. In their outline of the pact of guarantee they had declared they were "fully persuaded" that a German war against France must be regarded as a matter concerning all the peoples, "involving inevitably and directly the states of Europe and indirectly, as experience has unfortunately and amply demonstrated, the world at large." [42]

But what did this logically imply? An advanced bastion of civilization is also the military responsibility of civilization. Those who want to take advantage of the bastion must contribute to maintaining its garrison, an adequate garrison, ready to fight at the right time. Wilson and Lloyd George shied away from this logical implication. With regard to this attitude of theirs, Clemenceau's feelings were no more indulgent or approving than Foch's. He, too, was filled with that resentment which from now on was to be rampant throughout France, and which was to prove fatal for the world: resentment at having been ruthlessly prevented by his own allies from reaping the only worthwhile fruit of victory: security against future aggression; resentment at being ruthlessly abandoned to bear the all-too brutal risks of an all-too delicate experiment. Clemenceau passed harsh judgment upon the competence of those world leaders who, he realized, had stored up future miseries for their own countries.

But could anything be done about it? If they refused to give France serious military cooperation of their own free will, they could not be compelled to give it. What could be done?

Take independent action, advised Foch. But that will be permitted us by the treaty itself, replied Clemenceau. If Germany violates any of the terms, we shall be able to act on our own, with the approval of the other signatories. Why not obtain this approval before taking any action? Why do something which today may offend our Allies, while later it will have their explicit approval?

Because there is all the difference in the world between now and later, Foch answered. Because we do not know what will happen in five, ten or fifteen years. Because we do not know in what moral and material situation we may be then. Because we do not know in what situation our Allies will be, and whether or not, despite the pact of guarantee, hell will not break loose against us. Because we do not know in what situation Germany will be. Today we can act. We do not know whether we will be able to act later.

This was true. But it was only part of the truth. Many different truths can apply to one set of circumstances. No one can say whether the course of history would have been smoother if Foch's judgment, instead of Clemen-

ceau's, had been followed. Clemenceau's opinion was:
should France, in five or fifteen years, be so low materially
or morally as to be unwilling or unable to do what the
treaty permitted her to do, she was lost in any case. Then
America and England would be the only remaining reserves of France. And in that case it would be fatal for
her if she alienated them in advance.

The various points of view crystallized, the camps
formed. It was not a choice between good and evil, but
a choice between two evils. On April 25th, when the text
of the treaty was submitted to the Council of Ministers,
Foch was invited once again to state his reasons for rejecting it. The mood of the meeting was tragic. Many
wavered. It was felt that the ultimate decision depended
upon Poincaré. If the President of the Republic threw
his entire weight on the side of Foch, then the Council
would probably vote for rejection of the peace terms.

Foch made an impassioned plea, bringing forward all
his most potent arguments. General Maxime Weygand,
his adjutant, sat behind him taking notes. When the marshal finished, Poincaré remained silent. Clemenceau said:
"The Council will deliberate. *Monsieur le Maréchal* may
retire." Foch left the room.

The Ministers did not deliberate. They listened to a
speech by Clemenceau "which made their hearts heavy."
They saw the old man turn his face to Poincaré and conclude: *"Monsieur le Président,* you are much younger
than I. In fifteen years I shall no longer be with you.
In fifteen years, the Germans will not have carried out
all the stipulations of the treaty. And in fifteen years, if
you do me the honor of visiting my grave, I know you
will be able to say to me: 'We are on the Rhine, and we
shall remain there.' " [43]

The President of the Republic, "amidst general emotion," failed to support Foch. He put the matter to a vote. The treaty was unanimously accepted.

Twelve days later, the document was submitted to the Germans. They protested and made counter-proposals. There were crises, the negotiations took six weeks. Then they signed it. The statesmen of twenty-seven countries took their copies and went home with them to face their parliaments. The campaign for ratification of the treaty began.

Clemenceau went before the Chamber and spoke: "You must not think that after such an upheaval we are going to bring you pages of writing, which one after the other will be voted, approved and ratified by the Chambers and that that will be the end of it and we shall be able to go home, all wrongs in process of being righted, all precautions taken against a new outbreak and everybody able to say: Verily we have a paper! Now we can sleep!

"No, nothing of the kind! The life of mankind is not a life of sleep. Life is but a struggle. That struggle you can never get rid of. . . . When a treaty comes before you, a treaty which has I don't know how many hundred clauses dealing with all kinds of questions, you must not forget that these so complex provisions will be of worth only by what you do. The Treaty will be what you make it. . . .

"If you go to peace resolutely, as our men went to war, you will give it life; you will make it worth while, you will make it of service to mankind. If you waste time . . . you will have given our country a thing of death instead of a thing of life." [44]

4.

What was the structure of the political universe according to this settlement?

High above all other agencies, omnipotent as a divinity, a new earthly Providence was to rule the world: the League of Nations.

The substance of the League was compounded of hypotheses: the hypothesis that from now on human nature would be the opposite of what it had always been; the hypothesis that peoples and governments would be willing and ready to face small discomforts, great sacrifices and apocalyptic terrors for the sake of justice and the peace of other peoples; the hypothesis that the solemn promise to behave in an ethical fashion would be kept, without any need to resort to compulsion, purely out of understanding and morality.

If these hypotheses were confirmed by reality, then the new earthly Providence would indeed be established. Then it would be all-powerful. Then, verily, he had come who was to establish the Reign of Law:

With righteousness shall he judge the poor,
And reprove with equity for the meek of the earth;
And he shall smite the earth with the rod of his mouth,
And with the breath of his lips shall he slay the wicked.
And righteousness shall be the girdle of his loins,
And faithfulness the girdle of his reins.
The wolf also shall dwell with the lamb,
And the leopard shall lie down with the kid;
And the calf and the young lion and the fatling together;

And a little child shall lead them.
And the cow and the bear shall feed;
Their young ones shall lie down together;
And the lion shall eat straw like the ox.
And the suckling child shall play on the hole of the asp,
And the weaned child shall put his hand on the cocka-
trice's den.
They shall not hurt nor destroy
In all my holy mountain:
For the earth shall be full of the knowledge of the Lord,
As the waters cover the sea.[45]

Could these hypotheses prove true? The United States
denied it in advance. It did not join the League. It refused to make a solemn promise to behave in accordance
with the tenets of the Covenant. Did the keeping of such
a promise depend on a decision of the Senate in 1919?
Would America have kept it if the Senate in 1919 had
ratified the League Covenant? Would the other powers
who ratified the Versailles treaty keep their promise?
Whether the new earthly Providence would become a
reality or a chimera depended exclusively upon the truth
of the hypothesis that from now on men and nations and
politicians and governments would be something they
had never been before.

If the new Providence became a reality, the conditions
it would have to control were of little moment. Any kind
of condition was then controlled. If it proved a chimera,
the kind of conditions which were to be controlled would,
on the contrary, matter a great deal. If no superior power
controlled the world, everything would depend on how
stable conditions were in themselves.

The general situation created by the settlement was

more precarious than any previous one. Relying upon the
new Providence, things were organized in such a manner
that if it failed, there would be no order, but only something approximating anarchy. Conditions of the utmost
instability had been created artificially and violently.
There had been nothing like it in any of the general peace
settlements of the past. The outraged statesmen and diplomats of the "old order" could turn in their graves.

The principles of self-determination and nationality
had smashed the old balance.

The German colossus had formerly been limited to the
south and east by two great powers. Both of them, Russia and Austria-Hungary, had been strong and capable of
defending themselves, had been centers of political gravity in their own right. The whole region was thus in a
state of balance. This time a region had been created of
the most obvious incongruity: instead of two great powers, there were now nine medium, small and miniature
states. Counting the indirect neighbors, of these nine,
there were fourteen or fifteen states, none of which was
capable of defending itself to any serious extent against
a Reich that rebuilt its strength. Such a Reich could, almost without risks, oppress, blackmail, brutalize and
threaten each of them in turn. Every local disturbance
would almost inevitably assume international proportions.

The principle of nationality, as well as various principles of "impartial justice," created crippled territories,
crippled constitutions and crippled state machines.

The Poles, instead of receiving a self-contained territory, with a few Germans in it, received, on strictly eth-
nographic grounds, the bizarre corridor through Germany which did not make the Germans any happier and

tormented the Poles like a disease. There were the little states of Danzig, the Saar, Memel, all of them to be ruled by the League, all of them to hang in thin air, if the League failed. That most important business of preventing Germany's rearmament was to be carried out by the League, and it could not carry out that task if it proved a chimera. There were the reparations payments, the amount of which had not been fixed yet, although, for the sake of justice or God knows what, it had already been limited in a manner which nipped in the bud any practical method of settling them. Among these limitations was the philanthropic rule forbidding any plan of payment which extended over thirty years. And to protect Germany from "exploitation," there was the rule that the marks paid over as reparations must never be reinvested in Germany. By these two rules alone the reparations were in fact made impossible, even while they were imposed in principle. Thus, dominating the whole picture, were all sorts of distorted, anemic, unrealistic, incubator products. And underlying each of them: crises without end.

All the Wilsonian principles taken together had everywhere prevented the establishment of firm and definite socio-economic conditions. Everywhere, there were provisional arrangements; almost every year delays expired or instalments were due; plebiscites, evacuations and non-evacuations filled the calendar of unsettled business up until 1935. Even world disarmament—which, successful or not, was sure to turn the whole world upside down—was officially put on the agenda for the coming years. The spirit of the settlements was anti-static, conducive to change. One of the basic conceptions of the Covenant was that not everything must remain as it was, that every-

thing could be changed. A world which had barely escaped the most frightful convulsions was entitled to a comfortable convalescence in an atmosphere of stability. But
as long as the world is not perfect, the spirit of reform will
have nothing to do with stability. The treaty provided for
and favored mechanisms of constant world improvement
—constant struggle against evil—constant changes in the
existing order. Instead of barring it, the way was opened
wide for some allegedly advantageous permanent transformation. It was wide open for "revisionism" and "dy-
namism" of an unexpected kind, which began rapidly to
creep into every crevice and to undermine the foundations of Europe.

If an omnipotent Providence floated over these uncertain conditions, dominating and controlling them, it did
not matter. But if its omnipotence was only a delusion,
these conditions would create a dangerous jungle in
which all sorts of monsters and horrors threatened to
grow.

But even this jungle could have been kept under control. If the new Providence failed in its task, there was
still the old method of power. The united power of the
three democracies was gigantic. The military three-power
alliance of the "pact of guarantee," the collective military
watch on the Rhine, were absolutely sufficient to maintain the new order by force. But the common watch on
the Rhine was limited to a few unimportant years. The
pact of guarantee never became a reality. The American
Senate did not reject it: it never even discussed it or
voted upon it. It evaporated into nothingness, without
leaving a trace, and the united power of the three democracies had no other instrument. Only the power of
France remained.

This power was quite extensive. Used at the right time, and in the right manner, adequately, preventatively and brutally, it could achieve the desired results. But this demanded that France be constantly ready to lead the "dangerous life." It demanded a strong will unimpeded by scruples, clear-sightedness without illusions, never-failing alertness and resolution—and absolute indifference and ruthlessness toward all advice and pressure, toward all opinions and consequences.

If France proved incapable of such an attitude or if miracles of transformation did not occur in England and America in time, then the jungle created by the settlement would in fact be controlled by no power at all. Then it was absolutely certain—and those who sensed it knew it, while those who did not know it, did not sense it either —that after the necessary lapse of time, the monsters and horrors would emerge out of this jungle. Then, the peace, this peace of principles, of the "ought," instead of the "is," this unprecedented peace which "misread and disregarded political experience in the maelstrom of abstract thought," was doomed to collapse in a total disaster.

Three years passed, only three years. In 1922, eighty-three-year old Clemenceau, now a private citizen, returned from a voyage to India, made for the purpose of study. He looked around and shuddered. His faithful chronicler, Jean Martet, received a black letter from him: "We are marching toward a catastrophe so complete that I find it impossible to see any way out of it. . . . Among us I see only the lowest kind of ambition and a lapse into total apathy." [46]

4: *Early Appeasements*

ADMIRAL VON REUTER who had given the order was treated by the English with respect.

They could have treated him and his officers according to the military penal code. He was in an English port, subject to English military control, and what he had done amounted to mutiny against this control. From the moment he entered Scapa Flow with the remnant of the German fleet which he was to turn over to the conquerors, his ships could be considered Allied property.

But the English were impressed by his action. On June 21st, 1919, one week before the signing of the peace treaty, when the unprecedented news came over the wires that this entire fleet had scuttled itself, the nation of seafarers par excellence reacted in a characteristic manner: they were more moved by the seaman's drama than resentful of their loss, and the defiance of their authority.

Eleven battleships, five battlecruisers, five cruisers, forty-eight destroyers—an armada more powerful than had ever been sunk in any single naval battle—rested in the watery grave of Scapa Flow. The admiral had plotted the whole thing with his officers; the crews had not been initiated into the secret. At the appointed moment, the officers had gone down into the holds of their ships and let the water in. The ships that were to be handed over to the English were sunk under their very noses. From the military point of view, the action had a kind of gloomy poetry about it. The English saw it in the light of the chivalry and romance of the sea, although it cost them a fleet. They bared their heads before this deed of valor. Without causing any further complications, they sent the admiral and his colleagues to an officers' prison camp. After the ratification of the treaty they sent them home along with all the other prisoners.

Yet their act was Germany's first revolt against the peace settlement. And this revolt was not for the purpose of saving Germany a loss. Its only purpose was to inflict a loss upon the old enemy. Stripped of military romanticism, it revealed an uncompromisingly hostile frame of mind and unshaken self-confidence.

The fact that this hostility and self-confidence were revealed by the officers' corps had special significance. The German officers' corps was never comparable to that of any other country. It had always been more than a professional group, and even more than a social "caste," with its own style and prestige, and its own, mostly unwritten, privileges.

Of all the organized groups in Germany, the officers' corps indisputably had the greatest number of efficient people. As far as first-rate individuals were concerned, many Germans were superior to the average officer. But as an organized collectivity, the officers' corps was superior to all others. No class, no economic group, no party or trade union, taken as a whole, had as high a level of ability.

The leaders of the corps, the Prussian general staff, that Mecca of all the pilgrims of the military career, was an admirable institution as a military machine, a mixture of scientific research institute, university, cloister and pontifi-

cate. Considerable demands were made upon this top
stratum of the hierarchy and great talents were trained.
Those under them, down to the lowest army officer, were
educated and selected according to standards as rigid as
those prevailing in the highest body. They all had to
study a great deal, for decades on end. Their intellectual
standards were impressive. A strict homogeneous mentality was achieved.

Under the Empire, this corps had no political life of its
own, it did not need one. Politics was the business of the
supreme officer, the monarch. And his collaborators were
Ministers and aides who had been officers themselves,
and who as civilians, like all other retired officers, still
belonged to the officers' corps. For the German political
chiefs, this corps was the supreme reserve of power, although it played no part in politics.

Now the Kaiser was gone. The Republic had come, and
with it, the defeat. The officers' corps saw its world col-
lapsing. Its very existence was threatened. If the army
was really reduced to 100,000 men, what would become
of the hundreds of thousands of officers? What would
become for instance, of a colonel, with twenty years of
service and study and aspirations behind him, who had
hoped to achieve a generalship, and who had enjoyed the
knowledge that he belonged to a class with particular
prestige and privileges? Would he now be compelled to
sink into the gray, unimportant and hopeless existence of
a wine merchant, cigarette vendor, insurance agent or
bank clerk? The threat was made acute by the possibility
that even in the new diminutive Reichswehr the imperial
officers might be replaced by new Republican officers.
Everything was at stake. Resistance was necessary.

Not only their personal interests were threatened.

There were also their class feelings and instincts to be considered. What kind of state was now being erected? What kind of undignified system would this be, in which one served not under chiefs from the respectable classes, who themselves had served and studied, but under saddlers, metal workers, trade union secretaries, artisans, lawyers, men of letters, journalists, bohemians and fools who had risen from nothing, knew nothing and poured dirt over everything sacred! What kind of lamentable Germany had been made out of the proud and mighty Germany of before? A Germany without magnificence or glory or respect, a Germany which was not the highest, but the lowest among the nations, a Germany to which it was no longer a distinction, but a disgrace, to belong. Could matters remain this way? Impossible! Resist these changes!

And in order to resist, in order to prevent the new order from establishing itself, the officers' corps went into politics. It did this not only with power and arms behind it, but also as that organized group in Germany which, as a whole, had the greatest number of first-rate people. It attacked this new field with furious enthusiasm and, as in everything else it had ever undertaken, it succeeded brilliantly.

In these days of the collapse and the defeat, the officers realized that they must at all costs get into the new institutions that were being formed. Their first objective, as the chief of the general staff, Groener, explained to Fieldmarshal Hindenburg at the very moment of the collapse, was: to see to it that a "supreme government power is formed with the participation of the supreme army command," rather than without it. Later, as a witness in court, he was to declare: "I was the first to advise the Fieldmarshal not to fight the revolution with arms. . . . I told him that the supreme command should ally itself with the Social Democratic party, because at that time there was no other party with sufficient influence over the people, and particularly over the masses, to restore government power in conjunction with the high command. . . . The old Fieldmarshal naturally disliked this solution, but as he had enough insight to disregard his personal prejudices, he declared himself willing. . . ."[1]

The two highest army officers had thus assumed control over the new executive power.

The new Defense Minister—his title was no longer War Minister—was a certain Gustav Noske. He was an uncouth and common character, closer to the lowest type of German factory worker than the highest. The officers assigned to his Ministry began at once to cajole, tame and direct him.

To begin with, the officers closed their own ranks defying the waves of transition which threatened to engulf them. They prevented every attempt to "republicanize the Reichswehr." Under the pretext that the Reichswehr must remain "free of politics," they prevented the investigation of their soldiers' republican reliability. They made the most of having suppressed a few weak local pro-Soviet rebellions, exploiting their role of "savior" to the best advantage. They founded all sorts of "free corps" and other irregular formations, in which all the troops were former Reichswehr officers. There were a "Luetzow Free Corps," a "Loewenstein Free Corps," an "Iron Division," an "Ehrhardt Brigade." They flaunted mysterious badges of all kinds, preferably the swastika cross. They sang songs against the Republic, the Jews and the "November criminals" of which no one knew the origin. Ev-

erywhere in the Reich, in fact, even on Polish and Russian
territory, their formations were active, fighting pointless
skirmishes, defending ill-defined objectives. They stubbornly and successfully resisted all attempts to disband
these irregular organizations. They were equally stubborn and successful in delaying the demobilization of
their regular formations and command posts.

They did more than that. They deliberately and me-
thodically expanded from the military to the political
sphere. They managed their own demobilization in such
a manner that the largest possible number of their retired
members went into politically useful positions: Reich and
provincial government offices, municipal administrations,
the police, political parties, societies, or newspapers. The
reduction of the astronomical war budget was compen-
sated for by the huge funds allocated to the demobilization; and the officer corps' entry into politics was facili-
tated by abundant finances. Next they created numerous
semi-military private organizations which paraded as
"civilian militia," and armed and trained them. They built
up various propaganda machines behind all sorts of
fronts, they hired spies and orators, one of them, a subal-
tern and obscure character in Munich, one Adolf Hitler
who hung around barracks, canteens and inns, receiving
his orders and his money from a captain in the Bavarian
War Ministry. They also began to subsidize newspapers,
to publish pamphlets, to finance meetings and societies,
to split and unify "movements," to encourage and coordi-
nate, from outside and inside, all sorts of parties, unions
and leagues, from student clubs to industrial organizations, from veterans' societies to peasant cooperatives.

There was no firm with an address called: "The Officers' Corps." There was nothing official, nothing tangible about its activities. There were simply a large number of individual officers who, seemingly on their own initiative, cautiously and under cover, were doing all sorts of seemingly disconnected things. Acting more publicly, there were many retired officers, who considered themselves on leave rather than retired, and numerous organizations of retired officers.

In fact, however, all of these groups and individuals formed a single unit. It would be hard to maintain that they had a central direction. The two high ranking officers who had, only the day before, politically ruled Germany still played a great part. There was General Ludendorff who had fled to Sweden in November but who was now back in Germany and whose aide was Colonel Bauer, a political expert. Though the influence of these men was great, they were not officially the directors of the officers' corps. Yet the corps acted as a unit. All the seemingly isolated actions of its members served the same purpose. And because of its really superior brilliance, the officers' corps soon became the pole around which all related forces and tendencies crystallized.

At the time of the conclusion of the peace, these forces and tendencies were growing everywhere, rallying and pushing ahead. They rapidly won over all those groups and classes which to any extent felt "superior" to the rest. They agitated against the enemy within: democracy and the republic; they agitated against the enemy outside: the victors in the war. They agitated against both with hundreds of special arguments which were born every day amidst a world in ruins. Their favorite one was that Germany, the magnificent Germany of yesterday, had in fact won the war, but, at the last minute, had been treacherously "stabbed in the back" and felled by the republican and socialist "November criminals."

But they did not limit themselves to this agitation. They went on a propaganda offensive among various strategic social groups. More and more, teachers began to expand their doctrines. More and more, judges and lower magistrates began to hand down decisions in accordance with their ideas. More and more, positions became closed to partisans of the new regime. The forces grouped around the officers' corps penetrated into every pore of the social organism and began to manifest themselves openly. Even the naked eye could see that this corps, now politically active, was the motive, planning and coordinating force, as well as the main bulwark of the nationalist movement. The German naval officers' act of defiance in scuttling the fleet was a symptom of far-reaching significance, to which the obvious romantic-poetic interpretation did not do justice.

But English public opinion willingly accepted such an interpretation. Even the government was pleased by this expression of the pride of the German officers. Such pride was useful, if Germany was to be a bulwark against Russia and an instrument for maintaining the balance of power against France. And, at any rate, the German people and the German government were not responsible for this act. There was no reason for attacking them. Moreover, it would have been unpleasant to have to attack them at the very moment when their representatives were coming home with the signed peace treaty. The value of the treaty depended chiefly on the value of the Germans' signature. To question their integrity would have been equivalent to questioning the achievement of the Allied statesmen. All unpleasantness must be avoided! Let us rather stress the very significant steps which justify confidence in the Germans and their government! Had not the National Assembly of the new Republic just completed that imposing democratic monument, the new Reich constitution? Was it not symbolic that the place chosen to promulgate it was not militaristic Berlin, but Goethe's Weimar? Was not this charter written by Professor Hugo Preuss the ultimate in democratic perfection, distilled from the best elements of all existing constitutions, with exquisite new improvements taken from the treasury of scientific abstractions? Were not the spirit, the ethics and the approach of this Weimar Constitution surprisingly similar to Professor Wilson's in his twenty-seven articles? Let us look forward to the future with optimism. Faith in success is the only soil on which success can thrive.

Optimism prevailed in Germany, too; but optimism of a different sort. The incredible ease with which the officers had carried off the scuttling of the fleet filled the really important political cliques with assurance. From now on, their hope of rapidly undermining the settlement by dint of spite and defiance could base itself on a concrete fact. The real leaders of Germany began to prepare for a test.

Their opportunity came soon; and it directly concerned the officers' corps. It was the proposed handing over of the so-called "war criminals."

The peace treaty provided for two kinds of personal justice. Article 227 called for the trial of Wilhelm II, "formerly German Emperor." He was to be tried for all the "supreme offences against international morality and the sanctity of treaties," [2] which he had committed as head of the government and supreme commander of the army. Article 228 called for the trial of a number of unnamed "persons accused of having committed acts in violation of the laws and customs of war." [3]

The proposed trial of Wilhelm II had aroused serious juridical objections. He could easily be tried, if the Allies could lay their hands on him, for all the acts falling under the provisions of the penal codes of the countries in which they had been committed. He could be held responsible for all the robbery and assault and murder and similar offenses which could be traced to his initiative. But on the basis of what laws or by-laws could he be tried for the acts arising from his position of supreme authority, above all for the unleashing of the war itself?

The jurists found this problem unsolvable, for one of the fundamental rules of all jurisprudence is: nothing is punishable that has not been forbidden by a law. And where, in 1914, was there a law forbidding the unleashing of a war? No human code had ever provided for the punishment of the greatest of all crimes against mankind; today there is no such law. There are laws against those who set a house on fire or murder another man; but no code provides penalties for burning whole cities and provinces or killing millions of men. The jurists of 1919 could find no legal basis for action against the sovereign who had unleashed a world disaster. And as no steps were taken to remedy this lack, the question will continue to be unsolvable for jurists of the future.

But the moral sentiments of the world of 1919 were unmoved by the helplessness of the jurists. In the words of Lord Curzon speaking before the British Cabinet: "Public opinion will not willingly consent to let this arch-criminal escape by a final act of cowardice. The supreme

and colossal nature of his crime seems to call for some
supreme and unprecedented condemnation." [4] And Lloyd
George himself said: "I do not think it is sufficient punishment for this man that he should get away with twenty
millions of money . . . I think he ought to stand trial." [5]

The juridical difficulties were finally circumvented by
the adoption of an "As Though" solution. In so far as the
trial was to deal with ultimate political responsibilities, it
would be juridical "only in its form, not as regards the
substance." [6] It was to be a moral trial in the form of a
legal trial. After this distinction had been made, all delegations to the peace conference were satisfied, and an article providing for the trial of the Kaiser was written into
the treaty.

But the German democracy opposed even this mild
attempt to proceed against the ex-monarch. They had already resolved to acquit the German Reich, including the
Kaiser, of all blame for starting the war. A powerful well-
endowed organization "for the struggle against the war
guilt lie" had already been formed. It flooded Germany
and the rest of the world with systematic propaganda.
The projected trial of the Kaiser which would involve the
publication of secret documents and the hearing of witnesses, was a serious threat which caused great concern
in Germany.

Much noise was made over this issue. The flower of
German jurisprudence demonstrated the juridical impos-
sibility of the trial in special memoranda. The German
delegation to Versailles protested vigorously. They proposed demagogically that a court be constituted to try all
the leaders of all the nations. In the German National Assembly, the plan to try the Kaiser was termed "a piece of
impudence which we reject." [7] Von Bethmann-Hollweg,

who had been Chancellor at the outbreak of the war made a beautiful and serious gesture: he wrote to Clemenceau, declaring that he alone was constitutionally responsible and offered, not without risk, to stand trial in place of the Kaiser. And Fieldmarshal Hindenburg aped the former chancellor by writing a similar letter not to the enemy camp, but to Herr Ebert in Berlin, a gesture which was less dangerous. He took this opportunity to resign from his command, which had ceased to be a pleasure anyway, and to retire to private life.

But the agitation against trying the Kaiser was purely theoretical. The culprit was in Holland. Nothing could be demanded of Germany in his case. The Reich government could neither do anything about him nor refuse to do anything. The question concerned only the Allies and Holland. In the end, the Hague government refused to extradite Wilhelm II, invoking the right of political asylum. The article in the treaty concerning the Kaiser thus became a dead letter without Germany's taking any steps against it.

The position of the other "war criminals" was quite different. They were in Germany, the German government had promised that it would hand them over to the Allies. It had pledged itself in writing to do so.

The "war criminals" were persons who fell under the ordinary penal law, who had given orders and committed acts which were not permitted by the recognized military law code, and who, as a result, could be treated as ordinary criminals. They had mistreated prisoners and given orders to mistreat them, plundered or given orders to plunder, deported civilians to Germany for compulsory labor, and committed all kinds of other brutalities. "Perhaps our demand for their extradition is a departure from the practices and traditions of earlier settlements," the Allies replied to the German protests. "But why not initiate such a departure?" The Allies and Associated Powers indeed consider that the trial and punishment of those proved most responsible for the crimes and inhuman acts committed in connection with the war of aggression is inseparable from the establishment of that reign of law among nations which is the agreed object of the peace to set up." [8]

Indeed, there was no plausible ground for not proceeding with these trials. It was an excellent idea to avenge the excessive bestialities of a war for the first time in history, so that the memory of the penalty would survive and check any attempt at imitation. A nation and a government which had dedicated themselves to the "spirit of Weimar" had no reason to fight against punishing those responsible for bestialities.

But the officers' corps had good reason to fight the idea. In February, 1920, the first lists of "war criminals" were to be presented to the Reich government, and they contained the names of 900 officers of all ranks, from lieutenants to generals and admirals, including Fieldmarshal von Hindenburg and ex-Crown Prince Wilhelm. Because the officers expected the indictments to spare nobody, their agitation against the projected trials had been strong even before the signing of the treaty. Later they went beyond all bounds, demanding the rejection of the entire treaty because of that single extradition article. As no effective argument could be brought forward against the punishment of those guilty of bestialities, the officers concentrated on the question of "honor." Count Westarp, the leader of the Prussian monarchists, issued a manifesto against "this humiliation, the like of which had never be-

fore been inflicted upon a civilized nation." [9] General von
Luettwitz, the new chief of the army command, issued a
proclamation to the troops stating that the article "was
incompatible with the honor of the Reichswehr and the
Fatherland." [10] And the Berlin government was so strongly
influenced by this campaign that its last struggles in Paris
before the signing of the treaty revolved exclusively
around this point.

But the treaty was finally signed, and the list of those
indicted was soon to be presented. Now, after the encouraging incident of the scuttling of the fleet, the Germans decided to make the trials a test of how far the victors would go in breaking resistance to the treaty.

They unleashed a campaign of unprecedented violence
in Germany and abroad. They tried to whip up the indignation of the German people. But above all they tried to
arouse the disquieting feeling abroad that the German
people had reached the point of boiling indignation. The
world must believe that a revolution—a real revolution!
—would sweep the German government out of office if it
dared to carry out the dishonorable deliveries. And the
attempt to carry them out would fail. Every one of the
60 million Germans would protect and hide the "war
criminals." Not one of them would be caught. Horrible
social convulsions would ensue, but no practical results
would be gained.

The campaign strove deliberately to inspire three emotions: fear before the incalculable consequences of an attempt to deliver the war criminals; hopelessness concerning the practicability of the whole undertaking; pity for
the tortured German people. This combination was destined gradually to destroy the whole peace treaty. To
arouse fear in the impressionable, resignation in the "real-

ists," and pity in the humanitarians turned the trick over and over. Now it was being tested for the first time.

At home and abroad the campaign was carried out with a shrewd strategy. It produced remarkable results. Five former army commanders published instructions to the threatened culprits on how to behave should it come to the worst: "We believe that it is not against the honor of a German officer to fly from the authorities of the German government or the Allies. In no case must we give ourselves up of our own free will." [11] Hindenburg wrote to Marshal Foch a dramatic letter appealing to his "sense of military honor." [12] Prince Heinrich of Prussia, the Kaiser's brother, appealed to his nephew, George V of England.

And while Rightists appealed to Rightists, Leftists appealed to Leftists. German democrats, pacifists and Socialists adjured their foreign friends not to create an unbearable situation for the German democracy over this really secondary issue. Their appeal was received with sympathy and more than sympathy. The Leftists of all kinds in the Allied countries were then about to sink into one of their most tragic errors. They were just beginning to discover that "everything had been different than they thought." With regard to the war, they suddenly discovered the mote in their own eye and began to overlook the beam in their neighbor's. They considered it their most important task to unmask the alleged war guilt and war crimes of their own "ruling classes." The extremists among them went almost so far as to acquit Germany of all culpability and charge their own countries with responsibility for the conflict. "For us to play the part of judges would be grotesque!" they said.

In November, 1919, the ground seemed sufficiently

broken to enable the German government itself to enter
the arena. It notified the Allied governments that the "entire German nation, regardless of class and political differences," felt the proposed trials to be incompatible with
its "honor and dignity." It was impossible to fulfil the
pledge that had been signed. "The officials who would
have to hand over their own countrymen would refuse to
do it. . . . The government would be powerless to deal
with such an attitude. . . ." Moreover, if the government
gave orders to carry out the delivery, it would "unleash
such a storm of indignation that it would find itself in an
extremely difficult position with regard to the country,
parliament and the Reichswehr. . . ." [13] It intimated that
on this point the peace treaty would have to be revised. A
few weeks later, toward the beginning of 1920, it indicated more concretely what these revisions must be. They
were only a detail, really nothing but a detail: The German Reich itself would institute proceedings to punish
the bestialities. The German Supreme Court would try
the accused.

Did anyone cast doubts on the impartiality of the Supreme Court at Leipzig? Was it not universally recognized as one of the strongholds of justice? Was it not one
of the loftiest, most respected juridical authorities in the
world? Were not its judges most enlightened legal minds,
had not their purity and integrity in the service of justice
been tested over and over again?

The German Supreme Court instead of foreign courts!
The trial of the accused in Germany instead of their delivery to the Allies—this was only a small, almost a micro-
scopic change, but what blessed consequences it would
bring in its train! The German people's honor and dignity
would remain intact. The verdict on the bestialities, if it

came from their own court, would have an incomparably deeper and more far-reaching effect than if it came from a foreign court. And the other terms of the peace treaty would be carried out in a completely different, a much clearer atmosphere, if the victors proved by this gesture that they, too, were ready to make concessions.

Meantime, in France, the Rightists were refractory. During that week, the two Chambers of Parliament met to elect a new President of the Republic. The *bloc national* refused to vote for Clemenceau, the "père de la victoire," because they felt that the peace terms were too weak. It had in fact embraced Foch's position. On the day of the presidential elections, Clemenceau resigned from his office as Premier, and withdrew from politics forever.

The new German demand had been presented while these incidents took place. The French reaction was negative. There was no point in giving in to the Germans. What was important was not the war criminals themselves, but the success or failure of the Germans' resistance to the terms of the treaty. To capitulate to it would not improve Franco-German relations, but would inevitably lead to new resistance, new campaigns, new demands. The French stuck by their principles.

The English reaction was different. In February, 1920, there was a debate on this question in the House of Commons, the first of a kind which was to be repeated many times during the next fifteen years. All the German tirades had impressed themselves upon the members of parliament, as though their minds were gramophone records. Practically nothing was said that had not been said in Germany. All the members, from Right to Left, had approved of the trials on the ground of their moral effi-

cacy, and continued to approve of them. But now, almost all of them from Right to Left, were convinced that
the whole plan had to be changed. Lord Robert Cecil, an
expert on world peace, whose position was between the
Right and the Left, was typical. He realized clearly that
the handing over of the criminals "must arouse every
spark of national feeling left in Germany." "If you succeed in your demand, you will run the risk of producing
a revolution." With a few exceptions, all the other speakers spoke in a similar vein. The German campaign had
borne fruit in England; it had changed people's minds in
less than nine months.

Its triumph in England led to its triumph pure and
simple. Lloyd George decided upon the course to follow:
no conflicts! Give in to the Germans, let them have what
they wanted. The French, although ready to face a conflict with Germany, were not ready to face one with England, and they gave in to their ally. In February Germany
was informed that the article of the treaty was in force,
but that an attempt would be made to handle the trials
according to the German proposals.

The test case was won. The Allies had failed to resist
Germany's resistance. The officers' corps and its satellites
had every reason to look forward to the future with increased confidence. How right they were to congratulate
themselves over the results of their campaign would become quite obvious once the German Supreme Court
began the "war criminals" trials.

This court took a whole year to institute proceedings.
Then, out of the 900 names submitted, it chose Heynen,
a sergeant, accused of having inflicted barbarous treatment upon war prisoners. His trial was carried out in an
unimpeachable manner. The attitude of the court and

the prevailing atmosphere were above reproach. And then, Sergeant Heynen was sentenced to ten months' imprisonment.

The next to be tried was a general, a certain General Stenger, indicted for brutal mistreatment of civilians. He was acquitted.

The French observer at the trial was recalled by his government. The English observer, Sir Ernest Pollock, remained. He later stated in the Commons that the sentencing of Sergeant Heynen was a grave humiliation of German militarism.

The Supreme Court tried a few other cases, slowly, ponderously. Acquittal, acquittal, six months' imprisonment, acquittal. Public opinion in the Allied countries began to make itself heard, parliaments clamored. But in the Commons, the Solicitor-General declared that the Leipzig trials were "a new milestone in the course of international justice."

The French felt that the whole thing was a mockery. They insisted that something be done, that the Leipzig farce be stopped, that the Allies resume their demand to have the criminals handed over to them. Negotiations were opened between London and Paris. They were reopened every few weeks or months, but no decision was reached.

And the German Supreme Court, ever slower, ever more ponderous, tried a few more cases. In one case, involving the deliberate sinking of a hospital ship with hundreds of wounded, they meted out a sentence of four years' imprisonment. It has never been ascertained whether the full term was actually served.

And then in 1922 the whole thing came to an end. No more milestones of international justice were erected at

Leipzig. The files gathered dust. *Comedia finita est.*
Twelve cases had been tried out of 900: six from the
English list and six from the French and Belgian lists. In
the six Franco-Belgian cases, one ended with a verdict of
guilty, five with acquittals. In the six English cases, five
ended with verdicts of guilty, and one with acquittal.
Justice must be impartial. The sentences given the culprits on the English list were not exactly adequate, but
still they were passed. In his preface to a book on these
trials, Sir Ernest Pollock insisted on their purity—"no
vengeance, but justice. These sentences were, to our esti-
mate, far too light, but they must be estimated according
to their value in Germany." [14] This value, according to Sir
Ernest, was enormous. According to Claude Mullins, the
author of the book, whom Sir Ernest had honored by his
collaboration, "the Leipzig trials may not have fulfilled
the expectations of the public which demanded them
when the Armistice came; but they were of very real importance and value none the less. They have made history." [15]

There can be no doubt about that: they *were* of very
real importance. They did make history.

5: *Troops on the March*

IN GENERAL LUDENDORFF'S eyes there was once
again a cold glint, as in the days when, surrounded by
maps and telephones, he directed great battles. His
mighty double chin jutted challengingly and ominously
over his collar.

In those days of February, 1920, during which the first offensive against the Versailles Treaty was victoriously carried through, he spent much time in conferences. His lips remained sealed even for his wife. "He told me that I must not know anything of what was afoot," she wrote later, "because what they were planning was dangerous. They might fail and in that case I must be able to declare with a clear conscience before any tribunal that I had no part in the political activities that went on in our home." [1]

His fellow-conspirators belonged mostly to a somewhat obscure organization called the "National Union." It had been founded by a restless and enterprising man named Captain Pabst. He had entered public life during the winter of 1918–1919. An indiscriminate murderer, he took a prominent part in the "salvation" of Berlin from a "Red danger," which was a danger for only one day. At the beginning of 1920, he was the chief of staff of the "Ehrhardt Brigade." Captain Ehrhardt's troops wore the swastika, paraded under the old Black, White and Red flag of the Hohenzollern and sang smutty songs against the Republic. This brigade was a thorn in the side of the government which had ordered it to disband several months before. But the commander and chief of staff had a different idea and failed to carry out the order. They kept their formation intact and said that anyone who wanted to disband them should come and try.

This was also the opinion of General von Luettwitz, "chief of the army command." Generally speaking, he was against disbanding any troop formation. The peace treaty provided for the reduction of the German army to 100,000 men. To supervise this and other phases of disarmament there was now in Germany the "Inter-Allied

Military Control Commission." It was headed by the French General Nollet, whose aide was the English General Malcolm. But this did not impress General Luettwitz. Had not the "war criminals" case just demonstrated that determined resistance could break down the adversary? And was not General Malcolm himself a living proof of the same theory? It goes without saying that General Malcolm had no decisive voice. He was only No. 2 man on the Commission, and nothing at all in English politics. But he was a kind of barometer of British public opinion. During the affair of the war criminals he had expressed his sympathy for the German point of view to General von Luettwitz. Now, too, he showed great understanding when Luettwitz began to hint that Germany needed at least twice as many troops as the treaty allowed. This was an encouraging symptom to the chief of the German army. He became firmly convinced that the reduction of the effectives must and could be stopped. He considered the Ehrhardt Brigade a part of the army; hence it should continue to exist.

The "National Union," founded by the brigade's chief of staff, was a small conspiratorial group, and accepted members only of the most radical tinge. It had connections with every influential enemy of the Republic, and, of course, with thousands of officers. It tried to establish even more important connections with foreign governments or influential individuals in foreign countries. The success of its plans depended upon support from abroad, for they were preparing a coup d'état. They intended to destroy the republic by a putsch and restore the old government in one form or another—the form did not really matter; this government would refuse to carry out disarmament.

Germany seemed ripe for such a move. Recently Ludendorff and Hindenburg had once again been cheered in
the streets of Berlin. A sensational trial had brought a further loss of prestige to the new masters. Erzberger, one
of the symbols of the Republic, vice-Chancellor until recently and the man who had signed the armistice, was
publicly convicted of having accepted bribes, miserable
little bribes in the petty bourgeois style which only made
them more contemptible in the eyes of little people. If
new elections were held now, the Weimar parties would
doubtless lose their majority.

New elections were due. The National Assembly had
completed its task of framing a Constitution and a normal
Reichstag was supposed to succeed it. But the Republi-
cans were so certain that they would be defeated that
they postponed the elections from month to month. New
elections was the main subject of political debates. It was
perfectly clear to everyone why the Right demanded
them and the Left delayed them.

Indeed, the gentlemen around Ludendorff were sure
that the majority of the German people were behind
them. A *coup d'état* would naturally crush the Weimar
"gang" more thoroughly than an election, but the majority would not object. The putschists saw only two possible obstacles: the workers—a minority which might
become active,—and the Allies. The conspirators decided
to neutralize the workers by obtaining help from Russia,
and the Allies by making use of England. They went to
the Russians and offered themselves as a bulwark against
the Allies. In return they demanded that the Bolsheviks
order the German Communists not to resist Ludendorff's
putsch. But the Bolsheviks were not taken in. They
warned Lloyd George of the impending coup.

With regard to England, the conspirators naturally represented themselves as a bulwark against Bolshevism. Submitting proposals to England was a delicate matter, and they entrusted it to an expert, a certain Trebitsch-Lincoln who seemed to them particularly well qualified. He was a native of Hungary—and the Hungarians are clever. He had managed to become a member of Parliament in England, and had many connections in British political circles. He was flexible and discreet. His mission was clear: "The chief thing was British neutrality." [2] He was optimistic.

It goes without saying that he could not submit his proposals in writing. He had to be careful not to expose his connections, because they were really important people. For instance, there was Major Ryan, obviously a person of consequence in London who had said of the peace treaty that he "was prepared to see that scrap of paper which had brought only trouble torn to pieces." However, he categorically objected to the restoration of Wilhelm II. Colonel Bauer reassured him: "There was no thought of that. The major seemed satisfied."

He had nothing against Ludendorff. Colonel Bauer told him that Ludendorff would be given the command of the army. "The major looked straight at Bauer and thought for a moment or two. He inhaled a couple of whiffs from his cigarette. 'Beyond question, the right man in the right place, as you Germans are so fond of saying now. But so far as the outside world is concerned, he must stay rather in the background. Will you promise me that?' Colonel Bauer promised." [3]

No doubt about it, the major was an important man. Yet he was, as Trebitsch-Lincoln said, only an intermediary, a connecting link with even more highly-placed people who, naturally, could not be named. Comforted by such assurances, the conspirators thought they had secured the approval both of Russia and England.

But there were other obstacles. The "National Union" was unanimously for the putsch, but the same was not true of all the upper circle of the enemies of the Republic. General Ludendorff had to recognize that many of these were laggards and waverers. The professional politicians, the leaders of the German National Party and of the German People's Party, did not see the necessity of a military coup d'état. The elections would come sooner or later they said; and would painlessly put them in power. Then they could do anything they pleased. Why, therefore, risk violent counter-measures by the Allies, or even the French alone? They were sure such measures would inevitably be taken, in spite of Trebitsch-Lincoln whom they considered a swindler. They felt that the Allies would probably permit the Germans to steal their victory from them piecemeal, but not all at once. They expatiated on the difference between a gradual "retail" whittling away of the treaty and a sudden "wholesale" attack upon it. For the first time the Rightist bloc seemed to be split into a heroic and an opportunistic camp.

Ludendorff must have felt great bitterness when he learned that opportunism was rampant even among high-ranking officers, like Major General von Seeckt, who was assigned to the Reichswehr command under Luettwitz. Ludendorff, a massive bulldog, had never liked von Seeckt, who was more of the greyhound type and the latter returned these feelings. Yet this man had once been the efficient chief of staff of an army. Was it possible that an officer with such a past considered a total solution superfluous and dangerous? There was too much talking and thinking, Ludendorff, Bauer and Pabst decided, and Luettwitz in the end agreed with them. Scruples can best be overcome by action. The putschists had everything: the troops, the mood of the country, assurances from abroad. To take care of the civilian façade of the affair, they even had a new Reich Chancellor ready—an elderly, reactionary and pugnacious bureaucrat, a certain Dr. Kapp from East Prussia. Why wait till everyone approved of the putsch? After the fait accompli, all Germany would jump on the bandwagon.

Then came the fait accompli, though not quite according to schedule. An accident transformed the furious offensive, which was to begin with the arrest of the entire government, into a weak defensive. In a new controversy with the republican authorities, General von Luettwitz committed the unpardonable mistake of sending them a formal ultimatum. "The most serious condition Luettwitz laid down before the Cabinet," said the Reich Chancellor a few days later, "was that the demobilization of the Imperial Army and the destruction of war material in accordance with the terms of the treaty must not take place, and that the Reich must prepare for a new war." [4]

The tone of this communication alarmed even Noske's childish mind. The government examined the information they had very closely, and decided to take it seriously. On March 12th, Luettwitz was formally dismissed. Warrants of arrest were issued against Bauer, Kapp and Pabst.

The putschists could not afford to wait any longer. On the night of March 13th, 1920, the Ehrhardt Brigade marched from the Doeberitz drilling grounds to Berlin. To the sound of martial music, under the naval battle flag of the Empire, they advanced toward the government offices. In the gray dawn, bedecked with all his medals, General Ludendorff awaited them at the Brandenburg Gate. Later, he was to declare under oath in court as a witness, not a defendant, that he had accidentally gone for a walk there. It had been agreed that he was to remain "rather in the background," which he did.

Were there no other troops, no Reichswehr regiments that could be thrown into the fray against the rebels? The government had asked for them. But General von Seeckt declared that this was impossible, that German soldiers would not fire upon German soldiers. So the Reich President and his Ministers got into their cars at the last moment and fled. Only the vice-Chancellor remained to watch the movements of the insurgents.

Herr Kapp seized the Chancellery. He issued a manifesto in strong language that the Reich of the November criminals had been liquidated, and that a new Reich based upon honor and power had come into being. He, Chancellor Kapp, had seized the helm of German destiny.

To the world outside, these events came like a thunderbolt, creating a greater stir than anything that had happened since the armistice and the collapse of the Empire. The Empire itself seemed to have returned. What would become of the peace? It was like the eruption of a volcano, the earth seemed to shake.

At that period there were no radios in Germany. The new rulers forbade the publication of the Berlin newspapers. Fragmentary news was issued to the country by telegraph. Chancellor Kapp gave out suppressed information as it suited him and so did the legitimate government in flight. But amidst all the confusion, a few striking changes took place immediately throughout the land from the North Sea to the Alps. The black, white and red flag, the discarded flag of the old Reich, suddenly reappeared in thousands of windows. As if by magic, all over Germany, civilians of yesterday were suddenly metamorphosed into officers who crowded the streets in their uniforms. The monocle, that traditional sign of pride which had vanished during the preceding months, suddenly began to glint again from tens of thousands of faces. The effectives of the regular and irregular regiments in barracks suddenly doubled and tripled. Well trained and well armed formations of civilians, calling themselves "temporary volunteers," suddenly emerged from universities, gymnasia and clubs and marched off to various places.

Less than two hours after Herr Kapp's proclamation, Germany was a different country. What would happen now? Who was for Kapp and who against him? Where and how would the Kappists gain control? The parties of the "Weimar Coalition" issued a call for resistance. Twenty-four hours later the Communist Party joined them. The putschists had not expected this. Resistance! Resistance! "Aux armes, citoyens!" Down with reaction! Down with the new war reaction is preparing!

But how and with what could resistance be organized? The Socialist members of the government had always believed and had taught the masses that the most powerful weapon in the social arsenal is the general strike. "All the wheels will stand still, if such is your strong arm's will." Against whom should the general strike be directed at this moment? Would paralyzing the entire country hurt Kapp more than his opponents? Never mind! There was no time for thorough consideration. One powerful weapon was available, and no other. The Weimar government and the trade unions proclaimed a general strike. The wheels stood still.

Strike call leaflets were dropped on Berlin from planes, and the capital, although under martial law, obeyed. Everything came to a standstill. Only one institution in Berlin functioned as usual: the hotel where the members of the Interallied Military Control Commission resided. The waiters and chambermaids of the Adlon wished in this way to show their solidarity with all the forces which opposed the return of the militarists. They made only one exception to this exception. While continuing to serve the French, American and Belgian officers, they refused to serve the English. They had seen too much of the activities of the English members of the Commission. Although there was no truth in Trebitsch-Lincoln's fairy tale about London's support of the putsch, and we have no proof that General Malcolm and his staff knew anything about it or encouraged it, the waiters and chambermaids had witnessed too much cordiality between the English and German officers.

The general strike began on March 13th. But even before it was proclaimed, an event of decisive importance took place behind closed doors. No sooner had Herr Kapp entered the Reich Chancellery than he discovered the fatal weakness of his whole enterprise: those professional politicians and officers who had opposed it during the conversation stage, continued to oppose it now. This was against all the expectations of the putschists. There the fait accompli was and yet these people refused to accept it. More than that! Up until the putsch they had regarded all the talk about it as a kind of game. They had expressed only abstract opinions, so to speak! Now, confronted with the real thing, they showed real indignation. Only madmen would have engineered the putsch, they said. Ludendorff must be crazy. For the first time, the suspicion was expressed among Ludendorff's colleagues that the former master of Germany was insane in the medical sense of the term. From the very beginning, they treated the astonished conquerors of Berlin as a frightful nuisance.

They reiterated their belief that the Allies would refuse to swallow this coup d'état, and that it was entirely unnecessary because the new elections would bring about the desired changes anyway—that is, if the putsch had not spoiled the Nationalists' chances. They branded the enterprise as a dilettantish, irresponsible and inexcusable disturbance. They refused to have anything to do with it at any cost. They had an entirely different conception of their task, and wanted to liquidate the whole clumsy adventure as soon as possible with as little loss of face as possible.

Major General von Seeckt came into the foreground. His chief of yesterday, General von Luettwitz, was later to call him "the soul of the resistance to me." [5] And so he was. A few hours before the putsch he had prevented the Reichswehr from acting against the putschists. But at the same time he had prevented it from submitting to them. He got on the telephone and appealed to the instinct for prudence which is not foreign to those bureaucrats who bear the title of general. Most of the high-ranking officers realized that for the time being it was advisable to steer a middle course and wait. Very few of them followed what was surely their heart's desire and openly joined the new government. In most cases, the generals in the provinces kept their troops on the alert and prepared for any even-

tuality. In Berlin, too, and this was most important, the
garrison, under the influence of von Seeckt and a few
other generals associated with him, at first remained simply on the alert. It did not obey Luettwitz.

This vitiated the entire undertaking. The military dic-
tators had no troops at their disposal! The formations
which marched into Berlin with them were far too small
to control the metropolis. They amounted to practically
nothing considering the presence of the far more numerous neutral troops in their rear. From the very first minute, the Ehrhardt Brigade was compelled to take the defensive. They stationed sentries at the main communication centers of the capital, protecting them by barbed
wire enclosures. They erected posts bearing the sign:
"Stop! Anyone attempting to advance further will be
fired upon!" And that was all they could do.

All the civilians upon whom the putschists had relied
also left them in the lurch. The very individuals whose
cause they wished to represent turned them the cold
shoulder from the very beginning. Every prominent politician of the two black, white and red parties refused to
enter the Cabinet Kapp tried to constitute. High minis-
terial officials refused to carry out the orders of the new
"Reich Chancellor." The Reichsbank and other large
banks refused to honor his signature. The board of the
Industrialists' Association decided to continue "collab-
orating" with the trade unions, despite the proclamation
of the general strike.

Twenty-four hours after they took power, the putschists
realized that they were floating in a total vacuum, and
Herr Kapp told his friends that he would have to "withdraw." Of course, he would have to withdraw! Or, rather,
give up! The opportunistic wing of the Right forces who

had full control of the situation wanted just that. It was essential that the whole thing be managed without excessively compromising the whole black, white and red movement.

And this movement which had been split into a minority of adventurers and a majority that refused to cooperate with them became unified once more. The majority began to cover the retreat of the adventurers in order to limit the amount of damage to the common cause. The whole situation was dominated by the Reichswehr which was still undecided, still manoeuvring, still threateningly standing by. The most important factor in the Reichswehr was the man who manipulated it: von Seeckt. He played the game to the end in the smoothest possible manner.

On the second day of the putsch, March 14th, 1920, everyone began to negotiate with everyone else: the political parties, Right and Left; the two Reich Chancellors and the vice-Chancellor; General von Seeckt and the other generals. By March 17th, everything was settled.

The black, white and red parties were granted a few of their demands, notably the setting of a date for new elections. In return for this, Kapp and Luettwitz agreed to "withdraw." The Ehrhardt Brigade marched out of Berlin in peace and honor, with its arms. The Supreme Court was directed to start a few painless proceedings. A few Reichswehr generals were pensioned, and von Seeckt became commander-in-chief. Thus was the world-shaking putsch buried after five days.

Out of it arose two legends which confused people's minds for many years: the legend of the "triumph of the German people," and the subsidiary legend of the "triumph of the general strike."

It is not surprising that these legends developed. The

defeat of the putsch was a fact but the causes of its defeat were a matter of interpretation. And wherever several interpretations are possible, everyone is prone to choose the one which best satisfies his interests and prejudices. Thus that version of the story prevailed which best suited the government which had returned to power, the Weimar Parties and the trade-unions: the version that the dragon of the putsch was slain by the militant people and that the telling blow which had done him to death was the general strike. Many Germans seriously believed this; and for reasons of domestic policy it was advantageous to make as many people as possible believe it. This version was also the most pleasing to the victorious Allies, for it had two encouraging implications. One was that the powerful German people stood ready to defend their democracy like a lion. The other was that the German people had a powerful weapon to use whenever democracy was in danger.

These were the conclusions drawn by almost all the Allied world from the liquidation of the Kapp putsch. Now they were sure there was no longer any reason to worry about Germany. The counter-revolutionaries and militarists had made a bid for power and had been definitely defeated. The German people would never tolerate an attack upon its democracy and its peace, and it evidently had the power to crush such an attack.

And all this was false. To be sure, certain sections of the German people wished to defend democracy and peace. But the outcome of the Kapp putsch had not been decided by them. To be sure, the weapon of the general strike had been used. But it had not determined the course of events. The adventurists had been outmanoeuvred and crushed by the main forces of the Right, exclusively by them from the very first minute of their putsch. And they had suppressed the small group of putschists not because they feared the people and their power, but because they feared the Allies.

There is no way of proving an historical hypothesis. No one can say what the outcome would have been if the the main forces of the German reactionaries had supported the small group of putschists instead of opposing them, and, after the entry of the shock troops into Berlin, they had supported the putsch with everything they could muster, particularly the Army. The course of subsequent events suggests that even then the united forces of the Right would have been sufficient to strangle any opposition in Germany.

But aside from all the ifs; the fact is that no actual conflict between demorcacy and reaction took place on the occasion of the Kapp putsch. What did take place was a conflict between two reactionary groups whose relative strength determined the outcome. There is not a grain of truth in the fairy tale that it was determined by the overwhelming power of democracy. Yet this comfortable fairy tale was believed by a well-meaning world, although to believe it demanded an almost super-human credulity. The immediate sequel of the putsch should have dispelled all these illusions.

To begin with, it was followed by a political somersault that only first-class and self-assured acrobats would have dared to attempt. As the Kappists marched out, without one moment's delay, the Rightists spread a new alarm: the Bolsheviks are coming! As the Left prepared to celebrate its renewed hold on the state power, the Right turned the organs of that power against the Left. Kapp himself, the putsch Chancellor, had the impudence to conclude the communiqué announcing his withdrawal with the warning that "the most urgent need of the fatherland was a firm union of all Germans against the frightful danger of Bolshevism." This was the fog behind which Kapp could retire with the minimum loss of face. The Right took the fullest advantage of it. The Bolsheviks are at our gates! They sent up the cry from every house-top, in every street.

Needless to say, there were no Bolsheviks to be seen. But there were workers who had been called into the streets to save the Republic; there were trade-unions which had proclaimed the general strike; there were many Germans who did not believe that the Republic had been saved by communiqués. They refused to go home and forget all about the putsch. They demanded a Republican purge of the Reichswehr and the administration. Some of the demands were more radical than others, some more intelligent than others; but those who put them forward were the same individuals who up until the night of March 17th had been called the "people," the "defenders of democracy."

On the morning of March 18th they were suddenly rechristened "Bolsheviks," and "Red Army." Once again the urgent necessity arose of saving the Republic, this time from its own saviors; and of unleashing against them the dubious troop formations against which they had defended the German democracy.

They were not treated with kid gloves. They were murdered as people are murdered only in a civil war, when one group of partisans takes revenge on another. Such was the first manifestation of democracy triumphant on the morrow of the "victory of the people." It was truly hard to be mistaken about what forces in this democracy held the real power.

But the Bolshevik bogy was not enough. Something else was required to wipe out the memory of the unsuccessful putsch, some gesture against the external enemy. Bolshevism was discovered in that fifty kilometre zone east of the Rhine which had been demilitarized by the peace treaty and which no German soldier was supposed to enter. At that very spot, in the Ruhr district, a particularly dangerous Red Army was found. What a menace to European civilization was that Red monster, squeezed into a space thirty miles wide between the Allied army of occupation and the Reichswehr! Europe must be saved without a moment's delay! Anyone could see now that demilitarization was a mistake. The Reichswehr must be permitted to move into the Ruhr!

One week after the end of the putsch, a new government was formed in Berlin, "a government," declared Lloyd George in the House of Commons, "which, as far as I can see, leans much more to the Left than the former Government." The new Minister of Defense was a certain Dr. Gessler. He made his début as a minister with an energetic speech about the democratization of the army and the extermination of all militaristic tendencies. The first act of the new government was to ask the Allies for permission to send German troops into the demilitarized zone.

The sparks began to fly between England and France. The French government and press denied that there was even a trace of Bolshevist danger in the Ruhr. They declared that the workers of that district were good if over-ardent democrats and socialists who naturally opposed the return to power of the militarist reactionaries. Plain good sense and fairness, they declared, forbade delivering them over to their enemies. Deputy Barthou, one of the most prominent French political leaders, sharply attacked Britain's attitude toward Germany, which, he said, unintentionally but effectively encouraged all her worst tendencies. He spoke of a "crisis in the Alliance." The French insisted that the German request be rejected. The British wanted to accede to it.

The Berlin government, representing the "victory of the people," cut through the Gordian knot of the discussion. On April 2nd it ordered the Reichswehr to march into the Ruhr without waiting for the Allies' authorization. The peace treaty stipulated that an act such as this was equivalent to an act of open war.

The international crisis became acute. Millerand's Cabinet inquired of Lloyd George's Cabinet what it intended to do. The English replied that they did not intend to do anything, that after having restored order the Reichswehr troops, it was to be hoped, would voluntarily withdraw from the demilitarized zone. Paris was bitter. The Cabinet debated the matter and resolved to act without their British Ally.

But what to do? March into the territory occupied by the Germans and eject them by force? Risk a new conflict, though no one could doubt the outcome? Millerand's Cabinet hesitated. It lacked the courage to brave the storm which would surely be aroused throughout the progressive, peace-loving world if France, which was armed to the teeth, moved against disarmed Germany. A weak alternative solution was finally adopted: a reprisal. If the Germans occupied one part of the demilitarized zone, the French would occupy another part and would stay there as long as the Reichswehr stayed in the Ruhr. The French occupied the city of Frankfurt and its environs.

This was by no means the action of a superior, but of an equal. It did not mean the crushing of the adversary, but only retaliation against him. The Germans were not impressed. If the French already treated them as equals, much had been achieved. They realized that France's solution of the problem revealed a certain paralysis of the will, whatever its causes. The Germans, nevertheless, took the opportunity to raise wild clamors protesting that they were being raped.

Lloyd George, for his part, did not even notice how weak the French démarche was. He was furious. Again, this unpleasantness! Of late he had justified his determination to pursue the balance of power policies against France on moral and emotional grounds. Now he seemed to have a real persecution complex. In conversations with his intimates he took it for granted that the French harbored dark designs of world conquest. "There is no doubt," he said to Austen Chamberlain, "that the French have strong military aspirations. They want to revive the Napoleonic ideal." Chamberlain contradicted him: "In my opinion, the French are not acting out of malevolence. Their action is dictated by funk. They think that if the Germans once get their heads up, they will advance at a much greater rate than the French, and will become a new menace."

But Lloyd George "did not agree with this." [6] He went to San Remo to meet Millerand, in a mood of aggressive Francophobia. "The French," he said, "regard the Germans as a beaten enemy who should be treated as such. The official British point of view is that the German nation was not responsible for the war, that the Junkers

have been ejected, that the German government should
be supported . . . and, that, generally, the Germans
should not be regarded with suspicion." [7]

By 1920 it was rather late to advance these theories
which had dominated the atmosphere in 1918.

The San Remo conversations were extremely unpleasant and almost ended in an open rupture between the
Allies. Then, as though sent by Providence, the new
German Defense Minister, Gessler, saved the situation.
In the course of the conference, on April 20th, he presented the Allies with a note demanding that Germany
be permitted to double the effectives of the Reichswehr,
and that the article of the treaty concerning the strength
of the German Army be revised. The Kapp putsch and
the Bolshevik uprising in the Ruhr, he argued, had amply
demonstrated that Germany required a stronger army:
200,000 men instead of 100,000 were the minimum.

Gessler's move re-cemented the Anglo-French alliance.
Lloyd George, "scattering chips on every number," resumed a pro-French attitude. He went walking in the
park arm in arm with Millerand not too far from the news
photographers. The Allies rejected Gessler's demands and
declared that Germany had repeatedly violated her disarmament pledges.

The officers in the Reichswehr Ministry were nevertheless satisfied with their new Minister. The man who represented "the victory of the people" was faithfully following the line set by General Luettwitz.

"The victory of the people" did not put the reactionaries at any disadvantage. The speeches about the democratization of the Reichswehr did not prevent its re-
creation in the spirit of the old imperial Army. The
putsch proved useful in this respect. There had been a

few officers, petty officers and privates in the rebel and
neutral regiments, who had tried to abide by their oath
of allegiance to the Republic. They thus exposed themselves. Many of them were sent to prison for disobedi-
ence; all of them were discharged from the army.

Finally, the Reichstag elections were held with the expected results. The defeat of the Republic would have
been more complete if that fool Ludendorff had not made
a mass of honest people uneasy with his putsch. But the
results of the elections were good enough. The two black,
white and red parties doubled their representation. The
"Weimar Coalition" lost its majority forever. One year
and a half after the "revolution," three months after the
"victory of the people" and the "victory of the general
strike," the Socialists disappeared from the government.
Why they and the entire Weimar Coalition were so un-
popular is hard to explain. Actually, they never caused
any serious difficulties to the real masters. But the masters wanted them out of the way. And now they had what
they wanted.

2.

Turkey—there was a country from which one could
learn. That General Kemal, he was the man. Do you still
remember the Dardanelles and the ups-and-downs at
Gallipoli? The German High Command had always recognized that Mustapha Kemal was of a different mettle
from the other Turkish generals. He had achieved his
aims.

True, he had been unable to get along with his over-
bearing German companions-in-arms. There had been
frictions, but never mind, that had been years ago. To-

day, he was even less able to get along with the over-
bearing victors of Versailles. Decidedly, Turkey was the
place. For the space of two years, German eyes were
fixed upon Turkey and Mustapha Kemal Pasha.

Toward the middle of 1920, after long resistance, the
Sultan agreed to sign the peace treaty of Sèvres. But
Mustapha Kemal rose against the shame of its provisions,
to tear it up and prevent it from being carried out. He
kindled a national movement in his starved defeated people. He planted himself in Asia Minor, in the town of
Ankara, which he had made the capital of his nationalist
movement, just as the German nationalists would soon
make Munich their capital, and defied the world. He defied the government of his own country and the victorious Allies. He challenged them with rebellion and sabotage, with regiments which he had reconstituted from
the defeated remnants of the Sultan's armies. Step by
step he moved closer to success.

Constantinople was occupied by the Allies. Allied
troops operated in Asia Minor, trying to suppress him.
But he resisted and grew increasingly stronger. He was
victorious on the battlefield and on the diplomatic front.
In 1921, at the same time that he exterminated every
vestige of Communism in his own territories, he concluded a pact of friendship with Soviet Russia. The text
of the pact contained no binding commitments. But the
mere fact that Russia and Bolshevism had placed themselves behind Kemal put him in another category. The
Soviet Pact,—there was something to be noted!

Something could also be learned from Kemal's clever-
ness in taking advantage of Franco-British rivalry. In the
case of Turkey, the usual situation was reversed: the
British were the intransigent ones. It was they who in-

sisted on enforcing the treaty and crushing the rebellious
nationalist movement, whereas, with regard to Kemal,
the French aped the British attitude toward Germany.
Whenever Lloyd George favored Germany, the French
favored Kemal. Whenever Lloyd George conceded them
something in the case of Germany, the French conceded
him something in the case of Turkey.

The Turkish liberator fully exploited this situation. He
chased the Sultan out of the country and established his
own dictatorship. He defeated the scattered Allied troops.
To crush him, it would have been necessary to send a
really strong army into Turkey. No one was ready to do
that. Enough of conflicts! In 1922, the World War victors
were so completely fed up with the Turkish problem that
they wanted to be rid of it at any cost. They informed
Mustapha Kemal that they were ready to revise the treaty.
A new peace conference with the new Turkey was called.

This was really a spectacle. Even the most miserable
defeated little country needed only to assert its will to
bring about the collapse of the policy pursued by the
greatest world powers. German political centers followed
every step of this process with joyful attention. Germany's position was, of course, different from Turkey's,
yet Kemal's success immensely increased their assurance
that Germany, too, could achieve similar results. Caution
—but let it be combined with tenacity! Create difficulties, arouse weariness! Weariness can have two results:
the opponent will become either soft or brutal. The likelihood in the present case was that he would grow soft.

The progress of the enforcement of the peace treaty
was as lumbering as that of a cart in a roadless waste.
Week after week, day after day, the Germans made every

conceivable difficulty on every conceivable point. And they never missed an opportunity to exploit these difficulties for all they were worth.

In 1919 it was estimated in Paris that the disarmament of Germany would be accomplished three months after the conclusion of the peace. 1920, 1921, and 1922 went by, but Germany was still "disarming." The reduction of the Reichswehr effectives to 100,000 men seemed an interminable affair, and as the official formations thinned out, all sorts of pseudo-civilian or "black" formations took their place. The General Staff, which was to be disbanded, doubtless continued to exist under cover. "If necessary," the writer of this book once heard Dr. Gessler declare to a small circle which received his words with jubilation, "we shall register it as the Institute of Textile Studies, Inc." The arms handed over to the Allies never reached the prescribed quantities, and whenever a delivery was made, half of it disappeared the next day. The machine tools for making armaments which were supposed to be destroyed either could not be found or were suddenly transformed into machines for purely civilian purposes.

The Allies had to fight and argue every step of the way. Often, a matter seemed settled and the Control Commission checked it off in their files, but one month later it would have to be reconsidered. The German courts meted out draconian sentences against anyone suspected of aiding the Control Commission. When a hidden store of cannon barrels was discovered in an armament factory in Berlin, the stock manager was accused of having revealed it to the Commission. A German tribunal sentenced this alleged traitor to life imprisonment. "How do you know that the Control Commission was informed of this by the stock manager?" the director of the armaments plant was asked. "An English member of the Commission told it to me confidentially."

It was never ascertained whether he was telling the truth and whether General Malcolm's officers had really helped to deliver their German informers to the vengeance of the German tribunals. Nor was it ever explained why the Commission's visits of inspection were often known in advance.

Resistance and sabotage were not limited to the field of disarmament. Germany was to begin her reparations payments by "deliveries in kind" of coal, chemicals, woods, etc. Later, no one would accept reparations in kind, and Germany would say: if deliveries in kind were accepted we would be glad to pay! But in 1920 and 1921 the situation was different. The destroyed factories and mines in the battle areas and the territories had not yet been rebuilt, and the victors sorely needed all sorts of goods and raw materials.

Germany, whose industrial power had remained intact, was perfectly well able to make these deliveries. Only recently she had produced for war purposes more of the reparations commodities than she was now supposed to hand over, and there was no technical obstacle to her continuing to produce them. The disorganization and "wave of laziness" which obtained could have been overcome after the war by an effort of will on the part of the government, the employers and the workers. If they had made such an effort, civilian Germany, in spite of the reparations deliveries, would have been better supplied with these goods than during the war. The pitiful outcry against the "vampire" exploitation of the poor German nation had absolutely no foundation in fact.

But the German government, employers and workers made an effort to default on the deliveries rather than to fulfil them. Without any previous arrangements, all showed a tendency always to do less than what they had been asked to do, to delay, reduce quantities, create shortages. There was no end to the frictions with the "Reparations Commissions."

In 1921, the Commissions drew up plans concerning the reparations proper, that is the sums of money Germany was expected to pay. Some people advocated low reparations and some advocated high ones. Twenty years later it was clear that both groups, above all, the so-called economic experts had been talking nonsense.

The partisans of low reparations payments were wrong when they contended in a humanitarian spirit that Germany could not pay very much. The plan providing for the highest payments was drawn up in January, 1921: it provided for payments of two billion marks a year for the first few years, gradually increasing to 6 billions in the nineteen-thirties. The partisans of minimum payments acted as though this scale of 0.5 to 1.5 billion dollars were sheer madness. Never, they contended, would the German government be able to squeeze such sums of money out of the German economy.

In the thirties, Hitler squeezed out of Germany 16 and 18 and 20 billion of marks for military purposes alone. In the few years preceding the present war, Hitler sucked out of his country a sum equivalent to the reparations payments planned for decades. We shall not even speak of production during the actual war years! With regard to Germany's potential, even the most exacting reparations schemes did not scratch the surface of her capacity to produce.

But the partisans of high reparations were equally wrong. For the "inner levy" did not solve the problem. It was not enough to obtain marks from the German government. Something had to be done to enable the foreign receivers of these marks to make use of them. The marks had to be "transferred," transformed from their German fictitious value into international real value, into gold, or foreign exchange, or foreign stocks, or goods, or anything that would be useful to the foreign countries. Germany's own stock of gold and foreign exchange did not suffice to transform even two reparations payments into international values. The value of German exports covered only a fraction of these annual instalments. But no way could be found to make the marks usable abroad, because the receivers of the reparations themselves rejected the only possible solutions of this problem.

One solution would have been to use the reparations for increased purchases of German commodities. But no one wanted to increase German exports to any considerable extent. The British exporters particularly opposed such a solution. British industrialists drew up memoranda against it the moment it was suggested.

Another solution would have been to invest the reparations marks in Germany for the purchase or the creation of profitable enterprises. They could have bought stocks and shares, founded new businesses, built houses—all of which would also have given work and income to the Germans themselves. But this solution was rejected: the Germans must be protected from foreign "exploitation."

Thus the Allies themselves, in one case out of selfishness, in the other out of philanthropy, rejected the only two methods of obtaining real payments. They stretched out one hand and said: "Give!" while with the other they

made a forbidding gesture: "Rejected!" Those who advocated high reparations were right because Germany
could pay enormous sums, and even the highest amounts
suggested were still reasonable. But their plans were useless because the Allies refused to accept the only values
with which real payments could be made.

But in 1920, 1921 and 1922, all this was still in the realm
of theory and had no immediate significance. What was
in question was not how to empty Germany's pockets, but
to agree on conditional and modifiable plans for the future. In 1921, Germany had to pay only one billion marks.
This billion was entirely covered by a loan from London.
In 1922 she was to pay the trifling sum of 720 million
marks. This was later reduced to 270 millions, but even
this sum was not paid.

Resistance and sabotage, systematically, step by step.
Unceasing propaganda campaign designed to arouse sympathy, fear, resignation.

In the spring of 1921, when Germany refused to sign
any reparations plan, the German Ministers returning to
Berlin were received like conquerors. It turned out, however, that they had gone one step too far. The Allies sent
an ultimatum threatening to send an army into Germany
unless she agreed to the plan. Germany moved two steps
back. The Cabinet of conquerors resigned and gave place
to a "Cabinet of Fulfilment." This Cabinet signed the plan
and for a few months quieted the storm by demonstrations of goodwill. Toward the end of 1921, the storm had
sufficiently abated for Germany to default once more
upon her obligations. A political outsider, celebrated all
over Europe, was a member of the Cabinet of Fulfilment.
He had been given the portfolio of Minister of Reconstruction. No one knew exactly what this Ministry was

supposed to do. Nor could anyone tell what a man like Rathenau would do. Whatever he did would be full of brilliance and flair.

From his father, Walter Rathenau had inherited the chairmanship of one of the largest enterprises in the world, the AEG, the German General Electric. By profession he was an engineer and captain of industry. By inclination, he was a "bel esprit," a man of letters, a man of the world, a philosopher, an esthete, an economist, a world reformer. He encompassed all culture, and lived in the most refined style; his intellect sparkled dazzingly. All he needed to become a super-Disraeli was a country like England,—and consistency.

Dr. Walter Rathenau's weakness was his over-sensitivity to changing trends. Every new current, no matter where it arose, evoked some response in his mind as though through a subtle capillary system, and, to a certain extent, permeated all his thinking. When it was intellectually chic, this Jew could even stray into a delicate highbrow form of anti-Semitism. At the proper moment, this democrat could become ardently enthusiastic for Prussianism and the Junker caste. This 75% Socialist was also an aristocrat and a nationalist. This cosmopolitan who once declared that if Wilhelm II won the war, "world history would lose all meaning," called for mass conscription a few days before the collapse of Germany. Aside from his brilliance and his ever present, carefully nurtured solemnity and dignity, there was no stability in the Minister of "Reconstruction."

It soon became clear that he was commissioned with the reconstruction not of Germany but of the world. His guiding principle was that "economics is fate" in contrast to Napoleon's feeling that "politics is fate." According to Rathenau, economics was at the basis of everything, and order in Europe and in the world could be created by organizing world economy. All his speeches and plans were dominated by this idea.

The period was particularly propitious for the propagation of his theories. The thesis of the economic as the essential factor was consistent with historical materialism, the core of Socialism and in those years Socialism held people under its spell as never before. Its chief formulations and hypotheses had penetrated even the minds of its adversaries. Even businessmen, millionaires and capitalists had swallowed the Marxist idea of the predominance of economic forces. Many among them were not a little flattered to be able to consider themselves important elements in the central force governing the world. Like any ordinary Bolshevik or "Red," these businessmen, millionaires and capitalists spread the gospel that everything depended upon economics and that all that was necessary to produce miracles was to entrust them with the task of its organization.

But not only capitalists and Marxists tended to see everything in the light of economics. Economic insecurity was what the public at large felt most immediately in their own flesh. Every country was suffering from unemployment and depressed business conditions, from inflation, rising prices, strikes, disorganization. It was said that Germany suffered worse than the others. For most people the chaos of the post-war world took the form of economic manifestations. The conclusion was drawn that economy was the crux of the whole matter, and that world recovery had to begin with economic recovery,

from which all other readjustments would automatically
flow. If the people and the voters thought this, there was
all the more reason for the Ministers to think it.

After six months of "fulfilling Germany's obligations,"
Dr. Rathenau went to see Lloyd George and expounded
some of his large-scale plans for the "depolitization of
politics," for its replacement by economics. The most
ambitious of these was his plan for the so-called reconstruction of Russia. To put that country on its feet again
would be one of the greatest tasks ever undertaken. A
mammoth German-Allied consortium must be organized
for the purpose. The Allies would supply the capital,
Germany the workers and engineers, Russia the "concessions." The factories of all countries concerned would
receive immense reconstruction orders. Russia would
blossom again, and normal trade with her would be resumed. German reparations payments would be somehow worked into this grandiose plan. Thus several beneficent results would be achieved at one stroke: orders and
work for everybody, the recovery of Russia and Germany
and the settlement of the reparations nightmare to the
satisfaction of both debtor and creditor.

Rathenau developed this and other similar plans. Lloyd
George was extremely interested. This would be the right
thing to do, he thought. This would be attacking the
problem in a most magnificent style. A conference of all
the nations of the planet could be summoned—why not?
—a gigantic conference under the chairmanship of Lloyd
George. At this conference, politics would be discarded;
the debate would be passionless and concern itself only
with the economic reconstruction of the world. Soviet
Russia would have to attend, too. What a sensation, the
Bolsheviks participating in an international conference!

Magnificent, unprecedented gains might result. Depolitization, economic reconstruction—that was the thing!

Rathenau returned to Berlin and Lloyd George plunged
into the task of trying to bring about the great international conference. This was in November, 1921. The next
event toward the beginning of December, 1921, was the
declaration of the "Cabinet of Fulfilment" that it would
be unable to fulfil anything during 1922. A long moratorium was necessary, they said. The news Rathenau had
brought from London had convinced the German government that it could afford once more to substitute refusal for "fulfilment."

In January, 1922, the French Chamber of Deputies
forced Briand to resign under particularly dramatic circumstances, at the very moment when the Allied Supreme Council in Cannes was deliberating upon the German request for a moratorium. In the midst of a conference the French Ministers received a telegram informing
them that they were no longer Ministers. The meeting
broke off, the delegates went home. Ex-President Raymond Poincaré formed a new French Cabinet. He was
France's strongest figure and there was no doubt what his
accession to power foreshadowed. His political position
was crystal clear.

In reply to this French move, Germany appointed
Rathenau Foreign Minister. Neither he nor Wirth, the
Reich Chancellor, displayed the moderation they had
shown six months before. They made more and more sar-
castic, sharp and intransigent speeches against Poincaré
and the Allied organs entrusted with the execution of the
peace treaty. "The two men of 'fulfilment,'" wrote their
State Secretary, "became men who openly challenged the
Reparations Commissions." [8]

In the meantime Lloyd George's great world economic spectacle was fixed for the month of April in Genoa. From all the capitals of the world, battalions of delegates, experts, secretaries, journalists, typists and political globe-trotters streamed into Genoa. "The largest gathering of nations that has ever met in the history of this world," [9] gloated Lloyd George. It is true that in private he said to Rathenau's representative: "I have no definite program for Genoa," [10] and the absence of a definite program has never been an asset to a conference, especially a big conference. But Lloyd George added: "They say Russia is my pet child. Well, Russia will be the feature of Genoa." [11]

The delegates of Lloyd George's pet child came via Berlin. It was somewhat disappointing that Lenin was not at their head, as had been expected. He had changed his plans at the last moment, and merely gave a special press interview on Russia's aims at the conference. This began with a pious tribute to the economic interpretation of the world crisis: "We have no intention of raising political problems at Genoa; we regard this conference as a meeting of businessmen, summoned to discuss business matters. We shall go to Genoa as businessmen. . . . I do not expect to conclude a political alliance which is impossible between bourgeois states and a Şoviet Republic." [12] Only at the end were there a few sharp pricks: "In all bargaining there is an element of bluff: we, too, know how to bluff." [13]

Although the Soviet delegation consisted only of Foreign Commissar Chicherin and his assistants, Litvinov, the expert for Western affairs, and Joffe, they were the object of extraordinary attentions during their passage through Berlin. They were given more than the usual

measure of banquets and receptions and remained for
several days—which was quite unusual for a party that
was merely passing through. And negotiations were bus-
ily carried on, "accidentally," as it were, in passing. Baron
von Maltzan, the permanent secretary of the German
Foreign Office was known to be an ardent partisan of a
pact with Russia on the Kemal Pasha model. In those
days he was very occupied and used up a great deal of
paper.

And then everyone went to Genoa. The guests installed
themselves in the villas of the adjoining Riviera. During
the first visits and return visits, everyone assured everyone else that he had really left all politics at home and
would talk exclusively of economic matters—which was
like saying that he had left his brain and spine at home
and would use his legs and hands. And then the conference opened.

Every self-respecting chairman of a delegation which
had any self-respect read a masterpiece of an opening
speech. Most of these speeches were printed and celebrated only in the countries of their authors. Rathenau
was one of the few whose remarks were given promi-
nence in all countries. He had prepared one of his most
brilliant literary achievements, and when he concluded
in Italian with a quotation from Petrarch, he received
much applause in the assembly hall and in the world
press. But, of course, all that was only ceremonial, show.
The real thing, of which no one knew the program, was
to follow, developing quite apart from the mill of rhetoric. From the very first day it was clear to all alert ob-
servers that something mysterious was going on between
the Allied Ministers and Lloyd George's "pet child."

Baron von Maltzan grew nervous, extremely nervous.

He hammered into the ears of his boss, Rathenau, his certainty that the Allies and the Bolsheviks were concocting something terrible. He was sure they were trying to reach a general agreement, who knows? perhaps even a resumption of the Entente Cordiale. He showed him the notes he had received, the information he had obtained. Rathenau, too, grew nervous. He tried to speak to Lloyd George, but failed. Maltzan tried to speak to the Russians, but he, too, failed. Both were overcome by a mood close to despair. What was to become of all the negotiations they had started with the Russians, some of which had even been put down in writing, if they now went over to the other side? What would become of the pact they expected to sign during the next few weeks? Before their eyes, the blue Mediterranean was scintillating in the brilliance of Easter Sunday, but in their souls was the desert, the dark night.

Then the miracle came. At 1:30 A.M. the sun rose. The telephone rang in Maltzan's suite. It was Joffe. He said that the great moment had arrived: now or never! The Soviet government was ready to conclude a pact with Germany. However, if the Germans still wanted it, it had to be signed that same day, now, immediately. No postponements, no wavering could be tolerated. If it were not done now, it could never be done.

"We, too, will know how to bluff," Lenin had said. One moment of cool reflection would have sufficed to show that the Russians had probably encountered an obstacle in their negotiations with the Allies, if these negotiations were serious at all. Their sudden urgency in the middle of the night proved that they had no choice between two possible pacts, but could conclude only one.

But Rathenau and Maltzan were too nervous to be able

to think clearly. Easter morning came. They jumped into a car and drove to Rapallo where the Russians were staying. That same morning Lloyd George telephoned to Maltzan, then to Rathenau, to invite them to have a talk with him, but the gentlemen in question had disappeared. On Easter afternoon, this largest gathering of nations that had ever met was stunned by the news that the Russians and the Germans, the Bolsheviks and the Boches, had inaugurated the proceedings by concluding a pact of defiance and threats.

The text of the pact mattered little. The most significant point in it was that both parties promised to "exchange ideas" before making any important decisions. But the very fact that Germany and Soviet Russia had become associated, changed the equilibrium of the world; and the manner and date chosen to announce this association implied an intention of mockery and provocation. Lloyd George and the entire conference were furious.

"Those who have not experienced it," wrote Bergmann, the German Secretary of State, "can have no idea of the excitement and bitterness among the delegates to the conference. No one showed any sympathy for the German move. Even the neutrals, particularly the Italians, stated with sincere regret that the Rapallo pact had completely spoiled the mood of Genoa. The sympathy the Germans had until then enjoyed in Genoa was by one stroke changed into its opposite. . . ." [14]

"I do not remember, even during the war itself, a sadder ending to an Easter day," Lloyd George's secretary, Edward Grigg, told later on. "We have never yet understood the motives which led the German statesmen to conclude the bilateral agreement at a moment when all the powers met together for the first time to discuss their

problems and their difficulties." [15] Even the Manchester
Guardian, a progressive newspaper full of sympathy for
the German cause, found that the manner of concluding
this pact was "not merely tactless and provocative, but
definitely opposed to the spirit of this or any other conference." [16]

Barthou's view was that the conference which had just
opened might as well be closed. The other French delegates even went so far as to break off all social relations
with their personal friends in the German delegation.
Lloyd George fumed, declaring that only the formal an-
nulment of the Rapallo pact would stop him from returning to England. But the next day he changed his mind,
realizing that a fatal end to his over-publicized conference would be fatal to himself. His Ministry had no solid
support to lean upon. He began to search for gentler solutions, and once again to preach moderation.

His volcanic eruption finally expressed itself in a
strongly reproachful note to Germany, which had no results whatsoever. The conference was saved.

The proceedings dragged on for another month, producing nothing but talk. It did not give birth to a single
proposal for the solution of any of the world problems
which it had been summoned to solve, much less a resolution or a deed. It degenerated into a hocus-pocus which
in the end became painful to everyone—and it would
have so degenerated even without the Rapallo incident.
Thus would all the other conferences degenerate, which
in the first period of conference-mania were summoned
dramatically, but "without a definite program." This was
particularly true of all the "world conferences" which attempted to cure an essentially political situation by
purely economic methods.

But what difference did all that make to Germany? She had her Kemal Pasha pact. True, her intimacy with Soviet Russia, the intimacy of "two pariahs," [17] as Lloyd George said, was never to be entirely free of ambiguity. But ambiguous as it was, German-Russian intimacy, which was formalized for the first time at Rapallo, was one of the Reich's most important and most effective assets in the decades that followed. Dr. Walter Rathenau knew as little as anyone else toward what goal those decades would lead the Reich. But his contribution toward its attainment, was as good as, and better than anyone else's! Everyone who after 1918 stood for any time at the helm of the German state contributed to its attainment.

Two months later Rathenau lay in a pool of blood in a street at Grunewald near Berlin. His murderers, a whole car full of them, had caught up with his car in a carefully prepared raid, riddled its occupants with bullets, and driven away at top speed in the bright morning.

Much later, when the police tracked down two of the murderers in an old castle in Central Germany, they first offered armed resistance and finally shot themselves. They had completely failed to understand that their victim—though by different methods and in a different style —had been marching down the same road as themselves. They understood this just as little as all the pacifists and "good Europeans" who believed that an apostle of their own religion had just been martyrized.

Most people's minds are like albums of old photographs. As a rule, their ideas about a given country are at best twenty years behind the times, their ideas about a personality, at least three years out of date. Rathenau was a Jew. That much was true, and to that extent, the cannibals who marched around Germany singing the new re-

frain: "Kill Walter Rathenau, the goddamn Jewish sow,"
were not mistaken. But they killed him not because he
was a Jew, but because they considered him a "traitor,"
an anti-nationalist. On the other side of the barricades,
too, he was considered an anti-nationalist—but these
were formulae of an earlier day! Many years later, Ed-
mond Vermeil, a French scientist, analyzing the intellectual sources of National Socialism, listed Rathenau
among its ancestors.

There was another tombstone to be erected. Lloyd
George returned from his disastrous Genoa enterprise
with a worn-out halo. The atmosphere of instability
which emanated from him was no longer acceptable. The
Conservatives left his Cabinet, and their leader, Bonar
Law, became Prime Minister. New elections gave them
the majority. For the first time, the leadership of His
Majesty's most Loyal Opposition fell to Labor. The Lib-
erals, Lloyd George's party, the glorious party of the
Whigs, collapsed.

Lloyd George nevertheless remained an important factor in British public opinion. Now freed of all restraint,
he was to plunge headlong into the most dangerous demagogy. He became an exponent of the most consistent,
most astonishing and most audacious complacency.

Were there clouds in the sky? This was because evil
people irritated the sky by talking about rain and asking
for their raincoats; moreover raincoats are expensive and
burdensome. Down with such people! Let us have sun,
not rain. Who speaks of rain? "The old world of national
blindness, national suspicions, national prejudice";
France, ever greedy for conquest; certain British reactionaries. Let us belong to the other party, which "be-
lieves with its whole heart that the welfare of every na-

tion depends upon peace, cooperation, a helping hand from the strong to the weak." [18] Germany apparently belonged to this party; Lloyd George surely belonged to it.

"The campaign for peace is only beginning," [19] he declared in the preface to a book about the Genoa Conference. He led that campaign. He led it for years, consistently using his authority as one who had for many years helped to guide the world, to deny every danger and recommend inaction. That was his position year after year, regardless of who ruled in Germany or what was happening there. His first great speech in Parliament after his overthrow was interrupted by calls of "pro-German!" [20] Fifteen years later, during a plebiscite held by Hitler, who was already busy murdering and incarcerating innocent people, breaking treaties and rearming, Lloyd George was shown on all the German billboards and newsreels speaking encouraging words for the good cause.

3.

An instance of eccentric heroism caused much comment in the European press. One Marek, a Viennese engineer, had insured himself for a rather high sum against injury. Shortly afterward he informed the insurance company that by accident he had lost a leg. It turned out that his misfortune had not been accidental, that he had deliberately hacked off his leg with an axe in order to get the insurance. In the end, instead of money, Marek got a term in prison.

In the eyes of Premier Poincaré, the German Reich was comparable to Marek. Poincaré was convinced that Germany was engineering self-destructive policies in order to prove that it could not make reparations payments. The Reich was deliberately destroying its currency.

From the enormous strain of the war and the defeat, the mark had emerged in surprisingly good condition. After the armistice it had maintained more than half its normal value on neutral stock exchanges. The mark had fallen to 6 to a dollar instead of 4. But this was only the beginning. The fall of the mark was not checked. On the contrary, it became precipitous. In July, 1922, 500 marks were equivalent to a single American dollar. Six months later the ratio was 20,000 to 1. The mark thus retained only a pitiful fraction of its previous value.

In the end, even this fraction became unstable. In the fall of 1923, the price of the dollar was to be 4,200,000,-000,000 marks. But in 1922, no one suspected that even German thoroughness would go as far as that. Ten to twenty thousand marks for a dollar was unbelievable enough.

These grotesque numbers concealed unimaginable realities. Every day, after the close of the stock exchange, shops and restaurants increased their prices in accordance with the latest financial developments: customers would often have to pay for their soup a price double what it had cost when they had ordered it. Small business men had no yardstick for determining their expenses, and each order of a dozen pairs of stockings gave rise to bitter disputes between manufacturers and shopkeepers. Wages and salaries had to be fixed every month, then every week, finally, every day.

One result of this state of affairs was the pauperization of all those whose existence depended, wholly or partially, upon savings or a fixed income. There was the widow with her children, there was the old man who had retired. They had lived on bank deposits, on interest from a mortgage or a few bonds, or on a pension. Now they were literally condemned to starvation. Their capital was not even sufficient to pay a single bus fare. If the pulverization of the mark was a kind of engineer Marek trick, the pauperization of the middle classes was an atrocity, a crime and "worse than a crime: a mistake."

Most people believed that it was a supernaturally or-dained plague. More than that—the interpretation propa-gated by the Germans themselves increasingly found cre-dence: that the fall of the mark was somehow a result of the Versailles Treaty, and particularly a result of those shameful reparations payments, which had not yet be-gun! Yes, odd but true: a large part of the world let itself be convinced that the mark of today was being destroyed by the reparations payments of tomorrow. Who under-stands the mysteries of financial alchemy? Who knows what inflation is, how it arises, how it can be terminated? Not one man among a million even suspects that any country can check inflation within a week's time, that any country can stabilize its currency in a week—if only it really wants to do so, if it places this task above all others.

In the whole world, there were probably less than two hundred men who knew this. And most of these experts refused to consider the monstrous assumption that the Reich was deliberately undermining its own currency, impudently indifferent to the tragic fate of millions of its own citizens. Experts ascribed the lack of stabilization measures to the inexperience of the new government. But Poincaré, that pedantic believer in documents and statistics who, four years later, was to stabilize the falling franc in 48 hours never doubted for one minute that the

Germans themselves had engineered their inflation, that they had failed to check it because they did not want it to stop.

Poincaré was right. It would have been simple to "stabilize the mark." All that was required to that end was that the German government raise the money it needed by rapid, energetic, even brutal taxation, instead of by counterfeiting operations. Such is the classical method, tested in many countries, amply proved. Germany herself would resort to it at the height of the catastrophe, and would be successful without aid from abroad, would be successful simply because the method is effective. There was no reason for not doing in 1922 or 1921 or 1920, under much more favorable conditions, what was finally done in the fall of 1923, no reason, except lack of good will.

The Germans pushed their inflation to the extreme, foreshadowing the things of which German extremism is capable. To unleash a war without real necessity—to wage it to the bitter end—to engineer an inflation swallowing that last billionth part of the last mark—if it could reach such a point in a series of increasingly insane tactics, one was forced to think that nothing was inconceivable to this nation without a *sens de la mesure*. That *furor teutonicus* which the Germans themselves liked to speak of, was obviously not limited to the battlefield, but could break out everywhere. It did not have to be a rage directed toward the destruction of the enemy: it could also be directed toward self-destruction. Those who understood this vicious, maniacal inflation farce could not feel optimistic about Germany's future.

Yes, M. Poincaré was right. A period of euphoria would later come in France, when everyone would be

carried away by the utopian prophesies of that fasci-
nating orator, Briand; when people would say: "Briand
knows nothing and understands everything—Poincaré
knows everything and understands nothing." Poincaré
knew and understood what was behind the mark frenzy.
At most he overlooked one nuance. He realized that the
German government's failure to take measures against
the fall of the mark was determined by its will to sabotage the reparations payments. He did not realize that an
even more criminal motive played a part in this affair, a
motive which, it is true, did not interest him. We shall
deal with this motive presently.

To shake off the reparations burden was the only motive inspiring the leader of the German-National Party.
Dr. Helfferich, who died two years later in a railroad accident in Switzerland, was one of the foremost financial
experts in the world. A respected professor of economics,
author of a famous work on "Money," he had been appointed director of the "Deutsche Bank" and had been
minister under Wilhelm II. Herr Helfferich knew how to
stabilize a currency. But he used his knowledge not to
achieve but to prevent stabilization.

"You are a baby," he said to a bank director who insisted that a remedy against the fall of the mark must be
found. "The remedy is there. But as long as we are not
rid of the reparations, we shall see to it that it is not applied." He used his enormous influence as a political
leader and financial expert to stave off all help for the
mark. With the most captious arguments, and often without arguments at all, he fought every proposed law or
measure capable of improving the situation. In the timid
"stabilization party" there was no one who could measure
up to him, and he always won.

He was firmly convinced that financial chaos in Germany, if sufficiently prolonged and acute, would rapidly induce the Allies to abandon their claims for reparations. The consequent destruction was part of the price to pay for this result. The lives that had to be sacrificed were war casualties. This was war. Helfferich had refused to join the Kapp putschists. Now he was staging his own financial putsch.

But there were others beside him whose motives were not precisely patriotic. Another black, white and red party, the "German People's Party," sat in the government and influenced its policies. To this party belonged a man whose name was now almost legendary, a man whose visiting card bore the undistinguished inscription: "Hugo Stinnes, Merchant from Muelheim-on-the-Ruhr." Herr Stinnes was a King Midas in whose hands even mud turned to gold. His transactions extended from one end of the earth to the other. His utterances were gospel truths for German industry and business. In addition, Herr Stinnes had gone into politics. He was a Reichstag deputy and to a large extent determined the policies of his party.

Herr Stinnes opposed stabilization. To be sure, he, too, advanced patriotic motives for his attitude. But it so happened that the destruction of the mark brought him huge profits, huger than any merchant ever made in so short a space of time. The secret was simple: one had to be in a position to borrow money. At the time of payment, every debt was reduced to practically nothing through devaluation. For instance, suppose you bought a factory for 10,000,000 marks. If you could borrow that sum for a period of six months, you still paid 10,000,000 to your creditor after this period had expired. But in the meantime that sum had become equal in value to a postage stamp. As a result, you bought a factory for a postage stamp.

To buy real values with borrowed money, then repay the debt with devaluated money: that was the trick which could turn the garbage of inflation into gold. Stinnes discovered this trick before any of the other big sharks. He naturally was imitated; there was an entire army corps of "inflation profiteers" but only after some time had passed. And none of his imitators ever reached his heights, because none could obtain as much credit. When Stinnes came to a bank, its treasure opened to him. When his debit account failed to increase in two weeks, the bank telephoned him asking him why he neglected it.

But he did not neglect the banks. He borrowed and bought. He bought coal mines and hotels, steel plants and newspapers, blast furnaces and furniture factories, electric plants and ocean liners, chemical works and film studios, apartment houses and air lines. Rathenau said of him: "There are men who go after every woman they meet; Stinnes goes after every business enterprise." Stinnes' firm became a department store of plants and businesses and stocks of all kinds and sizes, and he was still unsatisfied. Now there was a deal to be concluded, now another business to be bought. Hugo Stinnes' interest in the mark's continued fall seemed inexhaustible, he always wanted it to go on for another month or two. Of course, this did not influence his political views! Anyone who said such a thing would have found it hard to prove. But the fact is, that like Helfferich, he energetically opposed any measure that could alleviate the condition of the mark, let alone cure it.

In the fall of 1922, the diabolical procedure had not yet

reached its end, but M. Poincaré decided that things had
gone far enough. Each German violation of the treaty
taken separately could still be a matter for discussion.
Some excuse or justification could be found for each separate act of resistance with respect to disarmament, deliveries in kind, reparations. But taken in their entirety,
these violations had a clear meaning. The matter of the
mark, which had not been mentioned in the treaty, was
the clearest indication of all. On this point there was an
absolute difference of opinion between M. Poincaré and
a large part of the world. To most people, the sad plight
of the German mark was an extenuating circumstance;
because of it they pleaded for acquittal. To Poincaré it
was the most aggravating circumstance: it definitely
proved Germany's ill will, an ill will that did not shy before anything, not even before the impudent destruction
of the German middle class.

At this point, Chancellor Wirth, who had become a
"refusal" chancellor but of whom it was still remembered
that he had once been a "fulfilment" chancellor, was
overthrown. Herr Ebert replaced him by a non-politician,
a former middle-ranking government official who had recently been appointed General Director of the Hamburg-
American Line. As a government official, Herr Cuno had
been entrusted with investigating the Line's claims for
damages suffered as a result of ship losses during the war.
When this matter was settled he resigned from his small
government post and accepted the Directorship of the
Line. There was a time when Germany was a land of
honest bureaucracy, and such a thing could not happen
without resulting in unpleasant investigations.

All that was known of Herr Cuno, now a captain of
business, was that he was a pronounced black, white and

red, a "German-National." He was slender and elegant.
His face was smooth and empty; his utterances, too, were
smooth and empty. His only apparent virtue was that he
was a German-National. Thus, for the first time since
1918, a full-blooded monarchist, a total reactionary, was
at the head of the German state. And when he made an
opening speech full of bellicose lyricism, it became clear
that the German government had resolved to enter into
open conflict with the Allies, that it had abandoned the
policy of retreating two steps when resistance grew too
strong, and that it intended this time to move forward, to
push things to the extreme, to break through.

In December, 1922, Poincaré went to London. He told
his colleague, Bonar Law, that the time had come to use
force. It was impossible to get anywhere, he explained,
without using force. Germany had sabotaged the disarmament clauses, the deliveries in kind, the reparations, and
had even refused to put her finances in order and stabilize the mark. The Germans were apparently convinced
that platonic protests and diplomatic notes would be the
only type of retaliation. It was necessary to show them
that the Allies were capable of strong measures. Poincaré
suggested the common occupation of the Ruhr region,
the source of German coal, the center of basic German
industries. He argued that this forceful measure would
have a salutary effect.

Poincaré's suggestion was supported by M. Theunis,
the Belgian representative, and Signor Mussolini, who, a
few weeks earlier, had succeeded in getting himself appointed Premier of Italy. In Italy, Mussolini acted rather
noisily and bullied his parliament. Here, in London, he
was unassuming, more modest than his predecessors ever
were. And, of course, the English considered him to be a

dog on France's leash. In 1914, when he began his campaign for Italy's entry into the war, the French gave him
money to found a newspaper. Now he was nothing but
Poincaré's yes-man. "Poincaré has put the question on a
realistic basis. There is no time to lose, because the machine for printing bank-notes is working at full capacity." [21]

Bonar Law was not another Lloyd George. Bonar Law
did not assume that the French were motivated by the
Napoleonic ideal. That was what his predecessor cried in
a voice resounding through the country, as soon as Poincaré's proposal became known; and the entire Left held
the same opinion. Bonar Law was free from this absurdity. Nevertheless, his position was, in point of fact,
hostile to France, in accordance with the definitely
adopted British policy. Balance of power in favor of Germany was still the watchword.

He declared that the occupation of the Ruhr was no
"military picnic," [22] but a most dangerous undertaking.
He confided to Poincaré that the Leftist agitation sufficed
to make the proposal inacceptable, that if he yielded to
it, the Conservative Party would be crushed in the next
elections. And he developed the theory which was, from
then on, to define the official British position: the theory
of the fundamental difference between "voluntarily undertaken" and "imposed" obligations. Why did the Germans constantly violate the treaty? Only because it had
been imposed on them at Versailles. Their behavior
would change radically, he said, if we wisely replaced the
"Diktat" with new agreements, concluded on a voluntary
basis. That was the solution to be desired.

This theory was clearly fallacious. To achieve victory is
precisely to create a situation in which the enemy can be

coerced. To be defeated is to be coerced. Whatever the peace of 1919 should have been, it could only be a peace of compulsion. And whatever elements of that peace might be deleted now, the remainder would still be a product of compulsion. Germany would agree to that remainder only because and when she was compelled. Phrases such as "voluntarily accepted agreements" were only window dressing. Were the Allies willing to declare that the outcome of the war was a mistake? If not, no settlement was possible which Germany would not regard as, and which would not actually be, the result of compulsion. For a logician like Poincaré, the difference between "compulsory" and "voluntary" agreements was purely fictitious. He did not believe that the settlement with Germany could be made more effective by more gentle and polite insistence, but by sterner and more vigorous police measures. Berlin was refractory not because it had been compelled to sign the treaty, but because it was not forced to abide by its signature. This is what he wrote in his instructions to the French ambassador in London: "Judging others by themselves, the English, who are blinded by their own loyalty, have always thought that the Germans did not abide by their pledges inscribed in the Versailles Treaty because they had not frankly agreed to them. . . . We, on the contrary, believe that if Germany, far from making the slightest effort to carry out the treaty of peace, has always tried to escape her obligations, it is because until now she has not been convinced of her defeat. . . . We are also certain that Germany, as a nation, resigns herself to keep her pledged word only under the impact of necessity." [23]

The London conversations brought no results. The clash between England and France was extended to an

opposition between England and the Allies. By the end
of December, 1922, the Reparations Commission officially
stated that Germany had deliberately failed to fulfil the
deliveries of wood, only the English members of the
Commission objecting to this statement. At the beginning
of January, 1923, the Commission issued a similar declaration concerning the coal deliveries; this time, again,
the English members were the opposition.

The Powers met again in Paris. Bonar Law suggested
that the German reparations payments be reduced to
one-fifth of what had been decided a year before. He
also suggested that the Reparations Commission be abolished and replaced by a new Commission under the chairmanship of the German Finance Minister: the debtor was
to collect his own debts. This was obviously a "new milestone," of the same kind as the transfer of the war criminal cases to the German Supreme Court. Poincaré did
not have to intervene in the discussion: the Belgians and
Italians were so angry that they said whatever had to be
said. On the last day of the conference it was clear that
France, Italy and Belgium would apply forceful measures
to make Germany adhere to its agreements. Italy, which
had no troops on the Rhine, sent a token force.

On January 11, 1923, the occupation of the Ruhr began. The Allied troops encountered no armed resistance,
and within a few hours the operation was completed. The
heart of German industry was seized as security.

The march into the Ruhr sufficed to provoke a political
storm. The meaning of Herr Cuno's appointment as
Chancellor was now fully revealed.

The Reich launched a counter-offensive against the occupation. It announced a war of a special, unprecedented
kind, which, however, like all wars, had victory as its

objective. Herr Cuno and those behind him were convinced that the time was ripe to fight against the articles
of the treaty, and also against the military forces of the
Allies. Cuno was convinced that the Germans would succeed in forcing the French to withdraw, thus definitely
annulling the Reich's defeat, not only on paper, but also
in fact. The black, white and red Chancellor believed he
could rely to a certain extent on the British officials. But
he also expected help from the progressives, liberals, socialists, communists, pacifists, utopians, post-Wilsonians
in England, America, France and everywhere. Herr Cuno
expected people of this type to remove the bayonets directed against him. The German reactionaries and militarists expected to triumph through the intervention of
the world's pacifists and progressives.

Chancellor Cuno declared that special war which received the name of "passive resistance." He issued orders
that all life in the Ruhr be extinguished—and not only
in the Ruhr, but also in the other parts of the Rhineland
occupied by French and Belgian troops since 1918. The
factories had to close down. Railroads were not to operate. No order of the occupation authorities was to be
obeyed. The occupants were to be confronted only with
obstacles, so that they would be unable to get any profit
out of the occupation. They were not to be permitted to
obtain a pound of coal or a bag of flour without the use
of force. The more force they were compelled to apply,
the better. The reaction of the progressives and humanitarians abroad would be all the stormier.

For, this must be kept in mind, "passive resistance"
was not presented as the work of Cuno's government. If
it had been so presented, overwhelming indignation
could not have been aroused. The struggle was presented

as "the spontaneous resistance of the population," particularly of the workers. The mines, factories and railroads were shut down by orders from above, but everything was made to look as though the "workers" by their own initiative had refused to work under the foreign yoke. In fact, the German government financed the idle workers, officials and employers; it paid them their usual wages, salaries or incomes. But, to the world outside, it was their patriotic passion that prevented the Germans from working when bayonets of foreign oppressors were pointed at them.

A decade later the world was to observe another wave of "popular anger." By order of their superiors, Nazis would gather and in an outburst of "spontaneous popular anger" murder people, burn synagogues, plunder and smash shops. This time everybody understood what was going on. But when Cuno's government organized and financed "passive resistance," a large part of the world saw only the pieces moving on the chessboard, while failing or refusing to see the players who moved them about.

Mr. Bonar Law defined the British government's attitude as one of neutrality, benevolent neutrality toward both parties, Germany and France. He spoke of the events as though their meaning and purpose were exclusively economic, as though all that was in question was the collection of the deliveries in kind and reparations; that is to say, the most efficient method of obtaining these from Germany. To be sure, he argued, the French, and all the Allies, are entitled to obtain the largest quantities of both in the shortest possible time, but the occupation of the Ruhr, he insisted, would not result in larger or speedier deliveries and payments. Hence, according to Bonar Law, the occupation was a false method, but the difference of opinion as to the methods to be applied would not affect the Franco-British friendship.

This was a typical example of the economic fallacy. The occupation of the Ruhr was no more intended to enforce the payment of reparations, let alone to speed them up, than the arrest of a swindler is intended to restore the losses of his victim. The occupation of the Ruhr was a political move intended to break political resistance; resistance not only in the economic sphere, but in all spheres. The old French demand for security was once again being asserted. Security had been the theme of her struggle during the peace conference; the Anglo-American alliance and the "guarantee pact" seemed, at least to a certain extent, to have satisfied her demands. Now the pact was relegated to the realm of legends. The prospects for security were bad, and they grew worse on the day the Reich openly and successfully demonstrated its will to "break the chains of Versailles."

Edward Grey, made wise by his experience as Foreign Minister at a critical moment of history, and his long contemplation of the international scene as a spectator, warned his British countrymen: "I would ask people in this country who are very apt to criticize France as having been restless, or aggressive, or contemplating strong separate action in this last year, I would ask them to bear in mind what would be their own feelings had they been Frenchmen." The real reason for the occupation, he proceeded to explain, was not greed for money. "I am sure that what the French want most of all is security in Europe. As long as you deal with these questions of reparations solely by themselves, and deal with them as though they were purely economic things, without facing the facts, I do not believe progress can be made. . . . You

will not really get economic recovery in Europe unless
you also get greater political security. . . ." [24]

But while Bonar Law may have privately expressed
agreement with these ideas, his country did not permit
him to translate them into practice. His country was now
actually in that state of mind which Wilson had, four
years before, attributed to all the peoples of the world.
It had lost all sense of the world as it "is," and indulged
in the deceptive belief in a world as it "ought" to be. The
majority of the English people were convinced that Europe wanted to remain at peace, but that it was harassed
by a militaristic France. They saw only an honest, suffering, and fundamentally democratic Germany bullied by
a sinister, terrorist, reactionary France. The very word,
"security," made them impatient; it became a joke, it
passed as a symptom of French selfishness. That security
was the foundation of peace, of actual, not abstract
peace, of every country's peace, not only France's, was
forgotten.

And Germany ran amok. All activities in the Ruhr and
in the Rhineland, except in the parts occupied by British
troops, ceased. The German government interrupted railway communication between Western Europe and Warsaw, Prague and Bucharest. Every device was employed
to arouse the population. Signs were distributed in cafes
and restaurants, with the inscription: "Frenchmen and
Belgians are not served." Newspapers ran accounts of
atrocities committed by French soldiers in the Ruhr and
on the Rhine. The most odious insult, the "black shame,"
was the presence of Negro regiments among the French
troops. The presence of these black soldiers was particularly revolting because they allegedly behaved like ani-
mals. Their main occupation seemed to be the rape of

German girls. The *Deutsche Allgemeine Zeitung,* which belonged to the great Stinnes and which claimed to be the German equivalent of the "Times," published an "eye-witness account" of how a Negro sentry in Essen, seeing a little blond boy, smashed the boy's head with the butt of his rifle and proceeded to eat the brains in the open skull.

Germany ran amok. Inevitably, the occupation authorities were compelled to use force against a population which had been exhorted to disobey all orders. People had to be sentenced and imprisoned. Yet the principle of legality was preserved: no one was made responsible for actions which he himself had not committed. There were no reprisals. No villages were razed. But whatever incidents took place were sufficient to supply the manufacturers of propaganda with raw material.

There was more than propaganda. The time for patriotic adventures had come again, the time for all those Landsknechts who were still roaming about in all sorts of irregular formations, and "black" troops, the existence of which, now that the military control commission no longer dared show itself in Germany, was scarcely kept secret. The time had come for all the vagabonds, desperadoes and neurotics to join the various "people's" groups—not the least of which was the rapidly growing party of Adolf Hitler, who now no longer wandered in canteens and inns, but owned newspapers, held meetings in halls and beer-saloons, and for whom a general staff composed of ex-officers had built an organization extending over all Germany.

The Landsknechts, vagabonds and desperadoes, no longer had to content themselves with individual murders committed in their own country, with victims such as

Erzberger, Rathenau, or small-fry "traitors" from their own ranks. They infiltrated the Rhineland, bringing weapons and explosives. They blew up bridges and French trains. There were deaths; there were imprisonments and courts-martial. One of these criminals, who derailed a train and caused the death of many people, was sentenced to be shot. He was a miserable fellow named Schlageter. He had been a swindler, thief and pimp and he was so patriotic that after his arrest, to save his skin, he gave away his accomplices. Schlageter became nevertheless the pièce de resistance of the German campaign intended to arouse the world's pity. He became a national hero; later Hitler had streets named after him and an imposing monument erected to his memory.

Germany ran amok. She waited the break-through of her auxiliary troops. The reactionary rulers of Germany awaited the intervention of foreign liberals. And the liberals intervened.

In France, they were timid at first. Aside from the Communists, who defended the German cause everywhere, only the Socialists openly opposed Poincaré's move. On the day of the occupation, their new leader, Leon Blum, declared: "You are going to give the world the impression that you act against international law, the real, living law . . ." [25] But only the Socialists and the Communists were clearly against Poincaré. Their bourgeois neighbors of the "Bloc des Gauches," the Radicals, were more cautious. Their leaders such as Herriot, Chautemps, Daladier, abstained from voting.

In England, however, there was a real mobilization of the liberals, They went to war for the abstract peace. The Labor Party swallowed the whole Berlin legend of the "spontaneous resistance" by the "Ruhr workers." The

Troops on the March

Laborites succeeded in persuading themselves that the fight was mainly conducted by their German fellow-workers. They solemnly announced solidarity with the Ruhr workers and they sent a delegation to the Ruhr "battlefield." They never once suspected that in this case the German workers fought not for the cause of the working class, but for that of the German militarists.

The Labor Party leaders made speeches which once again proved that they knew the Berlin propaganda tirades by heart. Ramsay MacDonald and Arthur Henderson spoke in exactly this vein. Philip Snowden, afflicted with a serious illness in addition to various monomanias, indulged in bitter Francophobia; he said that the Allies treated Germany like a "beast." Verily, even the "black shame" was swallowed! The same politicians and journalists who were ever ready to fight for equal rights for all races, now suddenly found the presence of Negro regiments on German soil a provocation.

The Liberals—the majority among them—did not remain quiescent. Lloyd George went into action and so did Sir John Simon, who was consistently pro-German. And even among the Conservatives there were many defections to Germany. The French action, it was argued, was unjustified. Peace would be secure for generations if Germany were not interfered with. At one session of the House of Lords, sharp words were hurled at Postmaster General Neville Chamberlain who carried on a tireless agitation against France and for Germany behind the scenes. The London "Times," was openly pro-Cuno and anti-Poincaré.

Herr Cuno was waiting for the offensive of his British, French and American auxiliary troops. Would they compel their governments to act? Would they repulse Poincaré, force him to withdraw? Time was short, Germany could not wait indefinitely. The cost of the Ruhr campaign in money, goods and human suffering surpassed even what the most exacting reparations payments would have entailed. The Reich had to pay, in paper marks printed without stint, millions to inhabitants of the Ruhr and the Rhineland, it had to import coal and many other commodities; it had to support its most important provinces while being deprived of any profitable returns. This could not go on forever. Intervention by the auxiliary troops of the liberals was urgent.

The auxiliary troops did everything they could. In France, they launched a campaign against Poincaré, accusing him of ruining the nation; they argued that the occupation of the Ruhr was costly and unprofitable, that it alienated foreign sympathies, and they demanded that it be replaced by an agreement with the German people.

In England, the auxiliary troops were even more vociferous. They demanded that the government give up its policy of neutrality. They demanded that England compel France to leave the Ruhr; that France be indicted before the League of Nations and condemned for disturbing international peace. The "Times" wrote that the mood for intervention was growing daily. Mr. Bonar Law was under steadily increasing pressure.

The British Cabinet took steps. It brought pressure on Italy and Belgium to break their ties with France. It began to assume a threatening tone toward France, and to adopt the popular view that the occupation of the Ruhr was a breach of the peace treaty. Then it acted like an umpire jumping between two boxers: it made energetic appeals for mediation.

This was a good day for Herr Cuno. Now it was clear

that he had calculated correctly. Germany expected M. Poincaré to give way.

But M. Poincaré refused to be terrified. He surrounded himself with a disquieting lack of concern for all threats and promises. He declared publicly that he had no use for mediation. Germany, he said, must submit without "any intermediary." [26]

The British Cabinet got in touch with Herr Cuno. Lord d'Abernon, the British ambassador, was more important in Berlin than the Reich Chancellor himself. German augurs called him the "Lord Protector." He told the Chancellor that Germany must make an offer, an offer of voluntary reparations payments, as soon as the Ruhr was evacuated. The Lord Protector himself collaborated in preparing this offer.

M. Poincaré replied that the German offer did not interest him so long as Germany continued to wage the "Ruhr war." To begin with, the Reich must capitulate. The British Cabinet sent Poincaré a questionnaire: what would France offer in return if Germany declared herself ready to stop the "Ruhr war?" Poincaré left the question unanswered. He said the British efforts "could be dispensed with." [27]

The British Cabinet advanced a new proposal. Assuming that Germany was willing to stop the Ruhr war, would M. Poincaré agree to pledge himself, in all secrecy, in a communication addressed only to the British government, to withdraw from the Ruhr? Poincaré replied: No. The occupation of the Ruhr and the Ruhr war could not be regarded as equivalents. The first was a police operation, the second resistance to legal authority. The Germans, he said, must give up their Ruhr war, unconditionally.

The German augurs became uneasy. They demanded

of Chancellor Cuno and Helfferich, his oracle; Where is your victory? What has the offensive of the auxiliary troops accomplished? If this Poincaré is impervious to pressure, if everything is stalemated by his repeated refusals, how shall we recover from this disaster?

For a disaster it was. As a result of the passive resistance in the Ruhr, not as a result of the occupation, Germany which had been recovering economically, plunged downwards once again with frightening speed. The mark was heading toward the final abyss. There were instances of peasants, manufacturers and businessmen who refused to sell anything for this money which turned to ashes in the hand that held it. Shops and markets were as empty as in 1918. There was a shortage of coal. Railroads were disorganized. There was a wave of hunger demonstrations and strikes. Government authority seemed about to disintegrate. Bolshevist, National-Bolshevist, National Socialist rebellions loomed on the horizon. In the seventh month of the Ruhr war, the country felt that it had once again been hopelessly defeated. Materially and psychologically the new extremism approximated the stage of total chaos. Now and then rumors still circulated among the augurs, which restored hope for a few hours. For instance, in the Reichstag corridors, deputies told one another that "England and America" [28] had decided to smash the French currency. Thus, in 1918, a few days before the German collapse, Ludendorff had said: "As a drowning man clutches at a straw I cling to the report that an epidemic of influenza has broken out in the French army." But all such rumors proved false. On July 27th, six and a half months after the proclamation of passive resistance in the Ruhr, the principal organ of the Catholic Centrist Party opened wide the sluices of defeatism: "Confidence in the Reich government," it wrote, "has been completely shattered."

Liberals abroad grew tumultuous. In England, they launched a pitiless campaign against Stanley Baldwin, who had succeeded his friend, now quite ill, Bonar Law. Would nothing be done to insure the triumph of the just cause? The British Cabinet drew up a very sharply worded note and sent it to Paris in August: a real indictment in 55 numbered paragraphs. In this note, England drastically declared herself for Germany. "The highest legal authorities in Great Britain have advised His Majesty's Government that the contention of the German government is well founded." [29] There had been much talk of expert opinion by undetermined "high legal authorities," and this was the first official mention of them and the last. Who these legal authorities were and what they had said was never made public. The "Times" observed that if such a note had been addressed to France twenty years earlier, the Foreign Office would not have forwarded it without having previously notified the War Office and the Admiralty.

At the very hour when this note was sent, something happened in Germany: the chancellorship of elegant Herr Cuno came to an end. The people and the politicians realized that the game was up, that the remaining few gallons of gas had to be used to organize an orderly withdrawal.

At the last minute Cuno gave another proof of his inflexibility by launching a blow at the English as punishment for their failure to do what he had expected of them. Cuno stopped deliveries in kind to England, too. Under-Secretary of State Tyrrell congratulated the German ambassador for this action. Fifteen years later the same Lord

Tyrrell would say with melancholy: "We have treated the French as though they were Germans, and the Germans, as though they were English."

Herr Cuno's fall was not a change of government. It was a device to which all nations resort when defeat is imminent. The old government is replaced by a new one which "appears" friendlier to the victorious enemy.

"Appears" is correct in this case. Dr. Gustav Stresemann of the black, white and red "German People's Party," was the average German par excellence: he came of a typical middle class family, was moderately well-to-do, had occupied no exalted posts, and was endowed with average intelligence, and average eloquence. He was a catalogue of what was most common to his people and his class. He retained a typical loyalty for the imperial house; the common view as to the goals a nation must pursue in order to be great and happy, and most particularly the German nation with its world mission. During the war he shared the German belief that Germany must annex large territories and in the end exert a beneficent rule over Europe. Like most other Germans he thought that the collapse and defeat of 1918 were only passing episodes, and that the "chains would soon be broken." During the Ruhr war he believed that this goal had practically been attained. Now that Germany was on the verge of another defeat, he inferred that she had merely to withdraw in good order.

Had Stresemann occupied Cuno's place at the time Cuno held office he might have pursued the same policies as Cuno. As fate had decided differently, as he had come to power after Cuno and under different circumstances, as heroic extremism had once again turned to dust, these policies were thrown overboard.

Stresemann's utterances were marked by caution, moderation and willingness to compromise. He tried, like his predecessor, to avoid capitulation, but this was impossible. Though Chancellor Stresemann went so far as to address himself directly to the enemy, Poincaré informed him that he did not think it advisable to soften Germany's submission. He refused to build even the narrowest bridge to enable the Germans to execute even the appearance of an "honorable retreat." On the matter of the Ruhr war, he demanded of Germany complete surrender.

Mr. Baldwin went to Paris. Poincaré had won, there was no longer any doubt about it. Nothing succeeds like success. London and Paris buried the hatchet and announced their "complete agreement" on all questions.

Germany was in a death-agony. The mark was reduced to a billionth and then a trillionth of its former value; the institution of money practically ceased to exist. Remnants of trade were still possible, mostly by means of barter; all kinds of foreign currencies crawled from their hiding places: pound sterling, dollars, francs, guldens, Czech crowns. Millions were starving. Winter was approaching and there was no coal. The political organism seemed about to burst asunder. In the East, the "Black Reichswehr," the appendix which the regular Reichswehr had added to itself, launched a putsch, and Herr von Seeckt had to crush it by armed force. In Saxony, a quasi-Bolshevist government was set up, which Berlin put down. In Bavaria, a supernationalist government broke with the Reich and contended for local power with the swastika cohorts under Marshal Ludendorff and his drummer, Hitler.

Two and one half months after his assumption of office, on September 26th, 1923, Herr Stresemann proclaimed Germany's capitulation. The Ruhr and Rhineland prov-

inces were summoned to end resistance of all forms and
to return to work. The French and British governments
were notified that a normal situation was being restored.
The French, Belgian and token Italian troops remained
in the Ruhr.

4.

In the French Chamber of Deputies, the government
parties passed a resolution in the classical Jacobin style
to the effect that Citizen Poincaré "had well deserved of
the fatherland." This was true. But the man, whom nobody liked, many hated and almost everyone respected,
the dry Lorrainer without grace and brilliance, stubborn,
so insultingly incorruptible, had rendered a service to Europe and the world, and most of all to Germany. It is not
too much to say that this forced capitulation was the only
good fortune that befell Germany in the decades after
1919.

The defeat of 1918 had not been deeply felt by the
people of Germany. Their standard of living had not
been reduced by defeat below the level maintained during the war. Despite the defeat in 1920 the average German was better off than in 1917; and in 1921 better than
in 1915. As it had not influenced the average German's
personal life, the defeat remained an abstract conception.

The collapse of the "Ruhr war" was something else
again. Every German experienced it personally, participating in the terrifying St. Vitus dance of the mark, seeing
hunger and misery and chaos rampant in the land. The
experience would serve as a warning—for some time.

Odd and unpredictable are the ways of the world. For
five years, humanitarians and progressives and would-be

psychologists of all sorts had been patting Germany on
the back, recommending that she be treated kindly. In
these five years Germany had not for a single month de-
sisted from war. These were years of continuous and increasing trouble. Then one man came and seized Germany by the throat, and as if by magic, six years of
relative reasonableness followed, years of order and hence
of prosperity.

M. Poincaré's successors spoiled the cure. Yet for six
years its beneficent effects continued, although Germany's
efforts to destroy the settlement of 1919 did not cease.
But this time she proceeded with caution, using under-
hand methods. The demon which drove Germany from
one extremist move to another, the murderous and self-
destroying "furor teutonicus," was contained for six years;
thus the only years of order and recovery—an astonishing recovery—which Germany enjoyed between the two
world wars, were the result of coercive action. So indirect
and "dialectical" are the causalities in this complex world!
If the lesson had been understood and taken to heart, the
relatively golden age that began immediately after the
German capitulation in the Ruhr conflict and lasted for six
years might have lasted for sixty.

The very first consequence of the capitulation was so
clear that it is a mystery why the lesson was not understood. At the very moment of the collapse of the Ruhr
resistance, the Reich did what it allegedly had been unable to do; it stabilized its currency and put its finances
in order. Germany's hope of "breaking" the Versailles
chains with the help of the inflation bogey had evaporated. Engineer Marek's method of cutting off his own leg
proved a failure. M. Poincaré whom the fall of the mark
had moved not to pity but to increased severity, was in-

disputably in the right. Now Germany put her house in order.

A certain Dr. Hjalmar Schacht, an ambitious banker, was entrusted with the job of stabilization. The "miracle" he performed was extravagantly publicized. But the alleged miracle was nothing but the classical remedy. The printing presses were stopped, the Reich government demanded and collected taxes. For many years it had been "unable" to collect the necessary funds by honest taxation, because of the general misery and the defeat; the deficit was covered by printing bank notes in the last stage to the extent of 99% of the budget. Now, suddenly, in October, 1923, in the terror and chaos of unprecedented impoverishment, the impossible suddenly became possible. Taxes were imposed and the presses stopped printing bank notes.

Within a few days, the mark was stabilized at one trillionth of its former value. A few weeks later, the Reichsmark was introduced. It was made equivalent to one trillion marks. Bills bearing the inscription "one trillion marks" were exchanged for bills bearing the inscription "one Reichsmark." And that was all.

Political order was stabilized as quickly and easily as financial order. The political basis of Germany was intact. The armed force had always been the basis of the Reich. It was employed to put an end to senseless political convulsions. In November, while chaos was everywhere being replaced by order, Hitler and Ludendorff committed a belated act of folly. Either they thought that the German chaos had reached its climax, or they feared that it was passing without bringing them any profit. They failed to realize that the real rulers of Germany had set their minds to introducing order. In a grotesque meeting at a Munich beer hall they declared the Reich government deposed, and they proclaimed the "march on Berlin." One salvo of the armed forces sufficed to put an end to this affair. For six years extreme nationalism vanished from Europe. It was another victim of Poincaré's energetic move.

Poincaré remained in the Ruhr. He had security in his hands, which he did not propose to surrender. He was faced by a Reich whose extremism he had defeated. He knew this defeat was not definitive, that France must always remain on the alert. When his Rightist partisans praised him, and his Leftist opponents reviled him, he said: "We are far from having overcome our difficulties." But now France could seriously begin to solve the remaining question of the peace.

Charles Evans Hughes, the American Secretary of State, had repeatedly suggested that so-called "unpolitical" economic experts be consulted on the question of reparations payments. Though America no longer had anything to do with the peace, he suggested that American experts sit on an international committee to discuss reparations. Poincaré did not seriously believe that important international questions could ever be non-political. He did, indeed, want American support. But just as he had refused everything that resembled foreign intervention, he flatly refused such a commission of experts while the Reich was waging its Ruhr war. Now, after the Reich's capitulation, the situation was changed. He felt secure. He was willing to hear the recommendations of a committee backed by the prestige of America and composed of the highest authorities of all nations.

On December 12th, 1923, the experts held a preliminary meeting in New York. The American delegates were General Charles G. Dawes and Owen D. Young. In January of 1924 the experts moved to Paris, and in April of the same year they published their findings.

The world as a whole was determined in advance to consider the recommendations laid down by these experts excellent, human, and businesslike. In fact, the Dawes Plan was regarded as representing the expression of the most complete wisdom, as distinguished from the complete madness that had hitherto prevailed. This was a myth, but a beneficent myth. The Dawes Plan was no new revelation. It did not express the fictitious contrast between fruitful science and destructive politics. It made hard, very hard demands on Germany. It was as open to attack as former plans, and it would have been attacked if it had been proposed before instead of after Poincaré's energetic move.

The Plan was not definite, it did not name a final sum. It only advanced proposals as to the German payments for the next five years. In the fifth year, the German payment was to be two and one-half billion marks plus indeterminate additions according to a "prosperity index" which could increase the original sum considerably. According to the Paris Plan of 1921, which had aroused a storm of indignation in Germany and in the world, the instalment paid in the fifth year would have been 3 billion marks plus supplements. The difference was far from being that between wisdom and madness.

On the point of securities, the Dawes Plan was more exacting than any previous plan. The yield of certain German taxes was to be impounded. A reparations mortgage was to be attached to all German industrial plants. The German Railways were no longer to be the property of the Reich, and their supervising board was to be internationalized. The Reichsbank was to be removed from

all interference by the Reich government, and its supervising board internationalized. A foreign comptroller of
all German finance and industry, bearing the title of "General Agent for Reparations" was to be appointed in Berlin. These were enormous encroachments upon German
sovereignty. The Plan did not even provide for the evacuation of the Ruhr; indeed, it mentioned further "military
occupation" in the event of "flagrant failures." The phi-
lanthropists, humanitarians and perfectionists could easily
have found all this as monstrous as any previous measures, and Germany had as excellent reasons for being in-
furiated as in 1921.

But there was no evidence of fury, all agitation was
repressed. It was agreed that this time the plan was something quite different, a pleasant contrast to the others.
Germany accepted it, and her foreign legions abroad accepted it. The French Premier was satisfied, too, and said
so. He was particularly satisfied because "no one demanded the evacuation of the Ruhr." [30] A special conference to be called shortly was to draw up a program for
carrying out the provisions of the Dawes Plan. In April
of 1924 for the first time since the war, Europe seemed
somewhat stabilized.

In May came the French elections. The Cartel des
Gauches won them. For the first time since the war,
France was to be ruled by a Leftist majority composed
of Socialists and Radicals. These parties had bitterly
fought against everything Poincaré had done, the intensity of their fight against his policies increased as the
elections drew nearer. They represented the very victory
he had won as fatal for France. Had he not brought
France to the verge of a break with England? Had not
France been reviled by liberals all over the world? They

themselves would use other methods. They were against violence. They were for peace. They were for the German people. The world could not be saved by the applications of traditional methods; one had to apply methods which were the exact "opposite, reverse, negation" of everything that had been done before.

Poincaré was forced to resign. Herriot, his successor, announced a "new policy" toward Germany, "a new policy of conciliation," [31] proceeding by gradual steps. Stresemann listened with bated breath. All the black, white and red elements in Germany were attentive. They would see how it would look in actuality, whether all this was meant as conciliation within a rigid framework, or as toleration of the extension and loosening of the framework itself. Caution! Silence! Wait and see!

Three months later, as the first token of his new policy of gradual conciliation, Herriot agreed to evacuate the Ruhr. Mr. Hughes himself came from Washington to Europe to induce him to take this step. Berlin realized its time was coming. Caution! Feel your way! No longer try to "break the chains"—that had proved much too expensive. But to stretch them, to bend them, in a friendly, conciliatory spirit, that was worth trying. This new method was to lead very far.

On June 1st, 1924, when Poincaré was overthrown, France's role as a great power came to an end. This could not have been understood at that moment. The truth was to reveal itself gradually.

From that day on, the Third Republic was never again to assert its will. France ceased to perform the task to which she had been summoned by the miserable peace treaty: the task of controlling the jungle on her borders, for her own sake and the world's. Instead of remaining on guard, France, from that day on, would lead a twilight existence of uninterrupted apathy; at first benumbed and paralyzed by the visions and dreams of the Left, and later by the visions and dreams of the Right. For sixteen years France would never once deviate from what, seen in retrospect, was obviously a fatal direction.

Part Two: Euphoria:
1924-1929

6: The Magic House of Paper

AMBASSADOR D'ABERNON, the Lord Protector, solemnly put on his horn-rimmed spectacles. Not without emotion, for that February 9th, 1925, was a memorable day, he wrote in his diary: "There is another condition necessary to success, namely to abandon the view that Germans are such congenital liars that there is no practical advantage in obtaining from them any engagement or declaration. On this assumption progress is impossible. Personally I regard the Germans as more reliable and more bound to written engagements than many other nations."[1]

On this point, the noble Lord exaggerated a little. He was one of those ambassadors who adopt a traveling salesman's attitude toward the country to which they are accredited. They never fail to praise their "customers" in their reports, because their own personal prestige is at stake. Even so, Lord d'Abernon went rather far in his praise, and his entry that day was written under the impact of real feeling. In a tone of irritation he took action against an unnamed possible opponent, perhaps his su-

perior, the Foreign Secretary (for in everything concerning Germany, Sir Austen Chamberlain was skeptical) perhaps the French government to whom the memorandum
was to be handed that day.

What was all this about? What was the great "step
forward" the ambassador now considered possible? Herr
Stresemann had sent an offer to Paris and London. At this
time he was only Foreign Minister. A certain Dr. Luther
was Reich Chancellor. Doctors Luther and Stresemann
had offered Paris and London something which, according
to the Lord Protector, was enormously significant. He himself had helped prepare the German note, and for this
reason it seemed all the more significant to him. "An immense step in the direction of pacification," [2] he termed
the offer in his Diary.

Stated bluntly, Germany was now offering to sell once
again something which had been sold before. Nothing
more than that. The "immense step forward" was her
willingness to sign for the second time what she had already signed. Certain pledges made under "compulsion"
were to be made again; this time "voluntarily."

The Lord Protector was aware of the origin of the
offer. It did not arise from Germany's generosity, but from
her desire to thwart a plan hatched by the French and
Sir Austen Chamberlain. Sir Austen had always believed
that the core of all European problems was the "security" of the West, of France. He had never believed that
things could be left as they were with the Anglo-American
"pact of guarantee" having become a mere paper recollec-
tion. France, the advanced bastion, must not be left alone
with her weak garrison. She must be assured of military
succor. "The only way" to stabilize Europe was, according
to Sir Austen, "to relieve French fear." [3] The need of secu-

rity for France," he said, "is great. Her right to expect something from us in that respect is recognized. Our interest and our duty to provide that security are recognized."[4] Toward the end of 1924, soon after he became Foreign Secretary, he attacked this problem, and began to work for a British guarantee to France and Belgium as compensation for the Anglo-American guarantee which had evaporated.

The news of these negotiations had immensely upset Dr. Stresemann. This was the last thing that should be permitted to happen! If England and France renewed their former close alliance, it would be impossible to play one off against the other, and even as much as to dent the "chains of Versailles." "Chamberlain had never been our friend," he wrote later. "His first act was to attempt to restore the old Entente through a three power alliance of England, France and Belgium, directed against Germany. German diplomacy faced a catastrophic situation."[5]

The diplomats of the Wilhelmstrasse tried to find some method of preventing this catastrophe. They concocted the memorandum which was now under way; "a laboratory product prepared with much care."[6] If France wanted security, the memorandum explained, the best way to obtain it would be from Germany herself, and Germany was ready to remove all conceivable grounds for a feeling of insecurity. She declared herself ready voluntarily to recognize as permanent the Western frontier which had been imposed upon her by the peace treaty; voluntarily to accept the imposed demilitarization of the Rhineland and a zone fifty kilometres east of it; voluntarily to pledge herself never again to attack France or Belgium; in other words, she declared herself ready to give again three pledges previously given. No one, the memorandum said, plainly or between the lines, no one could fail to recognize that Germany was making a great sacrifice on the altar of European peace in offering voluntarily this pact of non-agression and respect for the status quo. She thus renounced any future aspirations to undo the settlement of 1919 with regard to her Western frontiers. She renounced revenge. This was indeed an enormous sacrifice.

.For the time being of course Germany was incapable of revenge. She could not have modified the frontiers even if she wanted to. With the subtlest irony of which he was capable, Stresemann wrote in a confidential letter to to his friend, the Crown Prince: "The renunciation of a military conflict with France has only a theoretical significance, in so far as there is no possibility of a war with France." [7] That possibility could at best arise only many years later. Well, if that were true, the pact guaranteed France against the dangers of those later years; Germany was offering a pre-dated cheque. The value of this cheque would become apparent when she became strong enough to attempt revenge. Then she would be compelled by her own signature to renounce any such ambition. Surely this meant real security for France!

And Doctors Stresemann and Luther did not ask an expensive price for this sacrifice. The only compensation they wanted was a moral one. Should France, despite the security offered by this pact, receive an additional military guarantee, they demanded that Germany, too, be given the same military guarantee. That was all. Assistance to France in the event of a German attack and assistance to Germany in the event of a French attack. England would come to the assistance of France, Belgium or Germany, if ever any of these states attacked either of the other two. Thus all would feel secure, and all the states involved would be placed on a level of equality. The world would know that war had been conquered forever and that Europe was once again a family of nations living in harmony, equality and friendship.

As we have said before, this offer was intended to prevent a new "Entente" between London and Paris. In Stresemann's words, it was "an intrusion into international negotiations." [8] Austen Chamberlain's first impression was that it was a "somewhat clumsy German attempt to drive a wedge between Great Britain and France." [9] The German manner of submitting the offer aroused suspicions. "What amazing people these Germans are," he wrote in a letter. "First they hand a copy of their secret memorandum to d'Abernon and ask my advice about it whilst attempting to enforce the condition that I should say nothing to the French. I repudiated the condition, as you know, and one would have thought that they might have learned the lesson; but they next sent the same memorandum to Herriot . . . with the addition that they have told Herriot that he must not communicate with me. Herriot very properly responds to my confidence by giving me his confidence. But what earthly object do they think that all this tortuous duplicity would serve?" [11]

But even the declared motives of the memorandum scarcely justified Lord d'Abernon's emotion on the day the Germans sent it. There was no reason for crowning Luther and Stresemann with the laurels of peace. Yet in the weeks that followed more and more laurels were placed on their foreheads. In March, even Austen Chamberlain said: "The House, I think, will agree with His Majesty's Government that it is a signal advance that such proposals should have reached us on her own motion from

Germany." [12] Later, under the October sun of Locarno, Briand would echo this with chords from his own harp: "As the representative of France I would be guilty of injustice if I did not recognize and salute the courageous gesture which motivated this conference. I shall not forget the memorandum addressed to France by the German government on February 9th, on the initiative of Mr. Stresemann. It was the point of departure of our present efforts, and today we are recording the results of that step to which I wish to render homage." [13]

Something had taken place between February, when the whole affair began in a rather sour mood, and October, when it was ecstatically concluded: London and Paris had decided to turn the German proposal into a gigantic attempt to hypnotize mankind.

Actually, the pact offered by Germany was unimportant. It brought no tangible advantage or disadvantages. Germany's second recognition of the Western frontier drawn at Versailles was worth hardly more than her first. Her promise of future good behavior was a questionable gain; but it was surely no loss. The whole substance of the pact, as far as Germany's contribution was concerned, was neither useful nor harmful; it was just another piece of paper. But the powers decided to use it as a hypnotic remedy, to magnify it into an event of great historic significance, to force mankind to look upon it and declare solemnly over and over again: "This is the final peace! Now we are signing the final peace." If the operation proved successful, the statesmen seemed to think, if all the countries, particularly Germany, really succumbed to this hypnotic suggestion, peace would become a reality. For effective hypnosis is reality.

Such was the psychological effect which the Allied

statesmen hoped to extract from this meaningless pact. Briand had Germany in mind; Chamberlain: Germany and France. To achieve it, even before the pact was signed, the governments turned into advertising agencies. Never before with such insistence had a mouse been represented as a mammoth. The pact was concluded not for its own sake, but for the sake of propaganda. But its fatal consequences arose not from its content, but from the pacifist hypnosis for which it was used. This hypnosis was not uniform in its effect. Part of the world which succumbed to it was in the end reduced to a sonnambulistic state and became the dupe of the part which had not succumbed.

Its effect was enormous in England and France, where the news that a pact was to be signed which would save the world was swallowed like manna from heaven. Could a similar effect be hoped for in Germany? Nothing was more unlikely. Things were happening in Germany which sharply contradicted any hope that the Germans, too, would fall under the spell of the "status quo."

During the very period when the new pact was being negotiated, General Fieldmarshal von Hindenburg was elected President of the Reich. In previous elections the trend had been consistently reactionary, and this time, too, the people favored the symbolic representative of the traditional ruling groups, whose name headed the list of "war criminals." Could it be truthfully said that the Germans were passionately fond of the status quo?

The German National Party which nominated Hindenburg conducted systematic agitation against the pact. It was against recognition of the Western frontiers and in this it expressed the voice of the real masters of Germany. One frown from the leadership of this party was enough to make the most important German negotiator of the pact recant. Chancellor Luther was forced to tell his nationalist friends that the whole thing had been started behind his back, that he had not even read the memorandum. The chief German negotiator of Locarno drew in his horns as a result of the first little unpleasantness. How fond were the Germans of the status quo?

More than that. Germany's Eastern frontiers bordered upon Poland and Czechoslovakia. After adopting a cautious course in the West, she directed her attack against Poland. She complained that the "corridor" was intolerable. Her litany found a prompt echo among the British pacifists. The London "Times" published such strong articles against the corridor that Stresemann himself was forced to disavow them. Labor agitated in the same sense. So did people like Lloyd George's Philip Kerr. But if Germany refused to recognize these Eastern frontiers again, the new pact would certainly be valueless. Czechoslovakia and Poland were allies of France. France was bound to come to their assistance in the event of war. A pact limited to a guarantee of the Western frontiers would not even on paper prevent a Franco-German war.

But Stresemann absolutely refused to renew Germany's pledge to respect the status quo in the East, and England supported him.

And even this was not all. The most dangerous result of the representation of a worthless pact as an epoch-making agreement was revealed only at the end of eight months of preliminary negotiations. In October, 1925, the great men of Europe met to review the final draft. Out of consideration for Mussolini, they chose a little Swiss town on the Italian frontier as their meeting place. The enterprise did not concern Italy, but the other statesmen were eager to have Mussolini's company in order to make the occasion as impressive as possible. Mussolini, too, was eager to be present. He was still in the throes of the severe political crisis unleashed by the assassination of the Socialist leader Matteotti. He was steeped in the blood of Italian democracy. At that moment it was to his advantage to demonstrate that the representatives of the great European democracies treated him as a legitimate ruler, an equal among equals, that they received him with sympathy and respect. But he feared an attempt on his life should he set foot on democratic soil. For that reason, the place chosen for the meeting was Locarno on Lake Maggiore which is half Swiss and half Italian. Mussolini could come to Locarno from the Italian side of the lake whenever necessary, could have photographs and newsreels taken showing him with the other statesmen, and then return to the protection of his own reliable police.

The little town was packed. The lenses and microphones of two hemispheres were mobilized for the occasion. For fully twelve days, as long as the festival of peace lasted, every clearing of the throat, every facial expression, every word of the assembled great men was recorded. A mood of joyful expectancy was created throughout the world, as befitted the greatest historical event since the Armistice.

And in the hotels and city hall of Locarno, behind closed and half-closed doors sat the chiefs of state with their assistants and experts. Their conversations ranged from the future of the human race to the importance of a comma in this or that subordinate clause.

On the third day, Stresemann let the cat out of the bag and the world had its first inkling of what was really going on here. Chamberlain raised his arms in horror.

Briand, as Stresemann later wrote, "almost fell off his sofa,
when he heard my explanations." [14] Stresemann explained
that of course it could not be expected that Germany
alone should make sacrifices for the sake of peace. At this
moment, he said, everyone agreed that, thanks to her
noble initiative, permanent peace was at last dawning in
Europe. Hence there was no longer any reason to behave
as though anything still threatened permanent peace. And
if nothing really threatened it, the time had come for
changing certain things which injured and dishonored
Germany. For instance, Germany had no colonies: it was
time to give her some. She was still being daily insulted
by the presence of the disarmament control; it was time
to abolish it. Allied troops were still stationed on German
soil; it was time to end the occupation of the Ruhr, set to
last until 1935. Germany was still the only country that
had disarmed; it was time for the other countries to disarm and demobilize their armies and navies.

This was not a demand for compensation. Germany
had renounced any compensation for her sacrifices. No,
Stresemann was only drawing the logical inferences from
the restoration of security and confidence. Now that this
had been accomplished, all the measures that expressed
the previous feeling of insecurity and mistrust must disappear.

It was all clear enough. The results of inflating the pact
began to show themselves. Be on your guard, Stresemann's
voice seemed to say. Be on your guard, Sir Austen and
Monsieur Briand, against exaggerating the real value of
this pact. Be on your guard against representing the world
as different than it really is! You will be caught in the trap
of your own propaganda. You know what this pact is,
Monsieur Briand and Sir Austen. You know that it con-

tains nothing that Germany has not signed before; that she will sign it all again when, as you have decided, she enters the League of Nations. You know that the promises contained in this pact are only a third edition of the same promises, and have no real substance. You know this document has no practical value for the immediate future and only a chimerical value for the distant future. And you can see that for this theoretical draft on the distant future you must pay at once; for this cheap, empty, piece of paper you must hand over cash and plenty of it. And the more you blow up the pact into an event of tremendous significance, the more surely you will have to pay for it. The more thorough the hypnosis, the more surely your own newspapers and parties and constituents will stand up and urge you: "Why not? Why don't you give in, now that security and peace prevail? Why do you resist?" You know your own countrymen, Monsieur Briand and Sir Austen. You know how irresistible their desire for sunshine has become, how impatiently they stop up their ears when anyone mentions difficulties in the way of peace; even now they misinterpret all the facts and distort all the lessons of experience to spare themselves unpleasantness.

Think it over, Monsieur Briand and Sir Austen! Once you adopt as your official thesis the idea that the world can be saved through this piece of paper, you won't be able to stop. You can see through it. You know that this pact has not been conceived as a happy ending, but as a happy beginning. It is intended as a psychological pass-key to all the treasure chambers and arsenals where you have stowed the miserable fruits of four years of misery. Conclude the pact, which is harmless, but in the name of God abandon your fantastic plan to hypnotize the world into a sense of security based on this empty bubble.

Perhaps they did not notice the trap into which they were falling. Perhaps they were too deeply involved in their fatal campaign. In fact, Monsieur Briand was one of the hypnotized, rather than one of the hypnotizers. He had never been a rational character. And now in his old age he was less so than ever. With his grey artist's mane, his slightly stooped shoulders, his slovenly mustache and the cigarette perpetually hanging from his lips, he looked like a Bohemian. God had endowed him with seductive eloquence, in the most harmonious of languages; when he spoke it was like music. His speeches were a stream of beautiful sounds and melodies, so that often their contents did not matter, neither to his audience nor to himself. Some of his listeners did not know what he actually said: all they heard was the rhapsody. On several occasions in the middle of the night with a bottle or two of wine inside him he had been dragged over to the Chamber to save a situation; without knowing what the discussion was about or what had been said before, he would begin to speak in a sort of trance and produce a masterpiece of such beauty that the members were won over to his side.

Yes, Monsieur Briand, the most illustrious living rhetorician, emanated all the fascination of his art, and succumbed to it himself. As he advanced in mastery of words, words increasingly mastered him. At Locarno it became clear that the spell of the words of peace, which had flowed by him and out of him during the long months of preliminary negotiations, had taken complete possession. Monsieur Briand had hypnotized himself.

He adjured Stresemann not to cause difficulties at this moment. He told him that some vague hopes in accordance with his wishes could be expressed in the preamble of the pact, but that he must not disturb the general harmony; that the creation of an atmosphere of unity was the most important purpose of the entire undertaking; that this harmony would soon produce all the desired results. I understand your demands, he told him, I myself hope "that the pact will bring results in this sense." [15] But that is a task for tomorrow, which we shall begin as soon as the basis for this auspicious pact is secured. Let us, for the present, concentrate on creating that basis.

And Stresemann and Luther listened with satisfaction. This was exactly what they wanted: that the pact be a basis, not a peak. They formulated this idea many times over. Locarno must lead to further agreements—if that is clearly understood and promised, we shall by no means disturb the universal harmony. We shall be satisfied with the general terms of the preamble—but it is agreed, is it not?—that we are to benefit from further "effects," and "results." It is agreed, said Briand.

On October 16th, 1925, the pact was provisionally signed in Locarno; on December 1st, it was definitively signed in London.

The advertising machinery outdid itself. A wave of happiness and hope swept over the world. In Switzerland, which had had the honor of being the birthplace of the pact of perpetual peace, church bells rang out. Thanksgiving services were held from Sweden to Yugoslavia. Mounting enthusiasm enveloped the old continent and reached across the oceans. Religious fervor filled all hearts when Briand, in a melodious final speech, celebrated the "new spirit," "the opening of an era of confidence and collaboration." Stresemann came to the rostrum and thanked him for his unforgettable words. They shook hands under the glare of the flood lights. "No," said Briand, "do not speak of words. I shall prove to you that these were not words but 'future acts.' " [16]

The hypnosis grew every day. The dream melted all frontiers. "The spirit of solidarity," exclaimed Briand after the signing ceremony in the banquet hall of the Lord Mayor in London, "now takes the place of distrust and suspicion. Opposite me sit the German Delegates; that does not mean that I do not remain a good Frenchman, as they remain, I am sure, good Germans, but in the light of these treaties we are Europeans only. By our signature we declare for peace. The particularism of our countries is blotted out by this agreement and with it vanish unpleasant memories. If the Locarno agreements do not mean that, they do not mean much. If they are not the draft of the constitution of a European family within the orbit of the League of Nations, they would be frail indeed and would hold many disappointments in store for us. Our nations have often in the course of centuries come into conflict on the battlefield and they have often left there, with their blood, the flower of strength. The Locarno agreements will have been worthwhile if they mean that these massacres shall no longer take place. . . . We must collaborate in a common labor of peace and our nations which on the battlefield showed equal heroism, will discover in other phases of human activity means of emulation no less glorious. It is in that spirit that, as French delegate, I sign the treaties of Locarno. And here I make this solemn declaration, confident that I am spokesman for the immense majority of my compatriots: I am determined to extract tomorrow from these conventions everything they can provide against war and in favor of peace. I see in them the beginning of a magnificent work,

the renewal of Europe to participate, each according to
their special qualifications, to ensure a definite peace." [17]

In the greenish semi-darkness of the House of Commons, Sir Austen Chamberlain himself became lyrical: "A
turning point!" he exclaimed. "A turning point in the history of Europe, and, it may be, in the history of the
world. . . . An omen of the new international spirit." [18]
In the depth of his soul he had always distrusted the German politicians and would continue to mistrust them. But
he was not now trying to diagnose their psychological
abnormality; he was trying to cure it, and thereby the
fears of the French, by hypnotic treatment.

It was brilliantly successful in England, France, and the
world at large. But aside from a smattering of ritual
phrases, it was unsuccessful in Germany. At a banquet in
Berlin Chancellor Luther, without even trying to be discreet, stressed the fact that Germany was interested in
the whole thing only to the extent to which it helped to
ameliorate the situation created in 1918 by its concrete
"effects" and "results." "It is beyond doubt that even after
the signing of the Locarno pact we are still far from our
goal of restoring the German nation to the place it has
earned in the community of nations by its achievements
and capacities. We are certain that the German people
will inwardly and outwardly approve of the Locarno
agreement only when they concretely experience its practical results. Otherwise, it will not be possible to overcome
their deep distrust of all 'political' agreements." [19] Thus
spoke the chief German negotiator of the "pact of perpetual peace."

Luther demanded the evacuation of the Rhineland as
the first instalment. And in the confession Stresemann
addressed to the Crown Prince, he wrote: "The most im-

portant objective of German politics is the liberation of
German territory from foreign occupation. Our first task
must be to remove the strangler from our throat." He was
correct in saying "first:" for behind this demand were
numerous others. The Germans would demand, indiscrim-
inately and opportunistically, what each day suggested;
they would demand everything "in the spirit of Locarno";
in accordance with the "security" of Locarno, and the
promises of Locarno. And they would discover that the
word "Locarno" was a magic open sesame of extraordinary power.

The Locarno pact proved to be Germany's greatest
achievement in abolishing the defeat of 1918. Later, the
world would be astonished at the legendary successes
achieved by Adolf Hitler with his "non-aggression" pacts.
A dozen times and more, it would see him wrest the most
enormous concessions out of the other powers with some
empty, cheap little piece of paper promising peace. People would say: what marvelous invention! What a genius
at swindling!

Actually this invention dated from 1925. The first and
most colossal non-aggression pact manoeuvre, with all
the subsequent ones only weak imitations, was Locarno.
And Dr. Stresemann deserves the inventor's palm. Only
two years before it had seemed as if Germany were
doomed to die in agony as a result of her own self-destructive policies. Only two years! In this short time Stresemann succeeded in making the world praise Germany,
cover her with honors and ask her to name her wishes.

How was this miracle brought about? All that had been
necessary was to discover, during the period of peace imposed on Germany, the enemy's Achilles' heel. Stresemann was forced to proceed with caution; in his letter to

the Crown Prince he said: "German policy must at present be subtle and avoid great decisions." And he discovered that "being subtle" could be the most irresistible form of aggression. He discovered the most passionate desire of his era: its need to find the world beautiful at any price, and to avoid all unpleasantness. He discovered that the most effective policy was to concentrate on that desire, to feed, flatter and exploit it. Thus, he became the king among the one-eyed men of politics. And he created a masterpiece based on his discovery. With the Locarno pact he provided a fetish which a world eager for peace would worship for many, many years.

The Locarno hypnosis destroyed the last distinction between the realm of wishful thinking and the realm of hard reality in the victor countries. The era of the empty phrase began. Those who warned against believing in them, and there were some even in Germany, were publicly branded as eccentrics and trouble-makers. Steady progress toward perfection was now guaranteed. History was no longer history. Nations were no longer nations. A world of brotherhood, a world without violence and arms, was at hand. An epoch had begun in which no retrogression threatened, in which only progress was apparent. "Credo quia absurdum." During the preceding years the wave of complacency had risen higher and higher. More and more stubbornly a policy had been put forward, which, under cover of varied arguments, theories and gospels, was nothing but the policy of least resistance. Locarno was the critical point. Locarno marked the beginning of the age of complacency in the democratic Western world. The years of self-destruction began. After them would come years of paralysis. But first there were several years of euphoria.

2.

When ice breaks, it breaks in many places. When the earth covers itself with green, its buds sprout forth as far as the eye can see. In the weeks and months following Locarno the finger of God was raised at every crossroads.

The League of Nations, clothed in its power, haloed in its lofty mission, entered the lists for the first time. In that fall of 1925 two little countries had mobilized their armies. Greece and Bulgaria had marched against each other. The League cried "Halt!" By its magic word, both armies stopped in their tracks. What a miracle! What a tangible manifestation of the new omnipotent Providence on earth! In a world in which shooting and fighting had been a daily occurrence, the League of Nations had stopped a war for the first time. The first, and the last. Except for this one instance, it was never again to prevent or stop a single war. In this case it succeeded because of special circumstances.

Greece and Bulgaria were two starving countries, each with about 6 million inhabitants. The League of Nations really represented the power of England and France, the two dominating powers in Europe. Whenever two dominating powers wanted to prevent a war between two small powers, the miracle had taken place, many times over. The dominant powers had been able to enforce their will without any League of Nations. But this time the wish of the only two great powers in Europe donned the garb of the League of Nations. It was all a grandiose illusion. Now it had been demonstrated that peace was really secure. Now it was clear that it had been secured through the deus ex machina of Geneva, the magnificent

robot, the djinn conjured out of Aladdin's miraculous lamp.
The champions of complacency were jubilant. Had they
not always said that the only thing needed to fill the world
with sunshine was that trifle—a new international spirit?
The world is "going up and up," [20] said Ramsay Mac-
Donald.

It did go up and up everywhere. From the Balkans, the
scene of action shifted back to the German frontier. The
Ruhr, which Poincaré's sinister ambition had tried to take
away from the honest Germans, was now freed of its
troops of occupation; to that extent the new ideal had
been realized. But there was still the Rhineland, there
was still the Anglo-French-Belgian "watch on the Rhine,"
another militaristic discord in the new pacific harmony.
As long as the Germans were compelled to tolerate it, they
would be prevented from fully developing their own
pacifism. It was high time to remove it.

The evacuation of the Rhineland was to begin in 1925,
but could be postponed if the Germans violated the peace
treaty. Toward the middle of 1925, France and England
notified Berlin that the evacuation would not take place
because Germany had committed too many violations of
the disarmament clauses. But this was before Locarno.
After the pact, toward the beginning of 1926, these violations were forgotten. Why make an issue out of such a little matter when peace was at stake? The first of the three
occupied "zones" of the Rhineland, the largest and most
important, was returned to German rule. Another milestone on the road to peace! Formerly, German disarmament had been considered the most important factor in
the quest for peace. Now, it was considered extremely
important not to press the Germans to carry out their disarmament pledges. Formerly, the watch on the Rhine had

been considered a decisive guarantee of lasting tranquillity; now, the rapid abolition of that watch was considered the best guarantee.

Up and up and up. Even greater things took place in the fruitful year of 1926. Germany's entry into the League would soon become a reality. What a change! During the peace negotiations, Germany had wanted to be admitted at once, and was rejected. Now the roles were exchanged. From 1920 on, Germany had categorically refused to enter the League every time she was approached: the League was designed to preserve the status quo established at Versailles and Germany refused any share in that effort. But at Locarno Germany promised to join. Now, in 1926, her admission was on the agenda. As soon as she, too, signed a certain piece of paper, even the gloomiest pessimist would be unable to deny that a new world had been born. What Wilson had called the "definite guarantee by word against aggression" would then be realized in the strict military sense, and the conflicts engendered by the war would dissolve in a great world brotherhood. A wonderful prospect!

Dr. Stresemann's own ideas about the League were not quite the same as those of the enthusiasts. If the latter had known what he had written to his friend, the Crown Prince, they would have had to make strenuous efforts to preserve their illusions intact; but they would probably have managed. Several years later, after the publication of the German statesmen's letters they did manage.

The Reich Minister wrote to the ex-Crown Prince that Germany's presence in the League would have a considerable nuisance value. "All the questions which today preoccupy the German people can be transformed into as many vexations for the Entente by a skilful orator be-

fore the League of Nations." [21] He went on to explain to
His Imperial Highness that from now on all the League's
resolutions could be dictated by Germany because any
resolutions passed had to be unanimous. Germany, he
wrote, would now be in a position to cause difficulties to
the other members of the Council at every turn. She could
paralyze them by demanding concessions in return for
her vote, such as modifications of the Polish border, or
Anschluss with Austria. She could pose as "the spokesman of the whole German cultural community," and thus
provoke all the countries with German minorities, especially Czechoslovakia and Poland. Indeed, Stresemann's
fantasy reached out toward such objectives as the stir-
ring up of the Africans, Arabs and Indians and the destruction of the colonial empires. He saw that the fight
against "colonial imperialism" in which the Reich, although she demanded colonies for herself, could engage
together with the perfectionists of all shades, afforded
magnificent opportunities: "Our entry into the League
will, I am sure, be in no way detrimental to the great
movement now animating the colonial peoples who are
turning against their imperialist rulers." [22]

Such were Stresemann's ideas about Germany's purpose in joining the Great Club. That purpose was not to
further world brotherhood, but to achieve territorial and
political gains through sowing dissension and suspicion.
Those who were still capable of reflection could have
guessed this from certain signs. For example, Germany
made her adherence to the League dependent upon being
released from all obligations including the moral obligation of sharing any "compulsory measures against the violators of the peace." [23] Germany agreed to become a member of the League, but not to cooperate in sanctions

against aggressors. She explained her position as follows: as we are not allowed to maintain a large army, we cannot take part in such risky enterprises; we cannot even permit our territories to be used for the transit of troops or similar purpose. Herr Stresemann's demand that Germany be expressly exempted from these duties put Briand and Chamberlain in an awkward position at Locarno. The logical inference to have drawn was that Germany's membership in the League was useless, since she refused to participate in its most important activities. But the policies of the two Allied pacifiers were not based on logic. Their purpose was to achieve merely a "psychological effect." What was important to them was not Germany's actual duties as a member of the League, but her formal presence. So they wrote a note to Germany which they thought artfully nebulous in its promises but which fully satisfied Herr Stresemann. A member must share in the League's compulsory measures, they said, "only to that extent which is compatible with his military situation and which takes his geographical position into account." [24] With this official certificate of exemption in hand, Germany agreed to enter the League. Any one could see how she was entering; that she would benefit from the privileges but not share in the responsibilities of a League member. But to attach importance to such matters and to the frame of mind which they revealed, was asking too much of the enthusiasts and the hypnotized.

Another significant event took place at this time. The full meaning of Germany's refusal to accept the full obligations of a League member was revealed when she concluded a new pact with Russia, a "supplement" to the Rapallo pact. In this document the two states pledged themselves not only to "non-aggression," but also to "non-assistance to an aggressor." Coming at that moment, this pact was obviously intended to demonstrate to the world that Germany did not consider her liaison with the democracies as exclusive, that she meant to live in equally friendly concubinage both with the democracies and the Soviets, that neither must take too much for granted nor, on the other hand, fear her.

And it had an even more concrete significance. If the League for any reason ever wanted to take action against Russia, it would have to ask for the privilege of transit through German territory. Now Germany, having obtained a pledge from the democracies that she would not have to grant passage, promised the Soviets that she would not grant it if requested. In other words, Germany agreed to be a bulwark between Russia and the League. Out of her imminent entry into the League, she rapidly manufactured a by-product and sold it to another party. While preparing to sign the Covenant, she sold the promise that she would prevent League sanctions against Russia. This was a very profitable transaction even though another illustration of those "tortuous duplicities" mentioned by Sir Austen, another warning against too much idealistic ecstasy.

And there were other warnings. At the very moment when the solemn ceremony of Germany's admission into the League was to take place, an unexpected hitch developed. It had been agreed that Germany was to receive a permanent seat in the League Council. But three other countries, Poland, Brazil and Spain, which had hitherto belonged to the groups of "non-permanent" members elected each year, were to be granted permanent seats at the same time.

Germany refused to enter the world brotherhood, if

Poland was admitted to the Council. Upon which Spain and Brazil were also excluded from permanent membership, as that would help to keep open the possibility of excluding Poland. The German Ministers who had come to Geneva for the induction ceremonies were inflexible on this point. Briand and Chamberlain, their sponsors, were bitter about it. "Whenever we make a concession to you," Chamberlain complained to Stresemann, "instead of being grateful for it, you ask for more." [25] "By no means a bad system," Briand added.[26]

Their bitterness was all the more justified because this time there was no way of satisfying the new demand with new concessions. The Brazilians angrily dissociated themselves from the too subtle strategy of Whitehall and the Quai d'Orsay and lodged their government's official veto against Germany's receiving a seat in the Council. The whole enterprise was wrecked, and everyone had to return home. The French and English statesmen might have left justly resentful of the Germans whose eternal chicanery had spoiled their own triumphant entry into the League. But statesmen must not allow their feelings to influence a long-range policy. During the last sad session, Briand made a motion that the Assembly express its deep regrets at being unable to salute Germany as a member. And when Chamberlain reported to the House of Commons, he had calmed down to the point where he once again completely vindicated Germany.

And, as might have been expected, he carried his point. For a few weeks, the statesmen tried to find a solution which would satisfy all concerned. Finally, a new kind of Council seat was created in addition to the "permanent" and "non-permanent" ones: "semi-permanent" seats were offered to Poland, Brazil, and Spain. Berlin gave its approval to this plan. But Brazil was ungracious and rejected the offer. The statesmen decided that Germany was more important than Brazil, whereupon Brazil withdrew from the League. Thus, the sacred ceremony of Germany's admission to the temple of world harmony was marked by a disquieting exhibition of hostility toward Poland and the loss to the family of the largest South American state.

Another disturbing altercation took place, this time in secret. According to the League constitution, a state could be admitted to the League only after the admission committee had formally stated that it had fulfilled all its international obligations. The procedure involved a hearing and the submission of documents. You may apply this rule to any other state, said Herr Stresemann, but not to Germany. Great Germany cannot be expected to submit to the humiliation of proving orally and by documents that she is worthy of admission. If the League Constitution required this, it must be violated.

Once again, her demands were found justified. If Germany refused to submit to the regular procedure provided for in the constitution, the constitution must be ignored. "The Admission Committee," Stresemann later reported to the Reichstag, "resolved not only to omit the questionnaire, but also the hearing, and unanimously declared that Germany had fulfilled her international obligations." [27]

This new concession was more than a matter of mere form. Germany's disarmament was an important international obligation; and neither Germany nor her French and English sponsors wanted to risk any discussions about it. All the great powers were equally responsible for this astonishing sleight-of-hand.

When Germany applied for admission into the League, the Inter-Allied Military Control Commission was ordered to undertake a so-called "final inspection" of the status of her armaments. The Allied governments expected the commission to report that "everything was in order." Such a report would serve a double purpose: to demonstrate to the world that after seven years Germany had really fulfilled her obligation to disarm, and to supply the Allies with an excuse for satisfying the German demand that all controls be abolished.

But the plan went awry. The preliminary reports of the Commission showed that its verdict would have to be negative, that disarmament had not been carried out, and that, even in 1926, there were certain indications of rearmament. Sir Austen and Monsieur Briand were in a panic. What would happen to their long-range pacification policy now? What would be the reaction of the League Admission Committee, of their parliaments at home? This accursed "final inspection" had imperiled their entire program.

After some reflection they found a way of coping with the situation. Allegedly higher interests outweighed allegedly less important interests. They shelved the disturbing preliminary reports and, a few months later, also shelved the 504 pages of the definitive report in their secret files. They created the impression that the results of the "final inspection" had been favorable. In brief, for the sake of pacification they resorted to falsification concerning the most important prerequisite of peace. They concealed the truth both in their own countries and before the Admission Committee of the League. Such was the basis for the recall of the Military Control Commission from Berlin, whereby a new German demand, with par-

ticularly momentous consequences, was satisfied. And such
was the basis for the unanimously adopted resolution that
the Reich had fulfilled its international obligations and
that nothing now stood in the way of its admission to the
League.

This incident would have remained a secret if an English member of the Military Control Commission had not
violated military discipline and made the extraordinary
transaction public. General John H. Morgan, Adjutant
General of the Commission, gave the whole game away
by declaring that the sense of the suppressed final report
had been that "Germany had never disarmed, had never
had the intention of disarming, and for seven years had
done everything in her power to hinder, deceive and
'counter-control' the Commission appointed to control
her disarmament." [28] A Belgian senator named de Dorlodot confirmed these statements. During one session of
Parliament in Brussels he brandished a sheaf of papers
and exclaimed: "Here is the final report!" The Foreign
Minister prevented him from speaking further by invoking the secret nature of the document, but de Dorlodot
published an article in a newspaper in which he revealed
that Chamberlain and Briand had finally compelled the
Control Commission to weaken the style and text of their
"final report." [30]

Of all the incidents during this period of euphoria, the
manoeuver with the reports on German disarmament is
the saddest and the most baffling. Monsieur Briand's and
the French people's attitude is understandable. After four
years on the battlefield and five years of diplomatic isolation, France was a broken nation. She was tired of suffering and welcomed any illusion, any trick, that would permit her to veil her weariness with a semblance of reason.

During those weeks, Poincaré was again made Premier. But it had been agreed that he was being called to office only to stabilize the franc. He was not to have any hand in foreign policy. This remained under Briand's exclusive control and Briand was now a believer in his own oratory, which had become a faithful reflection of the mood of his countrymen.

Sir Austen Chamberlain's behavior was the most baffling of all. He had always been, and would be until his death, repelled by German policies, and the German nation as a whole. They inspired him with ineradicable distrust and fear. "We should be gravely mistaken," he had written after the World War, "and we should be entering upon a path of grave danger if we thought the ex-Emperor was the sole cause of offense in Germany. As long as he was successful the German people was behind him. He bears upon his soul responsibilities for great crimes against humanity, but he stands not alone, and I have no patience with the people who come whining to us to-day like a small sneak at school: 'It was not I, sir, it was the other boy. . . .' " [29] Austen Chamberlain was to make similar statements later, when Hitler came to power.

How could a man with such convictions pursue a policy based entirely upon trust of the Germans? The only plausible explanation is that the established course of British foreign policy got the better of the personal convictions of the man who directed it. The course chosen by Britain was to strengthen Germany as a counterweight to France and Russia, and to avoid any unpleasantness at all costs. Despite his personal dislike of Germany, Sir Austen followed this course.

However, the public at large was satisfied and knew

the ominous incidents in the background. In September, 1926, Germany formally entered the League. Once again, the flood lights flashed and the cascades of rhetoric flowed. The temple of peace through which resounded Briand's call "Down with Cannon," seemed to have been strengthened by a new pillar of granite. And any warning that this pillar was only a stage prop, and that the real trend of events was in the direction of war seemed more ridiculous than ever before.

3.

The economic man is a mythical figure in the materialistic dogma. In his economic activities, man must use the same intellectual apparatus as in his other activities. In this field, too, what is called reason is hitched to wishes, dreams, and emotions. Man can be as absurd in the economic sphere as in all the others.

Nowhere did the illusion of permament peace prove as effective as in the economic field. Locarno and the League seemed to insure the political stabilization of the world. Investors and employers need stability. In the beneficent climate of what was considered political stability, the capitalist system displayed its maximum productivity. Everywhere the indices of investments, building and manufacturing rose rapidly. People were filled with faith in an enduring prosperity. They looked for new fields of economic action, and discovered Germany.

Indeed, Germany presented a remarkable spectacle. Her intelligence, industry and efficiency helped her to achieve a miracle of economic recovery. By 1926 she had regained and even surpassed her pre-war standard of living. Although her territory had been diminished in certain fields, her production and trade outstripped those of 1913. She exploited every opportunity. As a result of the British coal strike from May to November, 1926, which paralyzed England's exports, she made powerful advances on the world coal and iron markets, although two years before she had declared herself unable to make any "deliveries in kind."

The material and economic devastation which was considered the most serious result of the war, proved the easiest to overcome in a world of unlimited technological possibilities. The "devastated regions" were rebuilt with one turn of the hand. What proved really irreparable was that more than 50% of all French males between 20 and 32 years of age had been killed in the war.

Germany's economic vitality, however, was more impressive than that of any other country. And the peace did seem secure. In addition, Mr. Parker Gilbert, the American General Agent for Reparations had been stationed in Berlin to see to it that everything proceeded in an orderly fashion within the Reich. Thus Germany was discovered. In the end she became a favorite child from the economic point of view.

German business needed capital: and everyone knew that money loaned to German business was profitably invested. German states and municipalities needed loans: everyone felt that they were deserving debtors, unlike the second-rate Slavic or Latin beggars. Foreign capital and money began to trickle into Germany. Investors became eager for German stocks which paid a high rate of interest. The Germans had always been industrious, solid, and serious of purpose, and now their honesty, too, was guaranteed. After they had been so mistreated, it was a kind of moral satisfaction to help their recovery. Germany became the best tip. The trickle of foreign capital soon swelled into a stream. Every new German issue went quicker than hot cakes, in London, Paris, Amsterdam, and particularly New York. The banks competed for German stocks. In the end, it could not be said that German business, states and municipalities were looking for foreign capital; they were being urged to take it. Representatives of American banks crowded the hotels in Berlin and the provinces, armed with long lists of corporations and municipalities which had not yet borrowed money, and offered them millions in loans. They were genuinely offended if a mayor or corporation manager explained that he did not need any money.

All this began at the same period as the peace hypnosis. In the five years of euphoria, from Locarno to the crash, about 30 billion marks, or 7,500,000,000 dollars in foreign money poured into Germany in every conceivable form: loans to public bodies, stocks and bonds, shares, new enterprises. And every dollar, every pound of this stream of money, astonishingly enough, was immediately doubled: it could be spent twice instead of once. The recipients could exchange the dollars or pounds for marks at the Reichsbank and spend the marks. The Reichsbank spent the original dollars and pounds.

These thirty billion marks further increased German prosperity. They were used for the systematic modernization, expansion and "Americanization" of German industry. The most up-to-date and large-scale industrial plant in the world, with the exception of that of the United States, was created; a plant which was in fact over-sized, too large for normal peace-time purposes. This brand-new industrial plant, built mostly with foreign money, would a few years later fall into Hitler's hands. With its help he would rearm and wage war against the countries which had financed it. Such was the ultimate result of the foreign loans.

The original dollars and other foreign currencies were used for world trade. They paid the surpluses of a tremendously increased importing business. All over the world enterprises were founded with this money, work was undertaken, credits were financed. One third of these 30 billion were used for reparation payments over a five year period in accordance with the Dawes Plan. The only reparations ever paid by Germany were paid with money borrowed from abroad, and in this respect, the plethora of foreign exchange even caused serious concern to Dr. Hjalmar Schacht. Famous as the great currency stabilizer, he now aspired to liberate his country from the reparations burden. For Germany did not give up her ambition to rid herself of the reparations even during her years of caution and good behavior. Dr. Schacht was annoyed by the indisputable fact that the great stream of capital pouring into Germany made it impossible to claim that she could not pay any reparations. His goal was to keep great streams of money pouring into Germany, yet not enough to leave a surplus for the payments. He made a few unsuccessful attempts to restrict foreign investments to just the right amount for his purposes. Even so a day would come when it could be stated truthfully that Germany had never paid a cent of the reparations; when it would be clear that even the five instalments she had made were actually paid by other countries. The end of the reparations farce was that Germany received three times as much from abroad as she ever paid.

But the awful economic, and still more awful political end was still far off. This was the age of euphoria. 1927,

1928, 1929. . . . Bankers and investors were still beaming over their flourishing investments, over the blessed security which, after all the years of confusion and misery, had at last been established. They beamed over Chamberlain, Briand and Stresemann, who had brought about the great miracle of pacification and who had all so justly received the Nobel Peace Prize. The economic men lived in a semi-somnolent state; no presentiment warned them what all this fun would cost. They believed what everyone else believed. "Up and up."

A new vision took shape in Monsieur Briand's mind. He began to say that a "faith" had to be created in the world, that peace could be made the object of faith, like nationalism or religion. On the tenth anniversary of America's entry into the war, he addressed a message to the American people and proposed a pact "which, according to the American expression, would outlaw war in these two countries." [31]

"To outlaw war" was indeed an American expression. It had been coined in 1918, at the height of Wilsonism, by Mr. Salmon Levinson, a Chicago attorney. A movement to outlaw war was born, as effective or as ineffective as any movement to outlaw sin. What this outlawing would consist of and who would carry out the verdict against the guilty parties remained a mystery. But the movement was a faith. The French Foreign Minister made it his own. A pact to outlaw war, he said, "would greatly contribute, in the eyes of the world, to widen and strengthen the basis of an international peace policy." [32]

Frank B. Kellogg, President Coolidge's Secretary of State, at first did not know exactly what to do about Briand's proposal. It seemed rather futile to him. Moreover, very soon the "ambassadors of Great Britain, Germany,

Italy and the representatives of other countries," [33] began to line up in his office asking him suspiciously what was being concocted between Washington and Paris, and against whom it was really directed.

In addition to distrustful diplomats, he also had enthusiastic visitors. Senators, Congressmen, delegations from pacifist organizations came to urge him to seize this opportunity. Then Kellogg somewhat modified Briand's idea. "It has occurred to me," he wrote the great statesman of peace in Paris, "that the two governments, instead of contenting themselves with a bilateral declaration, might make a more signal contribution to world peace by joining in an effort to obtain the adherence of all the principal powers of the world to a declaration renouncing war as an instrument of national policy." [34]

Nothing would please Briand more. Thus another unforgettable document in the archives of history came into being, an enlarged Locarno. It was to be signed by no less than sixty-one states with a golden pen, later to be placed in some museum. Such was the Briand-Kellogg Pact, officially, the "Pact of Paris." Mr. Kellogg, too, was to receive the Nobel Peace Prize.

When the text was published, some people might have been surprised. It was very brief. "The high contracting Parties solemnly declare that they condemn recourse to war for the solution of international controversies, and renounce it as an instrument of national policy." The solution of all disputes or conflicts "shall never be sought except by pacific means." [35]

That was all. The astonishing part about it was, first of all, that it had to be written down at all. For it was all in the League Covenant which more than fifty of the 61

signatories had signed years before. A powerful micro-
scope and a subtle juridical intelligence are required to
grasp the difference between the Covenant and this Pact.
Faith was required to ascribe more effective magic to this
document, which did not contain a single word about
measures to be taken against its violators than to the
Covenant, which at least mentioned vague "sanctions." It
must be admitted that when Mr. Kellogg was not speaking to the public at large he was inclined to be skeptical
about it. "I make no claim to perfection," he once declared. "All of the steps which have been taken to prevent
war, to improve the conditions of the world are of course
subject to the errors of judgment and the frailties of humanity. I do not say that this treaty will immediately accomplish all that peoples have struggled for throughout
ages." [36]

But although none of the gentlemen who used the
golden pen lacked a certain amount of skepticism, the
day in August, 1928, on which they put their signatures
to the document was marked by the usual ceremonies, speeches and mutual assurances of goodwill. In countries where the religion of peace had struck roots, it was
fortified; in the countries where it had not . . . but such
countries did not exist. Suspicions that Germany remained
untouched by the new gospel, and there were still some
stubborn people who harbored such suspicions, were
branded by Stresemann as pure slander. "The new guarantee of peace," he said in the Reichstag, "must effectively contribute to hasten general disarmament." [37] Could
anyone ask for more? What better evidence was there of
a truly pacific spirit than Stresemann's coming out for
general disarmament? What more progressive inference

could be drawn from the pact to outlaw war than re-doubled efforts to abolish the still existing armies and navies?

Indeed, world disarmament was the shibboleth of the perfectionists, and to win favor with them it sufficed merely to pronounce the words. After the First World War disarmament became a real Nirvana fantasy, in which all the other idealistic fantasies merged and flowered. It continued to delude mankind almost up to the beginning of the Second World War and even then one could never be sure that it would not emerge again.

The demand for general disarmament began rather modestly, decades ago. It was a demand of an economic, financial and social nature. The price of militarism was too high; it was argued that the same money could be spent for more useful things. Even this was not entirely true; to make it true it would have been necessary really to use the money saved by converting military expenditures for other purposes. That was never the case. Actually, the only results of the various reductions of military expenditures in England and France were decreased production and increased unemployment. But disarmament could still be defended on economic grounds.

Later, the disarmament idea acquired a significance far beyond its modest economic origins. The Bible promised that in the millennium of peace swords would be beaten into plowshares. The idealists inferred from this that to bring in the millennium of peace it sufficed to beat all the swords into plowshares. They confused cause and effect. They reasoned that gray hair is the cause of old age, and pass keys the cause of theft. They framed two theorems. Theorem No. 1: Wars occur because of the existence of large armies and navies. Cannon go off by themselves in some mysterious manner. Theorem No. 2: Wars are prevented through the abolition of large armies and navies. No one can start a war without having lots of cannon. These two theorems were based on a third: With regard to their ability to start wars, every army or navy is equal to every other army or navy. The German or French army, the Japanese or American fleet, all belong to the same class, all have the same properties, all generate war by their mere existence; and peace can be secured by their abolition.

These three theorems contained innumerable illusions and fallacies. The idea that large armies automatically generate war is untenable. Cannon do not go off by themselves, whether they are numerous or few. Nor do armies or navies beget wars, whether large or small. Wars result from human decisions. Of course it had become fashionable to pooh-pooh these simple truths. The progressives of the twenties were ardent debunkers of historical myths. They would not be taken in by fairy tales, like the official explanation of the war of 1914. They smiled scornfully at the primitive idea that man's will and instincts play a part in creating history. They denied the existence of "personalist" causes, and admitted only "objective" causes, anonymous occult "forces." They had a number of "objective" causes of war at their disposal such as "economic forces" or "capitalism." Nor did they forget the existence of large armies. You must realize, they argued, that when large armies confront each other, the cannon must go off in the end. But cannon never went off by themselves, they cannot go off by themselves, they will never go off by themselves. They are fired at somebody's order. And, as for him who gives the order, it is a matter of complete indifference whether he has only 100 guns against the enemy's 100, or 100,000 against the enemy's 100,000.

Nor is the second theorem, that small armies exclude war, any more tenable. Wars have been fought with armies of all sizes. It is just as possible to fight with 20 divisions against 20, as with 200 against 200. And, more important, it is possible to begin a war with 20 divisions, and expand them to 200 shortly before or during hostilities. This alone suffices to demonstrate the absurdity of the disarmament theory. Such an expansion of the armed forces will be best and most rapidly carried out by the country with the largest war potential, the strongest and most flexible industrial plant, the highest morale, the most effective secret preparations. If two nations with unequal war potentials are forced to reduce their armaments to the same minimum the result will be, under a deceptive appearance of equality, to render the potentially weaker country completely defenseless. If the potentially stronger country should suddenly begin to rearm, it would increase its strength tenfold before the other has even been completely awakened to the danger. General disarmament and uniformly small armies do not prevent wars. The opposite is true: they guarantee victory to the nation with the greatest war potential.

The conception that every army is the same as every other is false, too. While admitting that all armies are the tools of the nations and leaders behind them, the partisans of disarmament claimed that there was no difference between the various nations. All nations were equally honest, and all rulers equally suspect. The debunkers of the twenties were equalitarian and hostile to the idea of individual differences as a matter of principle. They rejected the popular "error," that revolvers or armies are neither good nor bad in themselves, and that they are put to good or bad use by those who fire or control them. They argued that revolvers and armies are always at the disposal of the same "ruling classes," and therefore always bad.

In practice the disarmament fetish served the purpose of German reactionary politics. It helped to weaken and crush the normal instincts and traditions of the Allied nations, and to weaken and crush these instincts and traditions was the main purpose of German politics. All the German "chain breakers" had to do to promote their own realistic objectives was to pretend to support the fashionable Utopian slogans. No government was as enthusiastic for general disarmament as the German.

Things were taking place in Germany which should have aroused grave distrust. There were signs that she was far from disarmed or as enthusiastic about disarmament as the prophets of general disarmament believed. But these enthusiasts were now in control of England's government machinery and the large Laborite majority in the newly elected House of Commons. After 1927, Messrs. Ramsay MacDonald and Arthur Henderson, the most passionate of all the advocates of disarmament, determined the course of British policy, one as Prime Minister and the other as Foreign Secretary. They must have been aware of the contents of the 504 printed pages of the vanished "final report" of the Control Commission. But there were other facts, which not only they but, to a certain extent, the public at large should have known.

It was quite obvious for instance, that the German army, theoretically 100,000 men strong, and in fact much stronger, had assumed a character different from that of any other army. Ten years before, Marshal Foch had vainly recommended that Germany be allowed a conscripted army of 200,000 men with one or two years of compulsory service, rather than a professional army of 100,000 men with twelve years of service. The first, he said, would be an army of ordinary soldiers; the second, an enormous non-commissioned officers' corps. The British and Americans, prejudiced against the very word "conscription," had stubbornly insisted on a professional army. The Marshal's fears proved even more correct than he had foreseen. The 100,000 members of the German Army of 1926 were not soldiers: they were 100,000 drill sergeants. And they were not sergeants in the French or American meaning of the term, men who perform their military duties and remain civilians in uniform. They were warriors to the very marrow of their bones, trained in the use of every kind of weapon, inspired to regard their present corps as the nucleus of a gigantic mass army in which the soldier of today would be a captain or a colonel. The German army was ready to multiply itself twentyfold, and it did not even conceal the fact.

Tanks, for instance, were forbidden to this army and during her period of good behavior Germany avoided too drastic violations of this restriction. But she built model tanks of wood and systematically trained her soldiers and commanders in the use of a weapon which had been forbidden by the peace treaty. Those who regarded this as only a game were mistaken.

Then there was the mysterious fact that the budget for this army of 100,000 men with limited equipment grew from year to year by leaps and bounds. It was almost as high now as the budget of the Prussian pre-war army of 600,000 men which had unlimited equipment. A detailed examination of the figures would have shown that every dustcloth and every pound of grease for cleaning guns now allegedly cost five or ten times as much as in 1913. The implausible figures of the budget alone proved what was going on in secret.

It was also disclosed about this time that the Reichswehr Ministry was engaged in trade in order to procure additional funds free of State control. The army and navy departments founded a secret corporation with money that had never been granted them. By the time the facts became public, they had acquired or founded three dozen firms. Among them were a film enterprise, several export businesses, a river navigation company, a bacon importing business, and many others. In the end they proved commercial failures and went bankrupt. But the fact that they had been put into operation at all was significant. If the Reichswehr Ministry was trying to gain independent sources of income it must obviously be making secret expenditures.

Then certain incidents which had occurred abroad became known. There was the submarine incident involving Captain Canaris, who was to become chief of German military espionage under Hitler. He founded a secret submarine shipyard in Vigo, Spain, the Versailles Treaty having forbidden submarine construction in Germany. The Spanish shipyard was too small for quantity production, but afforded an opportunity to keep abreast of airplane technical developments. Secret German airplane factories in Russia served a similar purpose. The Soviet Government had granted permission to its Rapallo partner to construct these factories, which were supervised by a builder of genius, who was certainly far from completely occupied by his world-renowned stove factory in Germany.

In the Reichswehr factories in Russia, Professor Junkers prepared to gain even greater renown by building airplanes, their construction within Germany having been forbidden by the peace treaty. In Russia he and his staff of engineers could follow the rapid technical developments in the aircraft industry. Unfortunately he was entirely lacking in self-control. He had several disputes with the Reichswehr Ministry as a result of the costs of his enterprise, and at one point went so far as to file a formal legal complaint against it. Under Hitler, he would have paid for such temerity with his life. Under Weimar, he only caused embarrassment to the authorities. His case was hastily adjudicated by a private court of arbitration under the chairmanship of the highest judge in Germany. But the indiscretion had been committed, and even the public at large now knew of secret German airplane factories on foreign territory.

Decidedly the Reichswehr showed no sign of disarming. But this did not prevent the Berlin government from enthusiastically promoting world disarmament nor the disarmament visionaries from regarding that government as genuinely interested in furthering peace and progress. Moreover, was not "the disarmament of the other party," a legitimate German goal? Were not the other powers, at least those which had signed the Versailles Treaty, bound to disarm? Of course they were! Part V of the Versailles Treaty, which dealt with Germany's obligation to disarm begins as follows: "In order to render possible the initiation of general limitation of the armaments of all nations, Germany undertakes etc. . . ." Could anyone deny that this imposed a definite obligation on the Allied powers? Could anyone maintain that it was only a vague mention of an indefinite future possibility? The Germans insisted it was a solemn pledge and when Germany spoke of solemn pledges, she spoke as an expert.

Anyhow, there was no reason to discuss the merits of disarmament. Fortunately, there was the great naval example to point to. The Washington Conference had taken place six years earlier and secured a general reduction of naval armaments. This conference was an object of worship for the devotees of disarmament.

As a matter of fact, extraordinary events had taken place during this conference. After a prayer by a minister who invoked divine guidance, President Harding's Secretary of State had made his unforgettable inaugural address. Mr. Hughes had come forward with an extraordinary proposal which went much further than the mere limitation of expenditures. Its principal object was to appease Japan. The Japanese were suffering from a fear complex. They feared the continuation of naval construction which England and America, with their huge building capacity, had begun during the war. He suggested that all three powers abandon building warships for the next fifteen years. In addition, he suggested the scrapping of existing warships on a grand scale. The United States alone was to scrap a number of old ships and 16 unfinished ones, in all some 845,000 tons. England was to scrap 583,000 tons and Japan 449,000. This really justified the phrase coined by Colonel Repington, the British expert: "In one speech, Hughes sank more warships than any admiral in a naval engagement." [38] The gesture was unprecedented: it meant that two strong powers would voluntarily reduce their naval strength out of consideration for a weaker power and, in addition, pledge themselves to remain on that lower level for fifteen years. The generosity of this gesture was all the more impressive because England needed ships in seven seas, the United States in two seas, and Japan in only one sea.

Yet the touchy Japanese had asked to be appeased a little more and had obtained further concessions. The United States obligingly agreed not to build new naval bases in the Pacific, in particular in the Philippines or on Guam. Great Britain made a similar promise with regard to all the islands between Australia and Canada. On February 6th, 1922, the pact was concluded. Through the scrapping of an enormous number of American and English warships, and a relatively smaller number of Japanese warships, the ratio of capital ships was reduced to 525:-525:315 thousand tons, ideal for Japan. This ratio of 5:5:3 was to be frozen for fifteen years. With regard to capital ships, for the building of which the English and American facilities were overwhelmingly superior to those of Japan, all new constructions were to be abandoned.

Liberals had always praised the naval pact as the most promising prelude to a new era. They considered its apparent effect in satisfying the Japanese as the most brilliant confirmation of their theories. True, that the military men wrung their hands in despair, whether they were British or American, orthodox experts like Admiral Sims, or heretics like General Mitchell. True, that many civilians, too, opposed the pact like Norman Davis who termed it "unnecessary and undesirable." [39] Prominent American writers deplored it. "Washington has not even grasped what the Pacific problem really is," [40] one of them wrote. "As a result of the Washington Conference," said another, "the intervention of foreign powers to halt the progress of Japanese imperialism on the continent of Asia is more impossible than ever." [41]

However, the partisans of ideal solutions to all problems of the world intoned Hosannas and Vivas. This was still the day of Lloyd George's ascendancy. In his Cabinet the post of First Lord of the Admiralty was held by Lord Lee of Fareham, one of his most uncritical admirers. Lord Fareham exulted over the pact: "There was much more accomplished than the material results enshrined in the Naval treaty. The conference produced a complete change in the attitude of mind of the nations there assembled. . . . As a result of the Naval Treaty, a bloodthirsty combatant of the future will find it exceedingly difficult, if not impossible, to get at the enemy for whose blood he is thirsty." [42] These sentiments were typical of the feelings of all the progressives about the pact of Washington.

Now, who could still resist the idea of disarmament? Who was still reluctant to reproduce the Washington experiment on a large scale and purge the world of armaments at one blow? Even the French ceased to resist this idea with their former energy and logic; for in France, too, the peace hynosis had produced results. After Locarno Briand was forced to admit that, once world peace was definitely guaranteed, military matters, too, could appear in a new light. France felt compelled to put the tip of its little finger into a machine which ended up by swallowing its whole body. It was agreed that it would be rash to call a world disarmament conference, but a "preparatory commission" for such a conference, it was argued, could be appointed at once. Its function would be to investigate and clarify the principles, standards and measures to be applied.

In March, 1926, this preparatory commission met for the first time in Geneva, with the participation of the United States and later also of Russia. It indulged in scholastic discussions. The French, cornered like Balaam's

ass between the old truth that they had experienced
and the new theories they had adopted, displayed a
lamentable weakness and schizophrenia. Instead of taking a firm stand, they resorted to impotent skirmishes
over details, to evasions and postponements. This earned
them the same ill-will from the enthusiasts that they
would have earned by determined resistance, but it was
without real effect. Everyone realized that the French
would be forced to give in and make concessions to the
German demand for equality. The pressure grew stronger
to put an end to the "preparatory commission" and begin
the real conference in earnest. Everyone was sure that on
this field, too, great pacifist achievements were at hand.

Up and up and up.

The reparations specified in the Dawes Plan were paid
on time. They never caused the slightest difficulties. Nevertheless, toward the end of 1928 it was a foregone conclusion that they would have to be further reduced. Suggestions in this sense came from the business leaders in England and America. The bankers and investors thought
that the interest of their 30 billion marks of investments
would be more secure if the German Reich's political
debts were reduced. Industrialists and merchants, for
their part, thought that as a result of the reparations arrangement Germany was becoming too strong a competitor. German exports were 33% greater than those of pre-
war Germany; in fact, they were second only to American
exports. Fanciful economists had discovered that this was
caused by the pressure of the reparations payments which
forced Germany to export huge quantities. Further suggestions and demands came ceaselessly from the fanatics
of peace who always and everywhere supported anything
that could alleviate the sufferings of the German people

from the "cruelty" of the Versailles Treaty. But whatever
the motives for these suggestions and demands, they
were all supported and utilized by the commander-in-
chief of the German reparations strategy, Dr. Schacht,
and S. Parker Gilbert, the General Agent for Reparations,
whom the Berlin augurs had long ago named the General
Agent against Reparations. A new international commission was appointed, under the chairmanship of Owen
Young. In the spring of 1929, it came forward with a new
"Young Plan" which brought further impressive advantages to the Reich. According to its provisions, the annual
instalment to be paid by Germany was about one third
lower than under the Dawes Plan; all international control agencies were to be abolished; all securities freed;
the Reich was to resume full control over its railways and
banks; and the supervision of the General Agent for Reparations over German finances was to come to an end.

In August, 1929, at a conference at The Hague, Germany and the Allies signed the Young Plan. This was another step upwards, an enormous step toward perfection.
But it was not the last. "Up and up and up!" Germany
had to be rewarded for her willingness to accept the concessions of the Young Plan. Monsieur Briand gave her the
highest reward in his power, the reward which, in the
opinion of the day would inevitably have the most powerful, the most placating effect on her: the complete evacuation of the Rhineland. According to the Versailles
Treaty, this was to take place in 1935, if Germany had
not committed any violations of her pledges. Briand now
promised to evacuate the province at once, in 1929, although there had been many violations.

Over this Rhineland, the fiercest battles had been
fought in Paris. At a critical session of the peace confer-

ence, Clemenceau had said of it: "In fifteen years, I shall be no more. In fifteen years, if you do me the honor of visiting my grave, you will be able to say, I am sure: 'We are watching on the Rhine and we shall remain there.' " [43] M. Briand had no intention of visiting Clemenceau's grave. He considered it the part of wisdom to stay on the Rhineland not more than fifteen years, but less. Of this Rhineland, Stresemann had written: "The most important objective of German politics is the liberation of German territory from foreign occupation. First, we must remove the strangler from our throat." [44] M. Briand granted this wish. Briand thought it wise to help Mr. Stresemann achieve his "first" objective to pave the way for what was to follow.

On September 29th, 1929, Allied troops and officials began to move out of the Rhineland. Once the evacuation was completed, the victors of 1918 held not a single German security in their hands. Nothing could be supervised any longer: not a single section of German territory, German population, German industry. Germany could now dispose of herself and her potentialities without any restriction.

It was now difficult for the Germans to discover pretexts for their periodic fits of anger. If this was not peace, what was? Ten years after the lost World War, six years after the lost Ruhr war, Germany was a respected, muchflattered member of the family of nations. Her living standard was higher than ever. Her economy was flourishing. She had been flooded with foreign money. The reparations had been reduced to a token. Interference with her internal administration had ceased. The military control had been abolished, and now the last foreign soldier had left German soil. No one could really maintain any longer that Germany had been harshly treated. She had come out of the misery she herself had created in better shape than could have been expected. Indeed, she had come out of it gloriously. Now the medicine of appeasement must work. The flask had been emptied.

M. Briand returned home somewhat disappointed. His magnificent gesture in favor of the evacuation of the Rhineland had not aroused the reaction he had hoped for. There was no gratitude or conciliatory spirit in Germany. She had accepted his gesture coolly as something she had a right to expect, like the payment of an overdue bill. But Briand's faith was steadfast. He did not allow himself to be discouraged. He sat down at his desk and drew up a still greater vision on paper: the project of bringing all Europe together into one single union. In September, 1929, he sent to all the capitals of the world a document urging the foundation of a "European Federation."

But he did not receive the answer he expected. The chords which had been harmoniously vibrating until then, broke abruptly. The world suddenly changed its face. It was like the story of the peasant and the ass. "What bad luck," said the peasant, "I'd just weaned the ass from eating when he died." Pacification had just reached its climax, when it came to an end. It came to an end at the very moment of, and a result of, the evacuation of the Rhineland. "First" we must recover the Rhineland, had always been Stresemann's program. The way was now open for something new. Moreover, another event pointed toward new times. One memorable day in October, 1929, the bottom dropped out of the New York Stock Exchange and the world was thrown into chaos. The liberation of the Rhineland and the beginning of the

great depression coincided. The first was the final point of
one policy. The second, the starting point of a new one.
Good-bye, euphoria. Good-bye, pacification. Good-bye,
"tricking."

And good-bye, Herr Stresemann. A third coincidence
was added to the other two. One night in that same week
of October, 1929, the Foreign Minister who had invented
"tricking" was preparing to go to sleep after a hard day's
work. Sitting on the edge of his bed, he had a sudden
stroke and died.

Part Three: Putrefaction:
1930-1935

7: Crumbling Structure

I AM NEVER mistaken!" thundered Dr. Schacht. His eyes gleamed angrily behind his pince-nez. His posture was rigid, dogmatic, and hostile. "I am never mistaken!" the President of the Reichsbank repeated.

He had been the official German expert and the leading negotiator during the preparation of the Young Plan. He had been one of the authors of this plan. Until it was signed (August, 1929) and even for some time after that, he had found it excellent, a plan marking a great step forward. He had accepted praise for his contribution to the Plan. The agreement had to be ratified by the Reichstag. And now in December, 1929, Dr. Schacht denied his own work. This quick-change artist suddenly issued a manifesto in which he declared: "In preparing the Young Plan, I have in good faith and with good will helped to conclude an agreement. . . . I must emphatically refuse to be made responsible for the enactment of this plan." [2] The lengthy manifesto attempted to establish a logical connection between Schacht's old and new attitudes. It argued that the "premises and intentions of the plan" [3] had been violated. But this was highly disingenuous.

The fact was that Schacht sensed a change in the political climate. He felt certain that old Hugenberg and his "Committee for the Preparation of a Plebiscite against the Young Plan" would sooner or later gain the upper hand. The agitational activities of this committee which, a few months earlier, did not appear to be very significant, now, with the evacuation of the Rhine and the onset of the world depression, had to be taken seriously. Indeed it seemed very likely that Herr Hugenberg's propaganda was the beginning of some new, insane adventure. Herr Schacht refused to be on the losing side, he refused to be completely identified with the Young Plan. He was in a hurry to join Hugenberg and to wash off a political stain which might one day prove fatal.

No one who looked at Privy Councillor Hugenberg, the strong man of German nationalism, would have suspected him of being what he was. His appearance was that of an honest, small-fry artisan; he might have been taken for a watchmaker. He was a cartoon portrait of the German philistine at his beer table: small, paunchy, with bristling hair on a square skull, with the mustache of an old-time Prussian sergeant, and with metal-framed spectacles on his nose. The graces were occupied elsewhere when he was born.

Although his outlook was limited, he was not unintelligent. He had distinguished himself as an official in the Royal Prussian service. He had earned a reputation as an agriculturist. He was the founder and owner of an important agricultural bank. He had been general director of the Krupp Works. An accomplished bureaucrat, agriculturalist, banker and industrialist, with many contacts in these fields, he went into politics at an early date.

He was the first of the Prussian conservatives and reactionaries to realize the meaning of modern propaganda. Even under Wilhelm II, he had founded an occult "National Consortium," which purchased newspapers at every opportunity. To bring other newspapers into line, he founded a large advertising agency which influenced them politically by buying advertising space from them. After 1918, he was one of the most stubborn partisans of the old regime and he was enormously active. He bought more newspapers and founded a large news agency. His various correspondents supplied editorials and features to half the German press. He even realized the propaganda value of moving pictures. During a period when cinema production was in financial difficulties he acquired the UFA, the largest German moving picture concern which completely controlled the movie theatre owners, and he used it to popularize what he found desirable. Like a spider, he sat in the center of a gigantic, almost invisible, web.

By the middle of 1929, Herr Hugenberg decided that the time had come for Germany to discontinue its more or less rational methods of political "trickery" and to run amok once again. He chose the Young Plan as the starting point for his agitation.

The Weimar Constitution provided for plebiscites with legislative power, but this process presented so many technical difficulties that in practice no plebiscite could be carried out; in fact, during the entire Weimar period, not a single plebiscite was successfully held. But Herr Hugenberg did not aim at direct result; what was important for him was the agitation. He formed a committee composed of the principal forces of German nationalism, of the new and the old variety: his own German

National Party, the Steel Helmet Association of Front Soldiers, the respectable Pan-German Party which had helped to bring about the war of 1914, and also Hitler's Nazis, although these people were unpleasantly plebeian and not very numerous.

This "Committee for the Preparation of a Plebiscite against the Young Plan" proceeded to create its own propaganda machine. Germans are characterized by the peculiarity of believing under all circumstances that they have been wronged. Even during the years of prosperity, even until the end of 1929, when the Germans lived better than ever before, they contrived to convince themselves that their situation was miserable. The middle class ruined by the inflation was to a certain extent justified in this belief; but those who engaged in production had never lived better; nevertheless they believed themselves very badly off. Herr Hugenberg and his committee began to tell them that their lot would be a hundred times worse as a result of the Young Plan. He contended, in the face of overwhelming evidence to the contrary that this plan would intolerably increase Germany's burden. The main feature of his propaganda was the fantasy of "slave labor." His agitators maintained that the plan provided for the deportation of millions of Germans to do forced labor abroad for the victorious powers and their capitalists. (Today Germany has herself adopted such a plan and imports labor from the conquered countries.) The theme was taken up by all the propaganda trumpets of the nationalists and millions of pamphlets spread the message to the remotest villages.

Actually the Plan did not contain the slightest hint of such a provision. The propaganda was pure fabrication. Nevertheless, millions of Germans believed it; over six million votes approved the plebiscite! And this was not under a dictatorship, this was not at a time when there was really only one vote in Germany, this was during a period of the fullest freedom of speech.

Herr Hugenberg talked and talked. He preached resistance, extremism, what amounted to madness. Let us tear the Young Plan to pieces and throw it in the face of "western predatory capitalism." [4] Germany had not yet taken to speaking of "plutocracy." "Let us finally become heroes!" [5] "We would rather be proletarians together with the entire German people, than taskmasters of our people for foreign capitalists!" [6] Moreover, neither he nor his allies concealed the fact that the "struggle against Versailles" to which they again summoned the Germans, was also to be a struggle against the republic, and against democracy. "Parliament must be abolished," [7] clamored Hugenberg. And his associate, the leader of the Pan-German Party, proclaimed: "In the last analysis we are fighting against the system. The struggle must not cease until the system has been done away with." [8] And that little fellow in Munich, that Hitler, said the same thing in his peculiarly plebeian rhetoric.

Before the evacuation of the Rhine and the Wall Street crash, Dr. Schacht had regarded this propaganda without concern. But after these two events, he saw the light. The man who was never mistaken saw that extremism, crushed in 1923, was raising its head again. Now that German territory had been evacuated, the *furor teutonicus* had greater opportunities than ever before. Moreover the deepening of the world depression might very well exasperate the German people and induce the rest of the world to accept nearly anything. He drew his conclusions and in December, 1929, declared himself against the Young Plan which he had helped to formulate. In March, 1930, he went one step further. With great fanfare he resigned from his office as President of the Reichsbank. He realized that to belong to a new dispensation one must dissociate oneself from the old.

From that moment on he became an agitator for extremist nationalism. He was asked: "What would you do if you were German dictator?" He replied: "Stop all foreign payments as of 8 A.M. tomorrow." He demanded "German initiative. . . . Our situation is so bad that we have no alternative but to seize the initiative." [9]

According to the speeches of this economic expert, the depression, which had dislocated the economy of even rich America, was not a world phenomenon. There was no world depression. There was only German misery. And this misery was caused by the refusal of foreign powers to grant Germany "living space outside her territory." "Unless we succeed in obtaining economic living space outside our frontiers, unemployment will become permanent in our country. For this reason we must demand again and again: Give the German people living space in the world!" [10] These words from a speech by Hitler were, according to reports, "stormily applauded." Why not? Herr Schacht was now openly for all the extremists. He called Nazism "a living protest against the internal and external restriction of our living space." [11]

Dr. Schacht was a man possessed by devouring ambition. Obviously he did not abandon one of the most important posts in Germany and adopt what looked like the wildest views without reason. He was one of the men best informed as to what went on behind the scenes. He did not harbor the delusion that his country's real policies were made by the voters. He knew that policies were de-

termined by a small group of important people behind
whom stood the officers' corps. Hence his sudden political
shift to extremism indicated that the most important people in Germany were tending toward abandonment of the
policy of international goodwill.

During those weeks, Dr. Heinrich Bruening, the Catholic Centrist, became Reich Chancellor. His closest associate was Minister Treviranus. Neither of these men were
partisans of Hugenberg or Hitler: Treviranus had broken
with Hugenberg whose social policies he found retro-
grade, and Bruening was to wage a constant fight against
the Nazis during his chancellorship. The truth is, that he
hated them. Nevertheless, the Bruening government, too,
expressed the changed mood of the real formulators of
German politics, who now wanted to put a stop to even
the simulation of international goodwill. Each German
government since 1919 had tried to return to 1914; only
the methods, the tone, the ideological make-up had varied. The Bruening-Treviranus government used more
provocative methods, had a more militaristic tone, and a
more aggressive ideology.

The new Cabinet stressed the fact that its leading
members were former army men, and introduced itself
as a "Cabinet of front fighters." [12] The term "front fighters" has been much used and abused, especially under
Hitler, and its exact meaning remains obscure; but there
can be no doubt that it intends to suggest something military. The charm of the new government was its aggres-
siveness, and Treviranus described its purpose as the destruction of treaties or, in technical languague, "an active
revisionist policy." This, he said, expressed the "feelings
of the generation of front fighters." [13] "We must be explicit," he shouted to the world. "Foreign countries will

have to get accustomed to the fact that we wish to interpret our European mission on the basis of the 'front fighter'
spirit." [14]

"Our hopes of reaching a peaceful agreement with our
adversaries have been painfully disappointed," lamented
Herr Bruening. He concentrated on systematically attacking every clause of the settlement of 1919 still enforced. His tone ranged from the whining to the threatening. In the beginning, he, too, refused to regard the
world depression as universal, insisting that it was a
purely German phenomenon caused by the reparations
payments. "The burdens imposed by the Dawes Plan
have increased the acuteness of our economic situation," [15]
he said, although Germany had not paid a cent of her
own wealth. Later, when he finally recognized the world
wide nature of the depression, he insisted that it was
more severe in Germany than anywhere else: "In Germany its effects are much more severe." [16] As a matter of
fact, the German depression was *less* severe than the
American. Even after the German economy had considerably deteriorated as a result of political madness, it remained more stable.

Moreover, the German people were "deeply aroused"
because "the promise given us that the compulsory disarmament of Germany would be followed by the voluntary disarmament of other nations has not yet been
brought closer to fulfilment." [17] Above all, there was the
question of the Polish frontier. With regard to this question, a resolute frenzy was displayed: threatening parades
and demonstrations along the frontiers, a sudden flood of
notes and complaints protesting against the alleged "terrorism" to which Germans living in Poland were subjected, and extremist speeches such as the one made by

Treviranus: "The eastern problem demands the unified action of the German people. We do not forget the partitioning of the lands along the Vistula, the unhealed wound in our eastern flank, the withered lung of the Reich. We think of the despicable pressure exterted on Wilson to make him accede to the unnatural mutilation of East Prussia. . . . Eastern Prussia's stagnation remains a European danger." [18] A few years later Treviranus told me that at the time he made those statements he had no idea what the consequences would be. But no single individual can be held responsible for events. If Treviranus had not, someone else would have spoken those words.

In Germany the depression deepened. Agricultural and industrial prices went down. Exports decreased. As everywhere else, capital went "on strike"; the investors were no longer interested in profits, they wanted only to preserve their capital, and anxiously sought to convert their assets into liquid funds. The depression now assumed its classical form. Prices, trade volume, stocks, investments, employment opportunities, incomes—all diminished.

The economic experts discussed methods of checking the depression. A modern school advocated government intervention, mostly in the form of energetic public spending intended to stop the deflation; we may call this the Roosevelt doctrine. The conservative school opposed government intervention, argued that the deflationary "purge" must be allowed to run its course, that the depression must be allowed to "burn itself out." This may be called the Hoover doctrine. Dr. Breuning developed a third method never tried out before. He intervened, not to stop the deflation, but to spur it on. By a series of "emergency decrees" enforcing radical restrictions in every economic field, he tried to hasten the process of deflation, hoping thus to shorten the period of travail. He interpreted his action as an attempt to relieve the situation. In fact, he aggravated it.

Despite all this, and despite additional political complications, the German depression was never as acute as the American. According to fairly incomplete statistics, at the height of the depression about 12% of the American population was unemployed. German unemployment, according to much more complete statistics, was never more than 9%. American national income dropped to 47% of the record figure, German national income only to 60%. But these peaks—or abysses—were reached only during the most acute period of the depression, in 1932. In 1930, things had not got so far out of hand.

In September, 1930, there were Reichstag elections. Their outcome stunned Germany and the world. An incomprehensible, unexpected event took place: a comet rose in the sky, a fiery, dazzling, swiftly expanding comet: the swastika. The insignificant party of that nonentity, Hitler, whom everybody had ignored, came violently to the fore. In the elections of 1928, this party had won 12 seats and 2% of the votes; now it obtained 107 seats and 18% of the votes. The Nazi organization moved from 12th, or last, to second place among the parties of Germany. This brutal caricature of Hugenberg's respectable "German National" party had suddenly developed into the largest of the organized extremist German groups. Hugenberg and his friends did not realize that by introducing a demogogic politics of desperation they had prepared their own exit. The Nazis were too serious politically not to win out over mere dilettanti of brutality. In the use of demagogy, those with the fewest inhibitions have the best chance to succeed.

This landslide opened a hectic period in German domestic politics. Chancellor Bruening refused to have anything to do with the Nazis. Morally and philosophically he was on a plane apart from these madmen. He was a devout Catholic and the bishops had already given orders that religious burial be refused to active members of the godless party. Bruening tried to rally all the conservative forces that were still available on the political stage and behind the scenes. But because of the bitter hostility of Hitler's and Hugenberg's parties on the one hand, and of the Communists on the other, the situation was precarious. There was no reliable majority in the Reichstag, and Bruening was compelled to proclaim a state of emergency in which President Hindenburg's signature could replace a parliamentary vote. He thus became dependent upon the signatures of the old, narrow-minded, increasingly senile field marshal whose whims and prejudices he had to flatter. And the prominent people behind the scenes were grouped around Hindenburg and influenced him; among these were Hindenburg's own son, his Junker friends and neighbors, generals of the old and new army. These were the people who had created the trend noticed by Dr. Schacht. Hindenburg's powerful intimates increasingly adopted the totally extremist domestic and foreign policies recommended by Hugenberg. They were still reluctant to let Hitler, the plebeian, play an important part in the game, but they did not object so much to using him in a subordinate role.

Chancellor Bruening put up a fight on the internal front. He fought the depression which nevertheless—or rather, as a result of his method of fighting it,—grew more acute. He fought the Nazis whose numbers were swelling to alarming proportions and whose expanding

Brown Shirt army enjoyed powerful protection. And he fought on the international front. As a "front officer" he had assumed office to further an active revisionist policy inspired by the "front soldier's spirit." His objective was the destruction of the remaining treaty provisions. A success of this sort on the international front was highly desirable, because it would win the approval of the old field marshal, and because it would "steal the Nazis' thunder."

The chancellor had considered all the forces arrayed against him and carefully sought a flaw in their defenses. He had intensified the campaign against the Polish frontiers and the campaign for the "disarmament of other nations." He had exploited the depression to urge the complete stoppage of all reparations payments even though the Young Plan had just been ratified. And he had discovered a new issue: Austria, the German "brotherland." He discovered the frontier which had not been drawn in 1919, which had always existed, which had only been confirmed by the Versailles Treaty.

There was never much love lost between Germany and Austria. The instinctive attraction between the two, celebrated in a rhetoric which convinced well-meaning but ignorant foreigners, simply did not exist. The Germans had always despised the Austrians as a soft, weak, semi-Balkan people. The Austrians had always had more hatred than admiration for the strong, presumptuous, hard-working Germans. A desire for unification had been manifested only by the Pan-Germans of Austria (not of Germany), and, during a short period, by the Social Democrats of both countries.

But after the defeat of 1918, the Anschluss appeared as the only possible compensation for other losses, the only chance for Germany to emerge from the war with at least something to show. This gave rise to a type of agitation as a result of which France, Czechoslovakia and the other "successor" states insisted upon and obtained the inclusion of a special clause in the post-Versailles treaties forbidding the Anschluss.

Dr. Bruening rediscovered Austria. What "active revision" more impressive than the destruction of this frontier was possible? The plan was sure to produce the greatest nationalistic feeling. It would unite German brothers, augment the Reich, tear up another treaty provision, and for the first time modify a frontier. With such an achievement, the "Cabinet of Front Fighters" would never again be refused the field marshal's support, and Hitler would be relegated to the role he clearly merited.

The Austrian Foreign Minister happened to be a Pan-German—a former police official named Schober, who stood in awe of the German Reich and readily agreed to play the part desired by the Bruening Cabinet. On March 20, 1931, in Vienna, a pact was signed which was to open a veritable Pandora's box. It started a chain of catastrophic effects operative even in Asia. Before the fall of the year, the terrible forces loosed by the pact signed in the spring, would circle the globe; because of the pact, 1931 was to become the "annus terribilis."

The pact had been engineered hastily and secretly. Only 48 hours before it was signed, the text was presented to the Paris and London governments, as final and unalterable. The blow was particularly bitter for M. Briand. Only a few days before he had illustrated the wisdom of his policy of pacification by pointing out how it had resolved the question of Anschluss: "I used to be told: 'You are blind. Tomorrow, or the day after tomorrow, the Anschluss will be achieved.' Months and years have passed. The danger, which could then be considered great, has gradually diminished." [19] Now, this pact *was* the Anschluss, only faintly camouflaged.

The camouflage was of an economic type. The pact stipulated that the customs border between the countries was to be abolished, and that measures would be taken to "merge their economic forces." This economic merger of the two countries officially bore the name of "Customs Union." But no one familiar with German history and the specifically German meaning of certain words could be deceived. Bismarck's Reich began by the creation of a "customs union" between the various states. For the German ear, the term "customs union" means the beginning of complete union. Moreover, the facts spoke for themselves. Little Austria with her six million inhabitants could not conceivably have any separate existence once it was economically united with the giant of 66 million inhabitants. Germany, Austria, and the neighboring countries clearly understood that the pact was intended to merge the two countries.

Premier Pierre Laval spurred Briand to action. But Briand was embittered and did not need any spur. As soon as he learned of the imminent conclusion of the agreement, he acted to prevent its consummation. "I immediately wired to Berlin, calling attention to the incompatibility of the pact with existing treaties. I have warned Henderson, my London colleague, who also declared to the authors of the project that they must abandon it." [20] On the day on which the pact was signed notwithstanding, the governments of Paris, Rome and Prague protested in a common note and demanded that the pact be annulled. The British government sent a separate note demanding that the pact be submitted to the League of

Nations. Unabashed, Bruening replied—and published his reply—that the Reich government "would follow with calm determination the path it had taken." [21]

As usual, the text of the pact was defended by the liberals. These people all over the world found the protests against the pact reactionary. They failed to see the reality: the German Reich of 1931. They saw only abstract universalist principles: the principles of nationality and self-determination. It was the will of nature that men speaking the same language unite into the same state: the larger the state, the better for peace. The right to self-determination is absolute, they claimed; those who object to the free decision of free peoples in the name of higher interests sin against an axiom of natural law. The progressives applauded the Anschluss.

But more realistic minds were dismayed. They realized that the process of doing away with 1918 was now out of hand. Frontiers were being modified. Germany was gradually recovering her position of power. The cry was raised that this must not be allowed. Prague saw that the very existence of the new Czechoslovakian state would be imperiled if Germany bordered it not only on the north and the west but also on the south. The British Foreign Minister found Paris "in a state of very natural perturbation." [22] Briand did not want to aggravate the situation; certainly he could not be accused of ill-will, or of trying to destroy the foundation of all his policies. But even he had to declare: "What is now being undertaken in Vienna and Berlin is illegal. We shall do everything in our power to stop them. It is obvious that we are forced to call for a temporary halt in German-French relations." [23] He brought pressure on Austria to annul the pact of her own initiative, and this she actually did a few

months later. He appealed to the Hague International
Court which, a few months later, decided against the
"customs union."

But these measures did not prevent the disaster which
followed the announcement of the customs union pact.
First of all the French and Czechoslovakian banks decided to withdraw their funds from Austria. Whether this
decision was a result of government pressure, or private
initiative, or merely normal capitalist unwillingness to
leave money in countries threatened by unrest, was never
made clear. The Austrian investors themselves joined in
the rush. Gold and currencies ebbed from the banks.
Seven weeks after the announcement of the customs
union, the *Nationalbank* was emptied. The largest Austrian bank, Rothschild's, became insolvent, to be followed by many others. The disaster was complete. March,
1931: customs union. May, 1931: Crash of the Austrian
money market.

From Austria the run on the banks spread to Germany.
England and America had billions of short term investments in Germany, and they began to withdraw them at
an increasingly brisk tempo. And the German bank customers joined in the run. Gold and currencies ebbed from
the banks. Dr. Luther, the new President of the Reichsbank flew to England and then to France, trying to borrow gold and currencies, and met with refusal. Hindenburg wrote a letter to Hoover asking him for help: he
explained the catastrophe as a result of the cruel reparations. Hoover wired to all governments proposing a one
year debt moratorium: all the countries involved would
renounce collecting reparations for one year, while America would renounce collecting her war debts for the same
period. The proposal had no concrete basis. It was in-

tended only as a "psychological" move. The reparations had no relation to the run on the banks; the annual sum of reparations was less than the funds withdrawn in one week from the banks. The Hoover moratorium was accepted, but had not the slightest influence. In July, there was a crash in Germany, too.

It was a truly German, truly extremist crash. Two big banks—and, it goes without saying many small banks—went bankrupt. All the banks suspended payments for weeks. But what was important was not the temporary suspension of payments—a similar step was later taken in America—but another measure, which became permanent. All foreign money and capital that were still in Germany were "frozen." Billions would not be repaid. Around Germany's frontiers, a wall of currency legislation was drawn, which ended the free circulation of money and capital. German self-seclusion, "autarchy," began. Now the German economic depression began to be really acute.

March, 1931: the customs union. May: the crash in Austria. July: the crash in Germany. But the series was not yet at an end. The British banks had invested billions in Germany. Their customers began to wonder whether they were still reliable. The run on the banks spread to England. Gold and currencies flowed from the Bank of England. A government, and then a parliamentary majority, collapsed. The Labor Party fell apart and on a gray week-end of September, 1931, the City of London, too, gave way. The English method of dealing with the situation was not like the German, but its effects were worldwide. The Bank of England went off the gold standard, letting the pound drop in value. England ceased to have a stable currency, and strictly speaking, would never have one again. And with England went the Empire and several other countries, among them the Scandinavian nations.

March, 1931: the customs union. May: the crash in Austria. July: the crash in Germany. September: the crash in England. The effect of the "active revisionist policy" was the bankruptcy that circled the world, bringing confusion and disintegration. But even this was not the last turn of the machinery of evil which was under way.

2.

Japan, too, had her "front officers," who had for a long time conceived an "active policy arising from the front fighter spirit." They were not yet all-powerful. The assassination of the Japanese Premier in 1930 was not enough to put them in power. Before they could succeed, two other Premiers and a few ministers would have to be murdered.

But they were already powerful enough. They completely controlled the army and navy. If the armed forces undertook something, it was already inconceivable that the government should not support them. Only the great white powers, particularly the sea-powers, England and America, stood in their way. But as they examined the world situation, the "front officers" grew more and more hopeful that these obstacles could be removed, and that the way would be open for military adventures.

The "annus terribilis" brought the long-awaited opportunity. The American depression had been encouraging. When the machinery of evil was fully under way in Europe, they decided that the time was ripe for action. In September, 1931, at the very moment when the convulsions that had started in Vienna reached London, General

Honjo, commander of the Kwantung Army on the Sino-Japanese frontier was given the green light. This signal caused a most lively night in the territory under his orders. An alleged patrol of this army discovered evidence of sabotage to the rails of the South Manchurian railway. And what is more, while the alleged patrol was examining the damage, it was fired on. The inevitable and logical result of this event was that General Honjo was at once compelled to order his army to march into Manchuria. What else could he have done? Before daybreak General Honjo had occupied Mukden and three other cities on a 200 mile front. In less than four months he had occupied all of Manchuria, a country of 35 million inhabitants, more than three times as large as Japan, blessed with one of the most fertile soils in the world, gigantic forests, and rich mineral treasures.

This exploit showed a total lack of consideration for China and the great powers. These powers had just appeased the Japanese for a second time. The first occasion was the Washington Conference. In April, 1930, a second naval conference took place in London and a second naval agreement was signed. This time, the procedures were dominated by the British Labor government. Both Prime Minister Ramsay MacDonald and Foreign Secretary Arthur Henderson were professionals at disarmament. Both seriously believed that the best way of securing world peace was to turn as many battleships into as much scrap as possible. Thus it came about that the phenomenally disproportionate scrapping of 1922 was followed by further unequal disarmament. England undertook to scrap five more battleships; the USA, three more battleships; Japan, only one. It was a new dose of progressive policy aimed at curing the Japanese of their in-

feriority and pacifying them by drastic proofs that they
were confronted by nothing more serious than a wish to
preserve peace.

No, it was not considerate of the Japanese to ruin the
policy of utopian disarmament. Moreover, by their invasion of Manchuria they violated a number of treaties. In
the Nine Power Pact of 1922, they had pledged themselves not to encroach upon Chinese territory. In the
Covenant, they had pledged themselves to submit all disputes to the League. In the Briand-Kellogg Pact they had
pledged themselves never to resort to war. The Japanese
had behaved very badly.

But the question was: how would the powers behave?
The Chinese at once appealed to the League of Nations
for help and protection and it was obvious that this was
the test case for the institution in Geneva. The party involved here was not little Greece or impoverished Bulgaria: it was a great power. The task was either to persuade or to compel Japan to restore the seized territories.

It would be well if persuasion were enough. But what
if Japan had to be compelled? The basic problem of the
Wilsonian institution was suddenly laid bare and this
problem related not to the wicked powers, but to the
good. Was human nature so constituted that the "good"
powers could not only refrain from evil deeds, but also
prevent wickedness even at the risk of serious sacrifices?
There had been sermons explaining what nations *should*
do, there had been prophecies as to what nations *would*
do. Here was the test.

It so happened that in this instance the chances of virtue were usually favorable. To be sure, in the League itself, only two powers were equal to the task of dealing
with Japan: France and England. More accurately, as sea

power was the decisive factor, England alone was up to
it. But, this time, the U.S.A., with her traditional interest
in the Far East, was concerned, too. China had appealed
to President Hoover, and the General Secretary of the
League had immediately cabled China's complaint to the
American State Department. Secretary of State Henry L.
Stimson immediately made it clear that in this case he
was willing to cooperate with the League, although the
cooperation was to be informal. Actually, the League's
attitude toward the Sino-Japanese conflict was to be determined by England, a League member, and the United
States, a non-member. All the other powers granted these
precedence in the affair.

Mr. Stimson's first cable advised a method of "discussion and conciliation." [24] He recommended tact and caution. There were, of course, militarists in Japan. But there
were, fortunately, moderates too. Foreign Minister Shidehara was one of them. The State Department gambled on
the hope that the moderate Japanese would force the
immoderates to back down. Hence, it applied the rules
provided for such cases in the book of recipes current in
the post-war period. These rules were: if you wish to
strengthen the moderates in a given country, be yourself
moderate; if you proceed with brutality, you strengthen
the extremists.

But did this method always work? Did not gentleness
often encourage savagery? And did not brutality sometimes induce moderation? Many years were to pass before such possibilities could be considered. In September,
1931, the State Department was still completely attached
to the progressive tradition. "It would be wise," went Mr.
Stimson's confidential reply to the General Secretary in
Geneva, "to avoid action which might excite nationalistic

feeling in Japan in support of the military and against Shidehara." [25] He urgently recommended a policy "of giving Shidehara and the Foreign Office an opportunity, free from anything approaching threats or even public criticism, to get control of the situation." [26]

Two months later, he would be disappointed, and admit that this policy had produced results directly opposed to those desired. Instead of strengthening Shidehara and the moderates, it strengthened the extremists. The Secretary of State would be uneasy at "the dark news as to the popular excitement in Japan . . . steadily rising as her troops moved forward. . . . Our Embassy in Japan reported that the Wakatsuki-Shidehara Cabinet was tottering and could not last long in the face of the excited populace." [27] In December this Cabinet would be overthrown. As was to happen repeatedly during the period that followed, the omission of threats and criticisms, instead of helping the reasonable elements, only brought triumph to the extremists. But all this was realized after the completion of the conquest of Manchuria by Honjo's army. When the case was opened, the State Department warned the League of Nations against actions that might excite nationalistic feeling in Japan.

The warning was superfluous. There was no desire for action in Geneva anyhow. And there was a positive desire for inaction. The Council sat under the chairmanship of M. Briand. The English delegate was Lord Robert Cecil, another priest of the religion of peace. The Council heard the Chinese complain that their country had been attacked and request the assistance provided for in the statutes. It heard the Japanese reply that the "protective measures taken by their army could not be regarded as a warlike aggression or a military occupation, and that their

government did not have any territorial designs in Manchuria." [28] Lord Robert Cecil declared that on this point
there was obviously a difference of opinion between the
two parties. But "both Japan and China are old main-
stays of the League and it may be trusted that they will
act in the spirit of the League." [29] Ten days later, the
Council requested both parties to hasten the restoration
of friendly relations, and adjourned for a month. The
Council failed to record that a warlike act had taken
place; it regarded the matter as an "incident." It failed to
designate the aggressor, and it did not even discuss the
possibility of helping the victim.

Mr. Stimson spoke to the Japanese ambassador, accusing the ambassador's government of violating treaties.
Mr. Shidehara's reply induced hopefulness, and Washington believed it could at least expect a halt to the invasion.
But the Japanese marched on. In October, when for the
first time they resorted to air bombardment, Mr. Stimson
became uneasy. The Japanese mentality, he thought, is
perhaps different from that of the whites. In a Cabinet
meeting he voiced the fear that "these modern treaties
initiated by western nations, and especially designed to
fit the exigencies of the industrialized world of Europe
and America, might not be taken very seriously in the
Orient." [30]

But he remained hopeful. It is true that he believed in
acting in accordance with principles: "If we surrendered
these treaties and permitted them to be treated like
scraps of paper, the hope of peaceable development in
the world would receive a blow from which it would not
soon recover." [31] But there was also the fact that the
American public evidenced a complete disinterest in the
whole question. "To a great many of our people, Man-

churia was an unknown part of the world and they wondered what we had to do with any controversy there at
all." [32] This was true not only of America, but of every
other country, including the members of the League of
Nations. The demand that something be done was dis-
quietingly weak.

To make matters worse, that part of the public which
was interested in politics was interested during those
weeks in a completely different question. It was interested in world disarmament; this was much more important, and much more conducive to comfortableness.
World disarmament was the wholesale panacea—the
Sino-Japanese conflict was only one of those details which
recur now and then. The path to peace via world disarmament did not require sacrifices; the path to Sino-Japanese
peace did require sacrifices, and the prospect was not at-
tractive. A General Disarmament Conference had been
called for 1932. To prepare for this conference was more
urgent and appealing than to settle the dispute over territories in Asia.

Thus, in the fall of 1931, the struggle for world peace
opened simultaneously on two stages, one imaginary and
one real; and the action on one of these stages was a
bloody mockery of what took place on the other. On the
imaginary stage, the *décor* was a world full of good will;
in it, all wickedness was frustrated by a sort of Aladdin's
lamp, an infallible charm named the League of Nations;
in this world, armies were senseless. On the real stage, the
progress of the Japanese invasion was demonstrating that
wickedness was as active as ever before, that the League
of Nations had no practical value, and that the only protection against aggression was armed force.

There was still a third stage, on which another drama

—also real—was being played: Germany. The final struggle for power over a country for the defeat of which half of mankind had been required, was nearing its end. It was not yet clear whether in the end power would be won by the plebeian or non-plebeian shades of militarism. But it was no longer doubtful that leadership would pass to a radical, aggressive militarism.

All these three stages were active simultaneously. On stage no. 1, the civilization that took itself for granted was bustling about, chattering gaily, recklessly rejecting all unpleasantness and sacrifice. On stages II and III, the primitive drive for power and conquest, whose suppression is the prerequisite of civilization, was marching on, sinister, booted, self-confident.

Mr. Stimson began to wonder whether action was not advisable after all. The League Council responded by presenting Japan with an ultimatum (on October 24, 1931) demanding that the Japanese evacuate Manchuria before November 16. The Japanese simply ignored the ultimatum and kept on marching. Mr. Stimson informed the League Council through his ambassador that if the League intended to use economic sanctions against Japan, the Amercan government was "anxious not to discourage them or to put any obstacles or difficulties in their path." [33] The British government was not over-curious to investigate the meaning of this cryptic communication. It was actually opposed to sanctions against Japan, which would result in Japanese counter-measures against Great Britain's trade in Asia—and England was in the midst of a depression. England did not want to increase the number of its unemployed. Moreover, who could foretell what other counter-measures Japan might take? It is easy to say: I do not want to fight you, all I want is to destroy your econ-

omy. But what if the other party resists? England had
many valuable possessions within Japan's reach, and
many colonies which would be imperiled as a result of a
conflict with Japan. In the last analysis, sea power was the
decisive factor in this crisis; and England would have had
to bear almost the entire burden of any action against
Japan decided by the League. Mr. MacDonald and his
new Foreign Secretary, Sir John Simon, wanted to avoid
war at all cost and without doubt correctly interpreted
the will of the English people. The English did not want
war or even the risk of war, and as a result, economic
sanctions were impossible.

Of course, something had to be done. But it had to be
something else. In December, 1931, three months after
China's call for help, the League Council decided to make
a thorough investigation of the incident. An international
committee, formed to this end, was to go to China and
to Japan. After its return, it would be possible to make a
clear decision on the basis of its report.

Meanwhile, the final mobilization of armament-busters
was taking place. England was in a condition of pacifistic
delirium. The "Conference of the Christian Churches"
summoned all churchgoers to impress the necessity of disarmament on every member of Parliament, orally and in
writing. Thousands of other religious groups, various
women's associations, peace leagues and League of Nations associations, and trade union locals held meetings
and passed resolutions. The enemy who had to be defeated was obviously France. To the English liberals,
France was, quite clearly, the real arch-militarist and enemy of mankind. Anti-French agitation in America was
equally violent. Senator William Edgar Borah, Chairman
of the Senate Committee on Foreign Affairs, lent this agi-

tation the authority he enjoyed as expert on international affairs. He made a speech in the Senate which contained epoch-making attacks on France. However, there were Frenchmen who also were heart and soul for the good cause. "Disarmament," exclaimed Leon Blum, the Socialist leader, "is the surest method of parrying the danger." [34] And he reassured those who refused to trust the surest method because of the domestic situation in Germany, by saying: "I do not think that Germany wants war. If the danger were imminent, the German people would react against this folly. We must have confidence in the working class, organized in the trade unions and the Socialist Party, which is an enemy of war." [35] Leon Blum, too, enjoyed a reputation as an authority on international affairs.

The great day came, the stage was set for General Disarmament. The curtain rose. February 2, 1932, delegates from sixty states met at Geneva. But the ceremonials of the peace lovers could not take place at the appointed hour. On this very day the news broke that having occupied all of Manchuria, the Japanese had launched a new enterprise. They had suddenly attacked Shanghai, a thousand miles from the scene of their previous "protective operations."

Even for the public-at-large, Shanghai was more than an "unknown part of the world." It was the capital of western trade in Asia, the city of the international settlements. The Japanese had been landing considerable masses of troops near Shanghai. And to show their respect for the Disarmament Conference, precisely on the day of its convocation, they bombed the Chapei district and railway station.

The ministers and representatives of the great powers assembled at Geneva asked President Henderson to postpone the opening of the conference for a few hours. They had first of all to reach an agreement about sending warships and troops to Shanghai. The U.S.A. dispatched her entire Asiatic fleet and some of the garrison stationed in the Philippines. The British sent warships from India and Hong-Kong. The French sent troops from Indo-China. Only after these measures had been taken, was it possible to attend to disarmament.

The official theme of the Conference was the limitation of all military forces. But navies were ignored; only land forces were discussed. Then, too, the land armies on other continents were ignored, and only European armies were discussed. But then the European armies were ignored, and only the French army discussed. In the end, even the French army was ignored, and only the relation between the French and German armies was discussed.

As it went on, the whole enterprise gradually changed its character and the change was not so much as noticed by the enthusiasts. After having sat together for weeks and months, the delegates spoke only of the absolute necessity of bringing the German and French armies to equality. This could be done either by reducing French armaments or by expanding German armaments. When the French asked, Who would guarantee the new balance?, they were told: the treaties and the League of Nations. They received the same answer when they inquired as to who would guarantee them against attack by a Germany with a superior war potential. The conference which had been called "to secure a substantial reduction and limitation of all national armaments" developed more and more into a conference to secure an approximation of French and German armaments.

On April 26, 1932, the first experimental step was taken

on this slippery path. In private conversation between Mr. Stimson, who had come to Europe, Mr. MacDonald and Chancellor Bruening, it was decided to confront the French with a plan for releasing Germany from all previous limitations on the type and number of her weapons, and for permitting her to double the strength of the Reichswehr. General Schleicher, German Minister of the Reichswehr, arrogantly disapproved of the plan: why bother about such obsolete procedures? The conversations were terminated. But although the scheme came to nothing, the fact remained that the two Anglo-Saxon powers had recognized the German cry for rearmament as in accord with the principle of "equality."

In the House of Commons, Winston Churchill, M.P., rose to protest. "He would much regret," we read in the official record, "to see any approximation in military strength between France and Germany, and to those who wished for it, he would say: Do you wish war? He was sure that the theory that they should be placed on an equal military footing was one which, if it emerged in practice, would bring them all within practical distance of almost immeasurable calamity." [36]

But Churchill was completely isolated. The vision of an equal military footing for France and Germany became a feverish pacifist dream. Everyone agreed on this point; a vociferous united front was formed to advocate this proposal of all progressive and resolutely anti-militaristic forces. That exemplary perfectionist and pacifist, General Schleicher, vowed in a speech to the German people, that the principle of "equality" would be enforced; he had promised, he said, to create a strong German army capable of fighting, and he would keep his promise. Lord Robert Cecil declared: "When Germans ask for equality of status with respect to disarmament, I think they are on strong, indeed on unassailable grounds." [37] And the Manchester Guardian, Lloyd George's progressive newspaper, wrote: "About the justice of Germany's claim there is nothing new to be said." And even that exemplary antimilitarist, Signor Mussolini, wrote in an article, for the English press: "Germany's right to juridical equality in the matter of armament must inevitably be recognized."

Herr Constantin von Neurath, the German Foreign Minister, then raised the question of time. Time was pressing. When would the principle of equality be finally adopted? Why have we come to the disarmament conference, if we are not granted permission to rearm? Neurath was not very brilliant, but pet children or favorite mistresses do not need genius to get what they want. Herr von Neurath was able to find the ruse he needed. He threatened to go. On September 18, 1932, Herr von Neurath was packing his trunks. Germany withdrew from the disarmament—or shall we say, rearmament?—conference. In a communication which combined complaints and threats, Germany announced that in view of French sabotage she could no longer participate in the discussion. Let no one say the conference was futile! Decidedly, world peace would never be secured without disarmament-rearmament conferences and agreements.

At the same time, world peace was being promoted in a somewhat different manner in Germany. Hugenberg, Hitler, Schacht and the Steel Helmet leaders formed a determined united "front." They vowed the definitive destruction of the Republic and the settlement of 1919. Presidential elections were held, and Field Marshal von Hindenburg received 21 million votes. The ex-corporal got 15 million votes. It was almost mathematically certain that Herr Hitler would have triumphed over any other candidate.

Influenced by Hugenberg-Hitler, the re-elected Field Marshal refused Bruening his all-important signature. Exit Bruening. He was replaced by a certain Franz von Papen who headed a "Cabinet of Barons." Yes, this was the same von Papen, of whom it was still vaguely remembered that as military attache in 1917, he had organized industrial sabotage in the United States. Now the wily Uhlan officer with the peculiar flat-skull was Chancellor of the German Reich.

To begin with, he lifted the ban on Hitler's Brown Shirts, decreed by Bruening a few months before. The SA and SS Troops, by the hundred thousands, established themselves amidst terrorism and murder, as a second, quasi-official police. Then Papen proceeded to yoke the press. Newspapers that displeased him were suspended for days or weeks. Finally, he staged a coup d'état in Prussia. The largest German state was under a government which included democrats and socialists—and among other things, this government controlled the police. One day, Papen declared it deposed. Soldiers with fixed bayonets removed the ministers from their offices. Papen appointed himself Reich Commissar of Prussia with unlimited powers.

This was the fateful moment which revealed the character of German democracy and the worth of the confidence put in it by the world since the "victory of the people" after the Kapp putsch. But nothing happened. One minister proposed to call on the people and the police to resist. The Socialist Police Minister replied that he refused to take responsibility for civil war. Nobody moved. The people of Prussia were not ready to defend their constitution, democracy and freedom by a general strike or other means. The "working class forces organized in trade unions and in the Socialist Party," in which M. Léon Blum had put his trust, were as frightened as any other group. Moreover, approximately a third of the workers were about to jump on the Hitler bandwagon. Electoral statistics were soon to reveal this.

Then, once again, Reichstag elections were held, and once again the Swastika triumphed, by a greater margin even than in 1930. In that year the Nazi vote had increased from 2% to 18% of the total. Now it reached 38%. The Nazis were easily the strongest party, they were almost twice as strong numerically as the shrinking Social Democrats, and two and a half times as strong as the stagnant Communist Party—a fact which incidentally suffices to characterize the theory of the "Bolshevik peril" in Germany.

The Reich President summoned the "Bohemian corporal" to appear before him and offered him the Vice-Chancellorship under von Papen. Hitler refused. He felt strong enough to demand everything. He demanded the leadership and more: he demanded single authority, and "the powers that Mussolini had after the march on Rome." The bloody red flag with the hooked cross now had the aura of success: the success already achieved and that still to be achieved. Whoever wanted to be safe joined the Nazis. Hitler's men, openly or in disguise, sat in every government office. His desperadoes paraded the streets shouting their songs: "We shall smash France. . . ." "Today, Germany is ours; tomorrow the whole world. . . ." A desire for disarmament could now be found only in the hiding places of the powerless. Such was the German scene in the fall of 1932.

During this time, the world was awaiting the League's moves with regard to Japan. The Chinese army, against all expectation, fought well, and barred the Japanese advance for weeks. There were also American and European troops in Asia, and an Anglo-American fleet. After a while, the Japanese gave up the venture. After four inglorious months, they re-embarked their troops and got out.

But in Manchuria, where they ran no risks except conflict with the League of Nations, they did not withdraw; and after the occupation of Manchuria, they continued their advance into Mongolia. The committee appointed by the League to investigate was active, and it was a good committee. Its chairman was the old colonial expert, Lord Lytton. But however excellent the committee, its procedure involved much loss of time. The State Department felt that stronger measures were urgent. It conceived a strategy which was to play a role in the following years: the doctrine of "non-recognition." Mr. Stimson notified the Japanese government that America "does not intend to recognize any situation, treaty or agreement which may be brought about by means contrary to the covenants." [38] This was true of the Manchurian case, and was to be true for all future similar cases. It meant that in the future the spectators would refuse to recognize any conquest as legal. They would call it illegal.

It is not known what effect this note had on the minds of the Japanese rulers. Mr. Stimson himself would later take into account the possibility that it had been "of comparatively little moment to the aggressor." At any rate,

the Japanese outwardly indicated indifference. And iron-
ically enough, they hastened to give a definite form to the
now unrecognized situation by proclaiming the transformation of Manchuria into a new state, Manchukuo, a
puppet state separate from China. To all appearances,
they regarded facts as more important than the manner
in which facts were being designated.

Mr. Stimson nevertheless believed that the doctrine of
non-recognition was an instrument capable of intimidat-
ing the Japanese, particularly if other countries employed
it. He succeeded in having this doctrine adopted by the
League: the governments belonging to that body passed
a unanimous resolution not to recognize Manchukuo. Mr.
Stimson tried to persuade himself that this resolution was
an effective contribution to the pacification of the world.

"When the American government took the responsibility of sending its note of January 7," he said in a speech,
"it was a pioneer. It was appealing to a new sentiment
and to the provisions of a treaty as yet untested. Its own
refusal to recognize the fruits of aggression might be of
comparatively little moment to an aggressor. But when
the entire group of civilized nations took their stand beside the position of the American government, the situation was revealed in its true sense. Moral disapproval,
when it becomes the disapproval of the whole world,
takes on a significance hitherto unknown in international
law. For never before has international opinion been so
organized and so mobilized." [39]

But however moral disapproval of the whole world
might work in the future, it remained without effect on
Japan. The strategy failed. Collective security did not become a reality by this word-doctrine, nor by words of any
sort. Collective security, the League of Nations and the

"definitive guarantee against aggression" were still without reality.

Winter, 1932–1933. Despair prevailed in Europe after Germany's withdrawal from the disarmament conference. The Archbishop of Canterbury, heading a delegation of churchmen, went to see MacDonald and Sir John Simon. "The promise given by the Allied Powers after the war should be fulfilled," they said. "The Government would have their enthusiastic support in fulfilling its declared willingness to give Germany a place of equality among other nations." The leader of the Trade-Unions made a similar pilgrimage. And Mr. Attlee, on behalf of the Labor Party, moved in Parliament for the complete abolition of all the military clauses in the peace treaty. Everywhere, a fanatical zeal arose to bring Germany back to the conference and to grant her equality of armaments.

Then, at last, M. Herriot showed himself to be reasonable. He had shown his reasonableness in an affair involving billions. The Hoover moratorium on debts and reparations had expired. What now? Herr von Papen was explicit: nothing at all! Germany had no intention of paying anything. The world, as usual, sided with Germany and M. Herriot yielded. Only one year and a half after the adoption of the Young Plan, he signed an agreement which buried reparations forever. As America had been particularly anxious to achieve this result, Europe took for granted that the war debts would be cancelled. President Hoover refused to cancel them, and M. Herriot again gave in. He was decidedly a most reasonable man.

Even Herriot, however, could not be quite so reasonable on the question of the French army. The instinct of self-preservation was still alive in the French people; discriminated against, they had been concentrating on maintaining their military superiority. But when the Washington, London and Rome governments made suggestions to M. Herriot, he did his best to be accommodating. In December, Herr von Neurath returned incognito to Geneva, and after a week of conversations between the representatives of the powers, a new project was ready.

This project recognized that France could not agree to equality as long as she had any reason for fear. But her fear could be removed. Germany would have to pledge herself not to wage war under any circumstances.

Another piece of paper, after the Briand-Kellogg pact, the Locarno pact, the League of Nations Covenant? How many times would that identical document appear? And why should it be more valuable the fourth time than the third? Quiet! Patience! The fourth time would be far from the last! The document would appear several times more. The more often, the better. And in this case, it was important as a beginning. If the German pledge not to wage war removed French fears, an understanding could be reached with regard to military "equality." The following declaration, intended to eliminate all future fears, was drawn up: "The Governments of The United Kingdom, France, Germany and Italy are ready to join in a solemn reaffirmation to be made by all European states that they will not in any circumstances attempt to resolve any present or future differences between the signatories by resort to force."

On this basis, delivered from uneasiness, France could really grant "equality" to the German army, without running risks. The whole thing could, for instance, be formulated as follows: "The Governments of The United Kingdom, France and Italy have declared that one of the principles that should guide the Conference for the Reduction of Armaments is the grant to Germany, and to the other powers disarmed by treaty, of equality of rights in a system which would provide security for all nations, and that this principle should find itself embodied in the Convention containing the conclusions of the Conference for the Reduction of Armaments."

Was this not satisfactory?

Something told Herriot that it was not. He was too much of a historian not to know that this declaration meant the end of the victory of 1918. But at least one half of his divided soul was complacent and prone to illusions. And the 100% illusionists and sun-worshippers belonged to his majority. He was confronted by their shameless agitation against his country, whose existence depended entirely on the friendship of other states. He was under heavy pressure from the two friendly governments of London and Washington. And he was a tired man.

On December 11, he signed. Germany had obtained a solemn document recognizing her right to military "equality." But "only in principle." Germany graciously returned to the conference. From now on, this conference discussed only one subject: the extent of German rearmament. And the world was entranced; people believed that this "equality" was important for collective security.

Let us look at the Lytton Committee, after its trip to Manchuria. It had seen and investigated many things, it had even seen the precise section of the railway where, many months before, the fatal damage had been discovered which had compelled General Honjo to march into Manchuria. The Committee's verdict was that Japan had committed an unjustified act of aggression; it held that she should withdraw her troops. But the Committee also found that there had been much mismanagement in Manchuria under Chinese rule. Hence, a Japanese withdrawal would not settle the matter. "A mere restoration of the status quo ante would be no solution," [40] stated the Lytton-Report. It recommended that, after the Japanese withdrawal, the League of Nations work out a new regime for Manchuria, which, among other things, would also take Japanese interests into consideration.

The League of Nations accepted the recommendations of the Lytton-Report and embodied them in a resolution. What did this mean? It meant that Japan was requested to evacuate Manchuria—exactly the same request that had been made a year and a half before, with something added. What was added was the promise that after the evacuation, Chinese rule would not be restored, but that under the aegis of the League a compromise solution would be adopted which would grant the Japanese certain advantages. They would get some profit from their aggression. There only remained to pray God that the Japanese accede.

They did not. Instead of acceding, the Japanese representatives walked out of the Assembly Hall when the League accepted the Lytton proposals (February, 1933). Japan resigned from the League. And that was that. President Wilson had not "entertained the slightest fear" that any state would ever dare to resign from the League. "It would become an outlaw," he had said.

This did not change the verdict nor its legality. As the Japanese refused to accede to the verdict, the League should have resorted to force. But force was not envisaged. In fact, the League dropped the whole matter. Summing up: An attacked member of the League had asked for help. The reaction of the League had been, after a lapse of six weeks, to demand that the aggressor withdraw from the occupied territory, and to repeat this demand after the lapse of a year and a half. The aggressor had expressed a disinclination to be disturbed. And that settled the matter.

This test of collective security, of protection from aggression through the medium of the League, definitely refuted those who, in 1919, had expected human nature to yield to the dreams of perfectionists. Clemenceau's definition of the League: "a parliament of super-parliamentarians without any instrument of authority" proved correct. The League was a talisman without magic. It was extremely unlikely that it would ever deter any aggressor.

Meanwhile, in Germany, what was called "the old world" in the days of utopian enthusiasm, disappeared from the scene, and an even older world, one no longer regarded as possible, was born.

For fourteen years, the real rulers of Germany had been taking the measure of their opponents. They found them incompetent beyond belief. Step by step the Germans had eliminated the effects of the defeat, and always to the applause of men of good will. The reparations were cancelled, German territory was evacuated, military equality was recognized as an irrevocable right. They could begin the final act of the drama.

There was no difference of opinion as to the character of that final act: it was to be the transformation of Germany into the dominant military power of Europe and the world.

Before this could be achieved, Germany had to go through a period during which she would be still inferior to other powers though on the way to superiority. To pass unhurt through the zone of danger, the maximum speed, maximum utilization of all resources, and maximum secrecy were indispensable. This in turn required a system in which the state had total power over the people, property, and all activities—all work, life, machines, wealth; a system of absolute power, absolute obedience, absolute secrecy: a total dictatorship. And it was indispensable to strengthen this dictatorship by arousing a spirit of enthusiastic fanaticism in the people.

Only Hitler could contribute this fanaticism, and the ruling powers in Germany, that is, the officers and their satellites, determined to make common cause with Hitler. Their determination grew stronger when, in November, at a new election, the Nazi party's vote receded slightly from its high point of 1932. It was obvious that fanaticism could not be kept on ice for too long a time.

The feelings of these German gentlemen were not unmixed. They were about to make common cause with plebeians. In order to exploit fully the fanaticism which Hitler contributed, it was necessary to give him a free hand: unpleasantness and brutality were to be expected. Nor could the sympathizers among the industrialists be sure that Hitler's promises to leave capitalism intact would be kept. Many regarded him as little better than a Bolshevik.

But the rulers of Germany calculated that they would organize a dictatorship in such a manner that in the last analysis the old forces would maintain control over the madmen. After some negotiations it was agreed that Hitler would be Chancellor, but that aside from him only two other Nazis would enter the Cabinet. The old forces would dispose of eight Cabinet posts, and thus have a majority of eight to three. They would control the President's power of veto. They would have the army. They would have the Steel Helmets against the Brown Shirts.

They thought that by thus organizing the dictatorship they would preserve their superiority and dictate the important decisions.

On January 30, the agreement was reached. From the Hotel Kaiserhof on the Wilhelmsplatz in Berlin, Adolf Hitler, surrounded by his paladins, moved into the government building across the square. He issued orders to begin the "national revolution." It was the only revolution in history which followed rather than preceded the seizure of power, and which was directed against adversaries who did not oppose it. There was no resistance, no defense, no general strike, not a single shot fired. Such was the scene in Germany in the winter of 1932–1933, the winter of the frightening disappearance of the fantasy of collective security, the winter of the festive baptism of German military "equality," the winter in which the German war dictatorship was established.

8: *Danger Zone and Reprieve*

O N JANUARY 30, 1933, fate gave the Allied nations another chance. For fourteen years they had been abandoning the fruits of their victory one by one. For fourteen years they had been the dupes of their own fantastic and complacent ideas about the real nature of Germany. Was it possible to be fooled about the real nature of Hitler, too?

The rise of Hitler in Germany was an opportunity for the Allies to realize their mistakes. It was as though fate said: Listen, I am going to do my best for you. I will show you German reality in all its bare ugliness. I will put it under your very nose. I will hit you over the head with it. You shall not be led to a miserable doom by politicians who look like honest burghers, or by generals who look like distinguished cavaliers. I will show you reality in a form which admits of absolutely no delusion. Once you see Hitler, you will no longer be able to make mistakes—or will you?

It was indeed inconceivable that anyone should make a mistake about Hitler. The man, the meaning of his rise to power, the character of his followers, were obvious. What, for instance, was unclear about words such as: "As I am a bad man, war and chaos please me more than the respectable bourgeois order." [1] Or "War arouses and develops the best forces of the nation. In the march of time it is a spiritual and material necessity for a nation which wants to survive and assert itself in this world." [2] Or: "Europe, the whole world may perish in flames; why should that concern us? Germany must live and be free." [3] Such were the pronouncements of doubtless the most important man in the whole Hitlerite enterprise: the organizer, educator and leader of the Brown Shirt army. And Herr Ernst Roehm had not said these things lightly, he had written and published them after mature reflection in a book intended as a confession. It was called: "The Biography of a Traitor." What kind of spirit animated all this? What was the meaning of this profession of faith in war, in war as such, for its own sake?

Then there was the Führer's own book. That he looked forward to the destruction of France and Russia was known to a certain extent—although it was not realized that he also foresaw the order in which they would be destroyed: first France, and then Russia. These two wars at least had a definite purpose: one was represented as a war of national revenge and liberation; the other as necessary to insure an immense supply of "soil and territory" that would be required "in a hundred years by a people of 250 million Germans." These two wars were within the framework of traditional ideas.

But there was something else in this book and in the mind of its author, and that something was the main thing. Hitler had ordered that his "political testament" be printed in bold-face type. The most important passage in it, in his usual untranslatable and illiterate style, ran as follows: "The political testament of the German nation concerning its activity with regard to the outside world shall and must forever read substantially: Never tolerate the coming into existence of the two continental powers in Europe. See an attack on Germany in every attempt to organize on the German frontiers a second military power, be it only in the form of the creation of a state with the potentialities of military power, and see in any such attempt not only the right but the duty to prevent by all means, including the use of arms, the coming into existence of such a state, or if such a state has already come into existence, to demolish it." [4]

This no longer meant war with a specific limited objective; it meant war with the general all-embracing purpose of destroying every state without exception, of rendering the whole world defenseless. It is true that the passage, interpreted strictly, applied only to Europe. But did the design for conquest stop at Europe's frontiers? The whole book is pervaded by the vision and the claim that Germany deserves to be "the mistress of the world." [5] One reads in it such sentiments as this: "The pacifist-humane ideal is perhaps quite satisfactory once the highest type of man has conquered and subjected the world, so that he is the only master of this globe." [6] The goal of world history is defined as a "peace, established by the victorious sword of a people of overlords which can bend the world to the service of a higher culture." [7] And if the reader was tempted to shrug his shoulders at such unrealistic follies, official commentators insisted that they were not so unrealistic as all that. Herr Ewald Banse, Nazi professor of "military science," explained: "Is it possible for the community of 90 million Germans in central Europe to achieve both hegemony in Europe and supremacy in the world outside? The fact that this riddle has not yet been solved, does not prove that it is unsolvable." [8]

Could anything be clearer? Fate was doing the world a favor. The Nazis' own frank utterances revealed to other peoples and governments what they had to deal with in Germany. This was not fate's only favor. She also took pains to show the powers with utmost clarity what it would mean to fall under the heels of these "overlords." After the Nazis took power there could be no doubt as to the consequences of the subjugation of any other country by Germany. The Nazis' behavior in their own country obviously set the pattern for their behavior on the international scene; it was evident that, once able to do so, they would apply on a world scale the principles, ideas, and morality they proclaimed and applied in Germany.

Their gospel had been set down in black and white; their course was clear to those who would see; their first measures as rulers were now being put into effect. These implied the absolute negation of whole chapters of the religious and ethical codes of civilized man; they represented the crassest, the most cynical adherence to the morality of success: "Right is what is useful to the German nation." The Nazis displayed ruthless contempt for "the self-evident truth that all men are created equal, that they are endowed by their Creator with certain inalienable rights, that among these are Life, Liberty and the pursuit of happiness." They abolished legality not only in fact, but also in theory. They practiced murder and terrorism and cruelty not as temporary and individual deviations from the norm, but as a permanent, organized system of intimidation and subjection. Was all this a purely internal German affair? Could the world disregard the doctrines, which the Germans were putting into practice, of the divinity of the state and the divinity of their race? Or their doctrine of anti-Semitism and its cannibalistic application? Or their denigration of the values of the Bible and their invention of a "Nordic Christ?" Or the Gestapo, the concentration camps and the abolition of the independence of the courts? All these manifestations of a people drunk with power were far from being a purely internal German affair. They were as important for the world as the character of each individual is for his fellows.

Yes, fate was merciful. By giving Hitler power in Germany, it did its best to throw a spotlight on Germany's spiritual and moral nature. With Hitler and his satellites in the saddle, Germany was being ruled by notorious liars and swindlers. Here, too, fate was merciful. The question: "Do they really mean it?" which could have been raised with regard to the previous German rulers, now made no sense at all.

To a certain extent, every politician and statesman can

be expected to be ambiguous and insincere. There is no mathematically defined boundary between the trustworthy politician and the political swindler; as in almost everything in politics, it is a question of degree and nuance. But in the case of Hitler and his Nazis, even before they acceded to office their insincerity had been proved beyond doubt. Those who knew them at all knew them as the very embodiment of falsehood. This was evident from all their newspapers, of which every issue was a huge mass of lies. It was evident from lesser phenomena, such as the fact that since 1919 Corporal Hitler had flaunted the highest German war decoration, the Iron Cross 1st Class, which no one had ever granted him; or that Dr. Goebbels, at the beginning of his career, had posed as a national martyr who had languished in Belgian prisons, until his claim was unmasked as pure fiction. The careers of the Nazi leaders were a long—and not a secret—record of swindlers' tricks. And at the very beginning of their reign the monstrous Reichstag fire frame-up, about which not a single diplomat or foreign correspondent in Berlin harbored any doubts, proved that their rise to power had not made them any less enterprising.

How could anyone rely on their word? It had been demonstrated a million times that the more solemn were their promises the less likely they were to keep them. A Bavarian Minister describes a conversation with Hitler shortly before the Munich putsch as follows: "He jumped up in the greatest agitation and beating his breast with his right hand, shouted: 'Herr Minister, I give you my word of honor that I will never make a putsch. Herr Minister, never in my life will I make a putsch.'" [9] He made the same melodramatic declaration to a general, a police chief and others. After he had broken his word, he said sententiously: "Forgive me, I did it in the interest of my country." [10]

The Nazi leaders have always shown the same conception of political strategy, and they have always been perfectly open about it. In 1930, during a session of the Reichstag the man who was then Hitler's chief spokesman stated it with a laconic simplicity which created a furore:

Deputy Hoegner: "Don't provoke me, or I'll remind you of a little incident involving your word of honor."

Deputy Gregor Strasser: "Go right ahead, I beg of you."

Deputy Hoegner: "You broke your word of honor by failing to deliver the weapons you promised to deliver to the Landshut police."

Deputy Gregor Strasser: "That is true."

Deputy Hoegner: "The breaking of your word of honor is obviously for you an accepted political weapon."

Deputy Gregor Strasser: "Quite so." [11]

No, nothing was left in doubt. Even a cursory checking of the record sufficed for a complete understanding of the new German rulers. On the threshold of the years of decision the situation was made crystal clear. Aside from this one factor, the appearance of Hitler on the scene did not change matters for the Allies; with regard to the outside world nothing happened because of his coming to power that would not have happened without him. Whatever novelties Hitlerism brought about in every other political field, in the field of foreign policy it was only the continuation of previous German policy. Hitler did not change this policy, although his advent probably did modify its tempo and certain details of its application. Even if the officers' corps and their hangers-on had not made an alliance with Hitler, even if Germany's political strategy had been guided by a general, by Hindenburg, or Schacht, or von Papen, Germany would have inevitably steered her course toward the restoration of her overwhelming military power and eventually toward war. The only difference would have been that she would have acted in a less repugnant, less conspicuous manner. The old-line reactionaries would have moved more cautiously, and in a more gentlemanly fashion. They would not have displayed Hitler's alarming cannibalism and would have moved forward with the winds of world sympathy strong in their sails. And perhaps—who can prove or refute it? —they would been a far greater danger for a deluded and complacent world.

At any rate, thanks to Hitlerism, all was now perfectly clear. The question was: would the world open its eyes? Would people now draw the necessary conclusions from the events in Germany?

"In this troubled and churning sea of uncertainty," I wrote in 1933, "there is only one firm island. Whatever happens in the future, one thing is sure even now: that among the permanent elements of the new era is the inevitable moral and material trend toward a new world conflagration. The only issue on which National Socialist theory is entirely clear is war, and from the very beginning it has taken a firm course toward war. . . . War is the only real religion of the Führer and his followers. There is no escape from this religion."

No gift of prophecy was needed to see this, no genius needed to understand its implications. Germany would now begin to arm as fast as possible, because the first stages of her rearmament would be the dangerous period. A certain amount of time was required to make her newly emerging mass army capable of putting up a serious fight. This period was also the period of reprieve for Germany's opponents, their last opportunity to stop her. It could be done only by force, certainly not by words or pieces of paper, but still without any real bloodshed.

Because of the large amount of preparatory work accomplished by the Reichswehr, the period of German dangers—and of reprieve for the outside world—could be estimated at two years at most. The supreme aim of German policy was not to be molested for these two years. Everything depended upon that.

The game for both sides was simple. For Germany and the other powers there was only one question: Should and would Germany be permitted to go through the period of military weakness unmolested? Or should and would she be forced to abandon her fatal path?

This is not a retrospective insight. In "End to Illusion," published in 1934, one year after the beginning of Hitler's rule, I summed up the situation as follows: "A few last months still remain in which to make good the mistakes of fourteen years. During these few months it is the world's foremost task to throttle the continuation of German rearmament at all costs. In this task is crystallized the rescue of the peoples, amongst them the German people itself. . . . This is the last moment for taking stock of the truth that in this case a threat of war, a brutal presentation of force is the only means to peace, the guaranteed means to peace. . . . The method is simple. It is based upon the fact that Germany will not for some months to come be in a position to cope with the concentrated military strength of France, let alone with that of a collection of states. During the short intervening period of incomplete armament—and only during this intervening period—she would with absolute certainty suffer annihilation if the cannons began to roar. This affords the categorical guarantee that the cannons will not begin to roar. . . . What is considered necessary to break the threat which is strangling Europe? The experts in warfare in the air and on land can work out the lists: A Europe which understands the hour, which knows how to speak in plain terms to the new rulers of Germany, will bring home everything that it wants on the points of its bayonets—without having to make use of one single bayonet, without spilling a single drop of blood. By force and yet without war Europe's rush towards a war of annihilation can be arrested. But only by force. And only for a few months more. War need not come immediately after the lapse of those few months; it might be postponed for a considerable time longer, perhaps even for years. After the lapse of those few months there will be nothing more to be prevented." [12]

Thus, the real problem during the period from 1933 to 1935 was the prevention of German rearmament. Anything else done to meet the crisis created by Hitlerism was sheer humbug, no matter under what name or by whom done. Would reason and the sense of reality triumph over humbug now, at the eleventh hour?

2.

We know today that humbug triumphed. The period of reprieve was wasted. The Germans passed through the danger period unmolested.

There was much indignation and much sorrow over what went on. People still vaguely remembered that eight million lives had been sacrificed to make the world safe for democracy. It was a bitter irony that democracy should now be crushed in the very country for whose democratic future these sacrifices had been made. The uneasiness of all democrats was aroused. It was aroused even by the first actions of the Hitler regime which seemed to be directed only against the Communists, even though anti-Communism was to a certain extent approved of. But the Nazi campaign of destruction did not stop with the Communists. One by one—never two at a time—it extended from one party or group to another. One day the trade unions were smashed; the next, the Social Democrats; a month later, the Liberals; then, the Catholic "Centre." As though to warn all those who aspired to form a coalition with him, Hitler did not, in the end, spare even his own partners. The calculation of the "old-line reactionaries" that they would forever preserve control over the madmen proved false. Even the Right, which, after four months of Hitlerism, had become in the eyes of the outside world the last remaining hope of German democracy, was exterminated as a political force. The freedoms of speech, assembly, and coalition ended for everyone.

The humanitarians were even more aroused than the believers in democracy. There was much anger over the concentration camps and the conditions prevailing in them. A wave of honest indignation over the horrors of anti-Jewish persecution swept all classes in the civilized countries. An attempt was made to check this barbarism by a boycott of German merchandise—it was unsuccessful; German exports increased: low prices made possible by the large-scale dumping policy of the German government proved more effective than appeals to morality. There were protest movements by Christian churches. There were debates in the English Parliament, during which Members and Ministers expressed their disapproval of Nazi brutality. The Berlin government, those eternally persecuted innocents, sent a strong note of protest.

But all this remained a matter of words and paper; they disturbed Hitler as little as they had previously disturbed Japan. And, important as all this public indignation may have been, it ignored the focal point: the German army. Did the world realize that Germany was arming, that it had only a short period of reprieve, that the unrestrained brutality displayed by the Nazis at home foreshadowed their behavior abroad? What would the world do?

It would do nothing at all. It would continue to do what it had done heretofore. What continued to preoccupy the world was the equalization of the French and German armies. The principle of equality had been granted to Germany: now was the time to carry it out in practice. Secondary events such as a change in the German government must not disturb the course that had been adopted. Six weeks after Hitler's advent, Mr. MacDonald prepared a plan for carrying out Franco-German military equalization under the supervision of the League of Nations. This won much public approval. Only that extremist, Winston Churchill, called the plan foolish. "MacDonald's plan," he said in a speech in the Commons, "has come at the worst possible time. It was a foolish moment to press it on France when there was a tumultuous insurgence of ferocity in Germany." [13] But his was an isolated voice. Under-Secretary Captain Anthony Eden called him the only unconstructive critic of the government in Parliament.

It was impossible to convince a "progressive" world

which in addition refused to face any unpleasantness, that
the Nazis would end by applying abroad the same methods they were applying at home. "There are two questions arising out of Germany's position," exclaimed Lloyd
George, "and it is a fatal error to mix them up. One is the
abominable treatment of the Jews in Germany, and the
other is the abominable treatment of the question of disarmament." [14] Mr. Morgan Jones, the Laborite speaker,
declared that his party felt the greatest repugnance for
the things that were happening in Germany. "But we
must measure these things with appropriate standards.
What goes on inside Germany is after all mostly the concern of the German people." [15] Sir Herbert Samuel, the
Liberal leader, demanded, "despite German attacks on
the race to which I belong," that "in this situation the
other nations offer Germany so much that her acceptance
of the offer will be a matter of course." [16] And Léon Blum
in France advocated the same course: "With regard to
racism we must not use nationalist weapons . . . lest we
thus reinforce German unity around Hitler. More than
ever, salvation resides in the organization of the peace.
Let us not sneer at the value of the world's conscience,
whose indignation has already forced Hitler's fascism to
retreat." [17] Lively applause on the Left welcomed both
Léon Blum's thesis and Hitler's alleged retreat.

Among the things happening "inside Germany," one
seemed, however, to concern the outside world quite
directly. "As long as every speech made in Germany,"
said Austen Chamberlain (in May, 1933), "as long as
every bit of their propaganda is menacing, inflammatory,
biased, one-sided, how can they expect that those whom
by this propaganda they menace should disarm in order
that Germany may be in a better position to attack them?

In fact, how could 'equalization' go on in the face of this unprecedented campaign of propaganda for war and hate?" [18]

But even a way of continuing with "equalization" was discovered: the Germans had gone mad, it was argued, for the very reason that they had had to live so long without equality. "Are you surprised," said Lloyd George, "that after waiting for fourteen years the Germans have got angry? We ought to have noticed in the swelling number of the Nazis that the young men of the nation were resenting it. We drive them to frenzy by injustice, and then we make that an excuse for not redressing the wrong." [19] To remove the Nazi inferiority and persecution complexes, one had to remove their cause, then the trouble would quiet down of itself.

MacDonald, too, expressed similar ideas. He explained the German excesses as a psychological reaction to the military restrictions imposed upon Germany which were "inconsistent with its self-respect and its honor." [20] This anti-militarist now simply closed his ears to Germany's violently militaristic propaganda. "I do not doubt Germany's motives. I have never doubted them and I hope that I will never be hasty enough to doubt them." [21]

No one disputed the fact of Germany's rearmament. It was made apparent by many signs. For instance, immediately after the "national revolution" German imports of raw materials indispensable for the production of armaments suddenly increased to a considerable extent. Before the end of 1933, imports of iron ore tripled. Imports of manganese were multiplied elevenfold. The large munitions plants, such as Krupp's, began to hire workers by the tens of thousands. The Borsig Works in Berlin which had gone bankrupt a few years earlier not only went into full production a few weeks after Hitler's accession to power but also began to build new shops. Certain important plants previously sold to foreigners were hastily bought back by Germans with government funds. One of them was the large Opel automotive plant.

And what was the state of the army? The Reichswehr had never limited itself to 100,000 men, as the treaty demanded. General John H. Morgan, former member of the Military Control Commission, revealed that as early as 1922 the commission has discovered that by an ingenious system of organization the Reichswehr comprised 250,000 instead of 100,000 men. When he made a report to this effect he received a telegraphic order from Lloyd George to resign, and only Marshal Foch's personal intervention saved him from outright dismissal. Now, in 1935, the exact number of the Reichswehr's effectives was unknown, but it was certainly larger than the prescribed 100,000.

In addition there was now the army of Brown Shirts one million strong. Its military value may have been low, but it could always be used as an auxiliary formation. According to official statistics, the Elite Guards numbered 200,000 men, and these were completely trained shock troops. Then the Labor Service was founded, numbering 250,000 men at the beginning. The very first public appearance of this formation of eighteen and nineteen year old boys revealed that they had received the strictest Prussian military training. No one could dispute the reality of German rearmament.

But no one realized its tempo and extent. People argued that governments could spend only a limited amount of money, certainly no more than the amount of taxes collected and bonds issued. And they felt that the German government could not possibly afford to build up an army worthy of the name in less than ten years. But this reasoning was based on obsolete premises. The Nazi government in actual fact was not limited by any budget, although in 1933 and even in 1934, it still published a half page of purely fictitious figures. It expended and collected whatever sums of money it needed. Its financial wizard, Dr. Hjalmar Schacht, who, under Weimar, had raised the cry of bankruptcy every time the government tried to spend a few hundred million marks above its regular income, introduced the Bolshevik system of state control of all capital funds for the benefit of the new dictatorial regime. The Nazis took the billions they wanted from banks, savings institutions and insurance companies, giving them bonds in return. The Nazi government which constantly complained of Germany's "misery," was able to spend ten to fifteen times as much as the "rich" democracies for war purposes.

But all this was beyond the imagination of the spectators. They could not and did not want to realize it. In the dining room of the House of Commons, I tried to explain the German technique and its consequences to a few M.P.'s. Both their facial expressions and their words demonstrated their courteous determination not to be talked into believing such things. "You know," said a sympathetic Liberal, "our ideas on these matters are a little more conservative." Germany's ideas were not conservative.

The democracies saw no reason for deviating from their carefully thought out policies: the equalization of French and German armaments; new non-aggression pacts; reconsecration of the League as the guardian of peace; pledges and signatures. And Germany did not object to any of this. Every month she gained brought her nearer to the end of her race through the danger zone.

In May, 1933, Chancellor von Papen caused a serious disturbance. He saw that the old-line reactionary forces were gradually losing their influence and feared that he would be dropped from the Cabinet. To strengthen his position he made a speech in which he derided the idea of a peaceful death, and proclaimed that death on the battlefield was the only one worthy of man; that war was as natural a destiny for man as giving birth to children was the natural destiny of woman. Although much less significant than many other things that were happening in Germany and which passed unnoticed, von Papen's speech unleashed a storm of protest. Even Sir John Simon called it "a terrible speech." [22] And this reaction was nothing compared to the indignation aroused in the press, particularly in France and Poland. Suddenly, the skies were overcast. "Enough! Let us put an end to all this!" was the cry. Now it seemed that the powers would at last intervene by force. Diplomatic circles were informed that Marshal Pilsudski, the Polish dictator, had suggested to his French ally to march into the Reich. Berlin was nervous. There was a chance that Germany would not succeed in passing the danger zone. This likelihood seemed so great that the President of the Reich, who was rather attached to his good night's rest, left a note to his staff before going to bed saying: "In this grave hour I shall naturally be at the disposal of the government at any time of the day or night."

Something had to be done. Five days after von Papen's demonstration of over-zealousness, Hitler summoned that assembly of automata which was still called the Reichstag, and made a speech against war, a speech for peace at any price. He declared himself a supporter of MacDonald's plan and of all the non-aggression pacts that could be conceived. He emphasized his experiences as a "front-line soldier," and this time "front-line soldier" was suddenly synonymous not with "fierce warrior" but with "eager pacifist." He had discovered that in other countries the associations of veterans were among the foremost proponents of peace and had read that a few weeks earlier a delegation representing eight million Allied war veterans had visited Arthur Henderson demanding "equality" for Germany for the sake of peace. Comrades! Brothers! He, too, was a war veteran, hence a pacifist. From that day on Hitler would constantly harp on his having been a "front-line soldier," and thereby confuse many more millions.

The sun broke through the stormy skies: Hitler was talking peace! What a miracle! How lovely to have unpleasantness again vanish into space. Hitler's words were eagerly lapped up. "A reassuring speech," [23] said Mr. Lansbury, chief of the Labor Party. Sir John Simon was ready "to go as far as I can to meet the newer and wiser spirit which the Chancellor seems to indicate." [24]

And now that Hitler had declared himself ready to sign all pacts, one could continue negotiations. Surely M. Daladier would not now seriously consider that crazy Polish idea of marching into Germany? No, M. Daladier would not consider it; he had never considered it. The French Rightists were for forceful action against Germany, but they never defined exactly what they wanted. But M. Daladier was a Premier of the Left Coalition. Military excesses like Marshal Pilsudski's plan were out of the question, more so after Hitler's profession of peace.

One shadow marred the brilliance of the new sunny weather, but no one paid any attention to it. German aviation had grown to such dimensions that some of it began to be noticed in the open skies. The gentlemen in

Berlin considered it politer to speak of the existence of a modest airforce under some harmless appellation, than to be entirely silent about it. One month after Hitler's peace declarations Goering, his air and police expert, published an entirely fictitious story about foreign planes that had flown over Berlin scattering leaflets. The only existing copy of the alleged leaflet was shown to foreign correspondents by the Air Ministry: it was a piece of paper carrying an irrelevant message stamped with a rubber seal. But this anaemic story served to justify the creation of a German "flying police corps." It was clear that behind this threadbare screen Germany would build her new Luftwaffe.

But, after all, the course of history could not be stopped by a few airplanes! Forward with "equalization," and the MacDonald plan! The plan provided for an army of 200,-000 men for France and Germany. What was Daladier's attitude toward it?

Daladier's innermost wish was not to have to commit himself. This weak, melancholy, timorous man was intelligent enough to recognize an absurdity when he saw one. But he had no idea what to propose in its place. "What policy do you intend to pursue?" a newspaperman asked him: "If I knew what policy we intended to pursue," he replied, "you would not have to ask about it, you would see it." He did not know what he wanted, nor what he should want.

He concentrated on details. He insisted that equalization must not be carried out too rapidly; that the organization of the League control had to be clarified first; that the dissolution of the German semi-military societies had to be completed. By these manoeuvres and temporizations he only succeeded in provoking the wrath of the "progres-

sive" idealists. Any child could see, they shouted, that
Daladier was preventing Hitler from making peace a
reality. Once again, British Labor entered the arena: its
leading newspaper wrote that France was the only dis-
turber of the peace in Europe. Captain Eden came to
Paris to exert pressure on the French government. He was
seconded by the American delegate to the disarmament
conference.

On September 22nd, 1933, M. Daladier, caught in the
blind alley of a plan which took his wishes into consideration, could no longer temporize. To avoid an avalanche of
unpleasantness, he had to say Yes, and he did. In the
course of three or four years, France was to reduce her
army by gradual stages to 200,000 men; during the same
period, Germany was to "increase" her effectives to the
same figure. During the following three or four years, a
similar operation was to be performed on French and
German armaments: France would scrap some, and Germany would build some, until the two countries equal-
ized their strength,—all this under League supervision.

A revolutionary development, indeed! M. Daladier was
congratulated by his colleagues. He sat there, small, depressed, fear in his eyes, disgusted with the world and
hating himself. My God, what would become of France,
of the peace, of his name, his Cabinet? He was saved by
a *deus ex machina:* Hitler. Verily, no one seemed to expect that he would say No. After all he had demanded
"equality," and now he had it. But Hitler and his gang
saw things differently. Behind the chatter about equality
Germany had safely traversed eight months of the danger
period. Of course, they could sign any rag of paper, but
if they signed this one, the precious theme of equality
would disappear from the world press, and a marvelously

effective stimulant of world discussion and world dissension would be thrown overboard, a development Hitler did not welcome at all.

Hitler was totally indifferent to "equality." He was only interested in having the talk about it continue. A few months of fog would be so many months gained for the safe completion of the rearmament program. The disarmers and pactomaniacs must be kept in a state of dissatisfaction, and stimulated at the same time. A year before, Herr Neurath had shown how to achieve this result when he had withdrawn from the disarmament conference. Herr Hitler decided to repeat this manoeuvre on a much larger scale.

On October 14th, the cry of a wounded dinosaur resounded throughout the world. Herr Hitler was howling that once again "equality" had been refused him. A proclamation addressed to his own people and the other peoples revealed the monstrous fact that the Reich government had been informed "by the official representatives of other nations that equal rights could not be granted to present day Germany."

The indignation and bitter anger that seized him in the face of this breach of the given word were beyond description. He would never sit at the same table with these perfidious people, never show himself at the disarmament conference or at the League of Nations. He sent letters giving notice. He withdrew. The alarming, sensational news spread around the globe: Hitler had withdrawn from the League of Nations. The tumult was enormous. Germany had broken with the civilized world. Why? Did she want war? What, in the name of Heaven, had happened? Sir John Simon rushed to the radio: "The British Government," he said, "is quite unable to accept the

reasons which Germany has given." [24] And Ramsay Mac-
Donald declared in Parliament: "This country can look
Germany in the face without any blush or without any
apology." [25] But Hitler did not care whether he was called
a liar or not. The grief of the deserted League of Nations
would not thereby be alleviated. An "outlaw?" The existence of the temple of peace depended upon his being a
member of it. Formerly, the powers had implored Stresemann to join the League. Now they would implore Hitler
to reenter it.

In addition to all this, as though refusing to take any
chances, he concocted something special for France—
after all the French still had an army. At the very moment
that he slammed the door in their faces, he made a speech
overflowing with the most ardent, most violent declarations of love for them. He doted on "Premier Daladier's
noble sense of justice." He acknowledged "with the most
hopeful emotion, the assurance that the French government under their present chief did not intend to offend
or humble the German people." He swore that he was resolved from now on to enter only "into a most noble competition with France," which has given mankind "all those
magnificent conquests of civilization, culture and art that
enrich and embellish the world of today." "As a nationalist," he declaimed, "I as well as my followers, in the name
of our national principles, renounce any ambition to con-
quer people of a foreign nation, who do not love us, at
the cost of the blood of those who are dear to us. . . .
Only a madman could conceive of the possibility of a war
between our two nations . . ." [26]

He gave them honey, he gave them morphine, and he
did not content himself with giving them only one dose.
He was prepared to repeat the treatment, and after his

speech, professions of love rained upon France like an army of bacilli. He had formed a brigade of peace visionaries, artists in international friendship and exploiters of human conceit and self-interest. Now they received the order to swarm into France.

You do not have to worry, General von Blomberg. You do not have to be timid, Herr Krupp. The Führer has managed to cross eight months of the danger period unmolested. He will manage to get through all of it. *On passera. On les aura.*

3.

The Prime Minister spoke to the House of Commons in a subdued tone. "The British government is not going to give up its attempts to work out a plan for disarmament upon which all can agree," he declared. "We ask Germany to come in!" [27] (Applause). Sir John Simon hoped that "in some form or other" the powers would achieve "the renewal of contact." [28] (Applause). Hitler lost nothing in England by his withdrawal manoeuvre. Just as he had foreseen, after a short interlude the powers would woo him more ardently than ever for his pacifist signature, his pacifist presence.

In France, the Rightists continued their agitation for a forceful policy—or what they considered a forceful policy. M. Georges Mandel, respected as Clemenceau's former secretary, called upon the government of the *Cartel des Gauches* not to remain in Geneva as a defendant. "You must appear at the League in the role of public prosecutor." [29] Such was their most radical proposal. The Foreign Minister replied that such action was no longer possible, that a motion to investigate German armaments could no longer rally a majority in the League. This was true. But if that could not be done, what could? The government of the *Cartel des Gauches,* which changed Premiers every few weeks, and was always composed of the same men, had no answer to this question. Amidst empty rhetoric and juridical quibbling, they let things drift.

Then a new factor complicated the situation. After a few years' delay, France, too, was in the throes of the economic depression. Unsavory political and financial scandals came to the surface. The average Frenchman felt with uneasiness that the victory of 1918 was disintegrating, that the defeated Germans were rising to new power, that their own country was sinking into impotence, that something was rotten in the state. The Royalists who condemned the very idea of the Republic found new followers. Others began to wonder vaguely whether France should not imitate the tricks of the Germans. Among the "young forces," as they were hopefully called in Berlin, a fascist current arose. The largest of the newly formed groups was called the *Croix de Feu.*

But the fascist current did not develop into anything serious. The *Croix de Feu* was anti-parliamentarian, but that was the only issue on which it was more or less clear. It wanted to be nationalistic, but not aggressively so, not racial, not bestial, not piratical. Its organizer, the retired Colonel de la Rocque, had no mass appeal. He tried to form a kind of Storm Troops, but only few Frenchmen were attracted by the prospect of marching in ranks. A few months later, this prerequisite for fascism was forbidden, and all the semi-militarist groups disappeared from the scene.

The only result of these pre-fascist attempts in France was to increase the general confusion and dissension. Hit-

ler and von Neurath went on making declarations of love
to the French nation, and the first political prostitutes of
Hitler's future French brothel made their appearance.
The most impudent of them, a certain Fernand de Brinon,
another "front-line fighter," published a sensational interview with Hitler. Daladier, the tragic Left-Wing Premier,
grew more and more bewildered, undecided and paralyzed.

And the vapors of disarmament talk continued to befog
the Cabinets, the Parliaments and the people of the world.
New false hopes were created by the diplomats' pious efforts to bring Hitler back into the League of shadows in
Geneva. Notes, speeches, conferences, memoranda. Mac-
Donald raised his bid: he now suggested 300,000 men
each for the French and German armies. He put forward
his whimsical distinction between "offensive" and "defensive" weapons. Everyone was to be permitted to have
fieldguns and light guns, which are purely "defensive."
Only heavy guns and tanks are dangerous, he said, for they
are "offensive" and produce wars.

More notes, speeches, memoranda, visits. The Germans
said: "No, but . . ." or, "Yes, if . . ." They offered France
a ten-year non-aggression pact (the sheaf of previously
signed pacts was supposed to have been valid forever)
on condition that Germany's repeated sacrifices be paid
for by concessions on the part of the French. They most
particularly desired the abolition of the demilitarized
Rhineland zone. The London "Times" considered that it
was unfair of the French to show so little enthusiasm for
this offer. "When a statesman known for always keeping
his word solemnly pledges himself never to make war
against France, such a gesture (ending the demilitarization of the Rhineland) would certainly facilitate a better

understanding between the two nations." [30] Mr. Mac-
Donald advanced the theory that a pact, no matter what
its content, was always better than no pact. "No agreement is no solution at all." [31] The fog was indeed thick.

A sharp gust of wind swept it aside for a few days: on
January 26th, 1934, Pilsudski and Hitler concluded an
agreement which seemed to undermine the whole political structure of Europe. It was a pact beyond reproach
from the pacifist point of view. The two parties guaranteed
to respect the status quo for the next few years. Was that
not wonderful? Since Versailles, Germany had not ceased
to rave against Poland. Its "bleeding frontier" with Poland
had been so unbearable for the German soul that a united
front extending from Lord Rothermere and Hearst to
Léon Blum, Lloyd George and Litvinov had always declared that it was unbearable, and even Stresemann had
been forgiven for not recognizing the Reich's eastern
frontier. Now Hitler had made peace with Poland; Hitler,
who had been the most rabid of the anti-Polish agitators.
Did not this prove his beneficent influence on the German
soul? Warm congratulations arrived from London and
Washington, and even the paralyzed Quai d'Orsay made
an embarrassed attempt to stammer out a bravo.

The truth about this agreement was quite different—
and it was obvious.

What it meant for Hitler had been made clear in *Mein
Kampf* in which he said that if a great injury could thereby
be caused to France, "no course should seem too difficult
to us and no renunciation impossible." [32]

Pilsudski's intentions were no less clear. He wanted to
pursue an isolationist policy and to discard "entangling
alliances." Neither alliances nor collective security had

any meaning with allies who lacked power or the will to use their power. Pilsudski gauged the trend of the times. He knew that Poland could never hope to be saved by anything named the League of Nations. "The League of Nations is dead," the Polish chief of State had told his people in December, 1933. And could any help be expected from France, a nation which had for years regarded no fiction too fantastic and no pretext as too foolish to accept as arguments for its suicidal inertia?

In November, 1933, Hitler offered Pilsudski a deal: Poland was to abandon her alliance with France and Geneva, and Hitler was to abandon his hostility toward Poland. Pilsudski was not fooled by Hitler's promises, but he welcomed a breathing spell. He realized that Hitler's adversaries would be further weakened by Poland's self-isolation, but he also knew that his country could not assume the role of guide to the Great Powers. When the real danger came, the Great Powers would either want to save Poland or not. If they wanted to save her, they would not be prevented from doing so by what Poland was doing now. If they did not want to save her, nothing she did would influence them. So Pilsudski closed the deal with Hitler.

With this action he served a ringing notice on the world that he considered the game of power already won by the Nazis. It was the first breach in the system of 1919, the first *sauve qui peut*. This attitude was bound to spread; the lack of will displayed by the Great Powers was bound to force the little powers to run for their lives. The rout had begun.

The collapse of the Polish alliance contributed to the February 6th outburst in Paris, when blood was shed on

the Place de la Concorde. The "young forces" marched
against the Chamber of Deputies shouting "Down with
the Cartel," and "Down with Daladier." Fearing a fascist
coup d'état, Daladier ordered his police to shoot and from
then on he was branded as the *fusilleur*. But after this
brief outburst of energy, he collapsed and resigned his
office. The President of the Republic summoned whatever
remained in France of the respectable "old forces," hoping that the "old guard" and the "elder statesmen" would
leap into the breach and stop the progress of disintegration.

But what was the real meaning of these events? The
German press deplored Daladier's departure and showed
itself hostile toward the Cabinet of "elder statesmen." It
can be questioned whether the February 6th riots constituted a serious attempt to establish a fascist dictatorship. The most accurate analysis of these events can be
found in the *Echo de Paris* of February 11th, 1934: "It is
true that the immediate motive for the riots was the
Stavisky scandal," wrote this newspaper. "But trouble had
been brewing for a long time as a result of the country's
anger over the weakness of our foreign policy . . ."

The new French Foreign Minister was Louis Barthou.
He did not belong to the "young forces:" he was seventy
years old. He had been Premier in 1913, when, against the
most rabid opposition, he enforced the raising of the period of military service from two to three years, a measure without which France would have been unable to
withstand the German onslaught of 1914 and turn the
tide at the Marne. Louis Barthou was not only a statesman, but a historian, a jurist, a bibliophile. He was a member of the French Academy and the author of books on
Wagner, Danton, Victor Hugo, Beethoven and Lamartine.

He had a wide knowledge of foreign countries and languages. In this confused period, he was the best man France and Europe could produce. But even he was not adequate. The experience of the past which was his strength was also his limitation.

His advent at the Quai d'Orsay ended the somnolent period of aimless though busy political inactivity, the passive drifting with the current which was the policy of MacDonald, Sir John Simon and the pacifist legions. M. Barthou had two convictions: Hitler must be made to suffer failures; and Hitler must be encircled.

The first defeat he intended to inflict on Hitler was in the Saar plebiscite which was scheduled to take place the following year. All the dogmatic complacent believers in perfection took it for granted that the best solution of the Saar problem was its return to the Reich. Were not the Saarlanders German? Did it make any sense to keep an independent state of 600,000 inhabitants under the protection of the League of Nations? Could such a situation endure forever? The world took it for granted that everything must be done to insure a favorable outcome of the plebiscite for Germany.

Barthou thought differently. He was not concerned with the principle of nationalities, nor with the subtle problems of the Saar's remote future. What he wanted was to inflict a defeat upon Hitler. And this did not depend upon God alone. Much could be done to influence the Saarlanders' votes for or against their continued separation from the Reich. M. Barthou was determined to put up a fight for the Saar with the sole object of inflicting a defeat upon Hitler. He realized that it was necessary to transform Hitler from a man of chronic successes into a man of failures. That purpose was more important than all the principles or arguments or merits of any given particular case.

In addition, Barthou was determined to build around him a ring of allied states. In 1914, a ring of military alliances had prevented Wilhelm II from subjugating Europe. M. Barthou had nothing but contempt for the professional falsifiers of historical truth, and their absurd contention that the "encirclement" of a threatening power decreases, rather than increases the general security. The old man boarded a train. It had almost been forgotten that there was in Europe a system of French military alliances. The preceding inert governments had completely neglected these alliances which had earned them bitter reproaches from the progressives. They hated to be drawn into all the difficult and contradictory problems arising from France's relations with Warsaw, Prague, Brussels, Bucharest and Belgrade. M. Barthou went from capital to capital to save whatever could still be saved.

These little alliances, however, were only stop-gaps in the encirclement. They did not represent much power; they had to be completed by understandings with the Great Powers. The circumstances were favorable. M. Barthou saw an opportunity to get Italy and Russia to join the circle. In private, Mussolini always spoke of Hitler in a tone of furious hostility. Even publicly, he permitted others to attack him. He was obsessed by the fear that Germany would grow strong enough to seize Austria and thus establish herself on Italy's borders. The struggle against the Anschluss became the prime objective of his foreign policy and he rallied all the forces that were opposed to it. "For my part," said Benes, the Czechoslovakian Foreign Minister, "I am entirely ready to follow Signor Mussolini's lead in this matter." [33] Austria was the key.

Italy could be made to join a sufficiently strong alliance
that guaranteed the independence of Austria against Hitler.

Russia's attitude seemed less clear. Stalin's policy up
until that time had been similar to that of England or
France. Moscow did not consider Hitler's rise as having
any foreign-political significance. The policy initiated at
Rapallo, which had for so many years helped Germany
in her task of destroying the order of 1919, was continued.
Throughout 1933, Russia supported the Franco-British policy of "equalization" at the disarmament conference. In
1934, Stalin defined Russian policy toward Hitler as
friendly, and unaffected by events inside Germany. "Certainly," he said, "we are far from being admirers of the
Fascist regime in Germany. The important thing, however, is not Fascism, if for no other reason than the simple fact that Fascism in Italy, for instance, did not prevent
us from establishing most cordial relations with that country." [34] For his part, Hitler, no matter how wildly he attacked communism, always emphasized his good relations
with Soviet Russia.

But behind closed doors, the Russians, too, began to
show uneasiness and fear. After conversations with the
Russian ambassador and Litvinov, Barthou was convinced
that the Soviets could be persuaded to join the encirclement front. They were ready to enter the League of Nations, after having denounced it as an instrument of imperialism for fifteen years, and to start negotiations for a
military alliance with France.

Barthou was a conservative Liberal, who disliked both
fascism and communism. He had not liked Tsarism either,
and yet decades before he had cultivated an alliance with
the Tsar against the German Kaiser. Four hundred years

earlier, the most Christian King Francis I had not liked the infidel Turk, yet he had made an alliance with the Turk against the German Emperor. When a country is confronted by a mortal enemy, it cannot afford to be fastidious about its allies. Italy and Russia were the only two powers on the continent capable of checkmating Germany. The Cabinet of the "elder statesmen," in which sat Doumergue, Pétain, Herriot and Tardieu, commissioned Barthou to negotiate with fascist Italy and bolshevik Russia.

For the first time in ten years, France adopted a definite policy. Unfortunately, it was no longer adequate. Although vastly superior to any previous undertaking by democratic statesmen, Barthou's plan was obsolete. Barthou was a man of 1910; and military alliances, which are instruments of calm armed preparedness no longer had the same meaning that they had had in 1910 when Germany and France were states of the same type, with approximately equal potentialities.

By 1934, the situation had changed. It was absolutely impossible for a state of the French type to remain the military equal of a state of the Nazi type. With her liberalistic peace economy, France was bound to grow increasingly inferior to Germany with her socialized war economy. France's air budget was 1,800 million francs, or 300 million marks. The new Cabinet prepared a "three-year plan" for air armaments which called for an expenditure of 980 million francs—160 million marks—a year. This was a huge sacrifice for a country with a liberalistic financial system, which in addition was in the throes of a depression. But compared to German expenditures for aviation, it was a trifling sum; the Nazi government spent 3 to 4 billion marks on the Luftwaffe—almost ten times as much as France. The same was true of other types of armaments. France could not afford to wait in a state of armed preparedness. To wait in this case meant to grow rapidly and increasingly inferior.

Barthou's policy of military alliances could not work. Alliances are not a matter of philanthropy: they break down when one of the partners grows perceptibly weaker. The alliances of 1900 lasted for ten, twenty or thirty years, because their military basis was relatively permanent. The French alliances of 1934 could not last because this basis was constantly changing to France's disadvantage. France could save herself only by crushing the evil at once, while it had not yet developed fully. It was now or never. Hitler's growing army must be smashed while it was still crossing the danger zone. Anything short of this was hopeless. Thus, in the last analysis Barthou's feverish efforts to give new life to the French alliances were doomed in advance to be a labor of Sisyphus.

Nevertheless, since the time of Poincaré nothing more forceful had been done on the European scene, and for a few months the world breathed with relief. The attempt to continue the disarmament conference without Germany failed. When Mr. Henderson again summoned it at Geneva, M. Barthou put an end to the farce. Sir John Simon was somewhat upset about Barthou's speech which he called "an ill-timed display of rhetorical fireworks." But now that there was French leadership, no less than fifteen states followed it. Litvinov, breaking radically with previous Russian policies, came out against disarmament without security. The conference was adjourned *sine die*. It would never be summoned again. Thus ended the ghostly hocus-pocus which had for so many years caused confusion and the loss of precious time, and which Ger-

many, before and after the advent of Hitler, had used to
the best advantage of her war machine.

Events seemed to be taking a bad turn for Hitler.

On June 30th, 1934, Germany's "supreme judge" staged
his St. Bartholomew's Eve. The slaughter was nothing
new in Germany; it had been going on ever since Nazism
had come to power. But this time the "purge" was open
and noisy under the pretext that a "conspiracy with foreign powers" had been discovered. A wave of horror
swept over the world. The London "Times" wrote: "In
the next years there is more reason to fear for Germany,
than to fear Germany." [35] But the rest of the world thought
differently: the feeling that Germany's "internal events"
were in reality a danger signal for the outside world
seemed at last to become general.

The June purge was not yet forgotten, when the Nazi
rebellion broke out in Austria. Chancellor Dollfuss who
had courageously opposed the voracious monster lay dead
in a pool of blood. Fighting broke out in all the Austrian
provinces, and an "Austrian legion" formed and trained
in Germany awaited the order to march upon Vienna.

Then Mussolini sent a number of his divisions to the
frontier. He was ready to risk everything. At that moment,
without papers and formalities, it was absolutely sure that
in this fight he would not remain alone, that Barthou's
France would come to his assistance.

Berlin was quick to realize the situation. At the last
moment, the Austrian Legion was recalled. The plot to
carry out the Anschluss under the mask of an internal
Austrian rebellion failed. Brute force, the threat of brute
force, frustrated it. This was Hitler's first defeat and a
resounding one. It could not be concealed by Germany's
hypocritical expressions of "sympathy," and "abhorrence."

It was well known that she had prepared, and even issued, declarations of an entirely different kind. "Evidence
came to my desk," noted Ambassador Dodd in his diary,
"that last night the government issued a formal statement
to the newspapers rejoicing over the fall of Dollfuss."
The whole world was filled with disgust and anger toward
the Nazis. Mussolini's *Popolo d'Italia* wrote of Hitler that
he was "not a dictator, but a liar." [36] Old Garvin in London wrote: "The hostility of all countries in the world has
been fanned to white heat. The monstrosity of the events
has caused public opinion everywhere to regard Germany as Public Enemy No. 1." [37] Even the "Times" lost its
calm and found that the Austrian adventure "is making
the name of Nazi to stink in the nostrils of the world." [38]

Only the Socialists and their followers seemed absolutely unaware of what had happened. On the twentieth
anniversary of the outbreak of the World War, the Second
International, to which the British Labor Party and the
French Socialist Party belonged, published a carefully
weighed manifesto in which they declared: "Only a few
days ago Italian fascism greedy for booty nearly unleashed a new war. The old warmongers of Europe have
risen again." [39] According to them it was forbidden to oppose Hitler's arms anywhere. On the same day Mr. Arthur Henderson uttered the profound thought that "the
most effective guarantee of the preservation of peace
would be the renunciation of war by all nations." [40] He
seemed to have forgotten that this most effective guarantee existed in several documents. On the same day, Mr.
Lloyd George flatly denied, in answering a question addressed him by a Paris newspaper, that there was any
danger of a new war. "Believe me, Germany is unable to
wage war." He declared himself ready to establish himself

as an insurance company and to give "all nations an insurance policy against any danger of war." [41]

M. Barthou had the reins of European politics firmly in hand. MacDonald, almost entirely isolated in his Coalition Cabinet, discovered his need for a vacation, and left London for a month before Barthou's visit, abandoning the field to his conservative colleague, Baldwin. The wall of encirclement which the French were building grew from day to day. The "Eastern Pact" with Russia, now a League member, was nearing completion. The "Southern Pact" with Italy depended only upon an agreement between Rome and Belgrade. To bring it about, King Alexander of Yugoslavia was invited to Paris. On October 9th, 1934, he landed in Marseilles and was welcomed by Barthou. As the automobile carrying the two statesmen began to move, a man from the crowd jumped up on the running board and riddled the occupants with an automatic rifle. The King died on the spot, and Barthou expired before he could be placed on an operating table.

The murderers were Croatians. Their organizer, Ante Pavelich, escaped. In 1941, he would re-emerge as "Premier" of the "Kingdom of Croatia." The trial revealed that the terrorists had been supported by the Hungarian government. It also revealed, though less clearly, their connection with Germany. Whether the murder of Barthou was part of the German program was never established with certainty. At any rate Berlin welcomed his death. The Cabinet of the "elder statesmen" appointed Pierre Laval to the post of Foreign Minister, and French foreign policy soon relapsed into the lethargy and paralysis of the pre-Barthou days.

Germany now entered upon the last stage of her danger period. She was nearing the point where she would be immune from attack. In August, 1933, the author of this book estimated the danger period at 20 months. "To squeeze twenty months more of peace out of the world is the cardinal objective of German politics." [42] In November, 1934, Foreign Minister Benes of Czechoslovakia declared: "By next spring Germany will be completely ready for war, ready even according to her own high standards of preparedness. I do not say that war will come, but I do say that beginning with next spring the peace of Europe will be at the mercy of any accident." [43] In the same month, Colonel Jean Fabry, Chairman of the Army Committee of the French Chamber of Deputies declared that France was suddenly confronted with a situation, which —and this was false—"no one could have foreseen, not even the most distrustful, not even those who studied this problem with the utmost care. . . . A year ago, the most pessimistic conjectures fell far short of the intensity, the extension, the tempo of German re-armament. . . . The gigantic efforts Germany is making can be compared to those of a country at war. If Germany were really preparing an attack,—and I hope that she is not—the tangible evidence of it would not be essentially different from that which we find today in every field." [44]

These were the last minutes! The last minutes in which the Allies, the victors in the war to end war, still controlled the destiny of Europe! What did they do?

Nothing at all! They resumed their hocus-pocus. Laval certainly was not opposed to inactivity. The surest and most comfortable course for him to steer was in the wake of Downing Street. But what was the course taken by Downing Street? As soon as Barthou's pressure was removed, the English Cabinet took the worst course of all. It began to make foreign policy the servant of domestic policy. Mr. Baldwin was to recognize later that in his foreign policy, too, he had been guided mainly by considerations pertaining to elections. And the elections meant a struggle against Labor.

And Labor? Did it indulge in an orgy of abstract pacifism when confronted with a Hitler who was obviously sharpening his knife, because it had fallen into complete spiritual impotence? Or did it pursue this policy which in actual fact served only Hitler against its better judgment? Did it pursue its policy without realizing the devastating consequences, only with the trivial object of capturing votes? On the European continent, closer to reality, despair gradually broke out over the attitude of the Labor Party. Even its few existing brother parties on the Continent ceased playing the pacifist game, with the exception of the French. In Switzerland, for instance, the Socialist press published comments like this: "What is in back of this monstrosity? Nothing but the hope of winning a few seats in Parliament in the coming election! . . . The present official policy of the British Government is, we fear, a misfortune for world peace. But what an even greater misfortune would be the policy of intellectual and moral blindness put forward in its stead by the British Labor Party! . . . Must not the policy of this party be described as 'moral insanity?' " [45]

But the English Labor leaders, and with them, the oppositionist Liberals, could not be stopped. They told the voters that universal peace was around the corner. All one had to do was to reach out for it, and then one would be rid of all dangers, all taxes for military purposes, all economic miseries. Hitler? A man who had been slandered. It would be easy to achieve world disarmament, collective security, serene sunshine by dealing with honest Germany. Only French militarism, explained these fanatics, stood in the way, with its incurable lust for conquest and its designs "to push the frontier back to the Rhine when occasion arises," [46] as Mr. Attlee put it. And why does no one speak of France? the fanatics kept asking. Why is not France regarded as a threat? The British government, they said, is a helot of the French; even worse, the British government itself is reactionary, militaristic, imperialistic, and out of its own wickedness plays the game in such a manner that Hitler is induced to stir up trouble. The purpose of the British government is to utilize this trouble in order to fill the munitions makers' pockets with millions. Down with this government, which sabotages peace!

The Labor Party seemed to be making irresistible progress with the help of this reckless pacifist propaganda. It won almost every by-election, every local election. In order to forestall a crushing Labor victory, the government seemed to have no choice but to oppose Labor with its own fantastic weapon.

What a spectacle! What a tragic incongruity! While Europe was living through months which irrevocably determined its entire future everything that was said and done in England was determined by petty electoral ambitions. Without any regard for reality, both the government and the opposition competed for ballots by exploiting the pacifism of the voters. Mr. Baldwin hastened back to the regions from which, a few months before, Barthou and Litvinov had rescued world politics. Even though it was now impossible to talk about disarmament—("Why not? We should take up disarmament!" clamored Labor)—it was at least possible to consider the "limitation of armaments." This was almost as good. Germany would be asked to state frankly the exact extent of her armaments;

and after she had made her confession, she would be granted absolution. Once this was granted, a world pact could be concluded which would at least for the future stipulate a certain maximum limit on all armaments. Mr. Baldwin set up as the chief objective of international politics the "limitations pact." For the next few months, the diplomats negotiated "limitation" with Hitler.

Hitler was not adverse to negotiating "limitations" or any other pacifist scheme with the Allies. On the contrary, he loved pacifism—in others. The machine of "front-line fighters" he had set up worked at full speed. More or less genuine presidents and representatives of veterans' associations sat everywhere with Nazis posing as world war veterans. Gentlemen of the "British Legion" went to Germany and received German gentlemen in England. French *anciens combattants* came to Berlin and held talks. A veteran named von Rippentrop came to Paris and talked. Everywhere they discussed the best means of insuring peace, and the Germans proposed one that they considered absolutely foolproof. "We former front-line fighters repudiate the inept diplomats!" [47] clamored the veteran Rudolf Hess. All important government posts in every country, demanded the Germans, must be given to presidents and delegates of veterans' associations. Could anything be more pacifistic?

In addition, the Germans exploited a theme which was popular not only with veterans: the theme that the "cannon merchants" cause wars. Be on your guard! See to it that they do not get any orders! An American Senate Committee named to investigate the munitions industry had just unmasked these poisoners and enemies of mankind. There it was in black and white. In the Committee's report one could read the question addressed by Senator

Clark to Du Pont: "Are you aware of the fact that the Skoda Works and Schneider Creusot have used Hitler's advent to spread fear of a new war in France, and thereby obtain new orders for munitions?" The munitions makers were behind everything!

Hitler's front-line fighters tirelessly denounced the war mongering activities of the munitions makers. In France they even helped an honest *ancien combattant* to found a newspaper mainly devoted to the unmasking of the "munitions industry, the gun merchants; the steel and concrete manufacturers." The "Militaer Wochenblatt," organ of the German army, bowed in admiration before such genuine pacifism. "The former front-line officer, Louis Thomas," it wrote, "is carrying on the struggle for the truth in the Paris newspaper 'Midi' with an energy which must arouse our admiration." Yes, Hitler was present wherever genuine pacifism was practiced. He was ready to negotiate about anything Mr. Baldwin wished. Only he had to settle that Saar plebiscite first.

And it was settled. There was no longer any difference of opinion as to the manner in which it was to be settled: Rightists and Leftists, in France and England, all agreed that a German victory in the plebiscite was desirable. A German defeat would only cause unpleasantness. Laval rejected Barthou's idea to use this opportunity to check Hitler. He never spent the few hundred million francs which had been constituted as a secret campaign fund for the Saar and no layman will ever know who got this money in the end. Everything was done to insure the desired outcome of the plebiscite. The League of Nations refused to promise the Saarlanders that they would be entitled to vote again at a later date. It refused to make public the constitution under which they would live if

they remained independent. The English police assigned
to supervise the voting showed marked sympathy for the
Nazis. And whereas during Barthou's ascendancy the
Holy See had recommended neutrality to the clergy, now
the local bishops and priests urged the population to vote
for the "German cause." The "German cause" obtained
90% of the votes, and Hitler entered Saarbruecken in triumph.

Now at last the way was open for negotiations. It was
announced that Sir John Simon would visit Hitler toward
the beginning of March, 1935, to discuss the limitations
pact and peace in general. To strengthen their special
envoy's hand, Baldwin and MacDonald published a White
Book which emphasized the importance of his mission. It
was a fact, the document explained, that Germany's rearmament had caused concern to all her neighbors; that
the spirit in which German youth was being educated
aroused apprehension everywhere; that all countries, including England, would be forced to rearm, unless a general pacification were brought about. The document was
actually an adjuration addressed to Germany, which, however, ventured certain criticisms. Herr Hitler seized the
opportunity to take offense. In exquisite, diplomatic style
the world was informed that the Führer's hoarseness prevented him from conversing with Sir John Simon. It was
obvious that Herr Hitler had other intentions than to chatter about armaments limitation.

But what a signal for the zealots and the demagogues!
What an opportunity for all the inventors of peace pan-
aceas to attack the shameful sabotage of peace by their
own governments! A real storm broke out over the White
Book.

"The most incredible document that has ever been pub-

lished by any government," foamed the "National Peace
Council." Lord Robert Cecil, its chairman, said: "I can
only regard the White Book as a deplorable document."
"The Prime Minister's declarations are one of the most
tragic events since the Versailles peace," said the Laborite
President of the London Municipal Council. "I consider
the publication of this White Book the greatest misfortune that has befallen us since the peace of Versailles," [48]
lamented Mr. Henderson's deputy in Geneva.

And why all this outcry? The News Chronicle, the Liberal London newspaper, stated with bitterness: "The consequence is a catastrophic increase of Germany's suspicions and fear of encirclement. In twenty-four hours, the
British government has immeasurably deteriorated the
entire international situation." "To publish such asser-
tions . . ." wrote the "Economist," "makes Germany a
scape-goat. . . . The document does not take the German point of view into consideration and creates the impression that England has joined in the encirclement
of Germany." [49] The Daily Herald, organ of the Labor
Party, was indignant: "Many sentences in the document
necessarily, though no doubt unintentionally, must sound
insulting to Germany, and in fact the conservative press
has termed them 'serious words' and 'warnings' addressed
to Germany. Germany is repeatedly accused of 'breaking
the treaty,' of 'aggravating the situation,' and of 'bringing
about a situation which imperils the peace.' . . . Let us
hope that the effects will not be catastrophic." [50] In another article they said: "The White Book is not only an
insult to Germany, it is also the rejection of the entire
system of collective security. But let the world understand—it is important that the world understand—that
this is not the voice of the English people." [51] "We hope,"

urged the News Chronicle, "that the British government will not spare any efforts to regain the ground lost by the publication of the White Book and to assuage the anger which is aroused in Germany." [52]

But Hitler assuaged himself. Without the assistance of his idealistic well-wishers in Great Britain and without much consideration for their feelings, he himself did what was necessary to soften his own anger. On March 16th, 1935, he issued a proclamation to his people and the world. He proclaimed the reintroduction of conscription, the repudiation of the military clauses of the peace of 1919, and the birth of a German army.

This was not, of course, the real birth of the new army. It was only the birth of its conscription phase. The secret methods of recruiting by which a strong army had already been formed were now replaced by conscription which could not be concealed. And the transition from secret to open methods meant that the time was past when Hitler had to be cautious, that he was strong enough to fight. Spring, 1935—the danger zone had been crossed. The period of reprieve had expired.

A world had collapsed. What was buried under the débris was not a volume of printed paper, not a piece of parchment, a treaty, a statute, but the whole structure of international cooperation. The very foundations of that structure had cracked; the meaning of the victory of 1918 had ceased to exist. What had been won by dint of the fiercest struggles and at the cost of millions of lives, not to mention the sufferings and sacrifices of hundreds of millions, had been squandered and lost.

Did they still parade in front of you, Unknown Soldier under the Arc de Triomphe, Unknown Soldier under the Cenotaph? Did they still salute you in tails or resplendent uniforms? You could no longer protest. You could no longer use your gun. But what you had won, they had lost. In sixteen years of lofty dreaming and low demagogy, the same generation that had won the prize had thrown it overboard foolishly, frivolously and complacently.

And now?

Four months before, the English government had agreed with the French and Italian governments "to consult on whatever matters may be required by the circumstances." [53] A few hours after Hitler's proclamation, the French and Italian governments requested that immediate consultations be held. The English government thought that pacifism was more important than their agreement. It left the Franco-Italian request unanswered; instead, it wired an urgent query to Berlin asking whether Hitler was willing to receive Sir John Simon and Captain Eden. Yes, Hitler was willing now. The two Ministers went on their peace pilgrimage to Berlin.

"I can naturally understand," said Sir Herbert Samuel in the House of Commons, "that our move has aroused reactions elsewhere. Unfortunately, we at present enjoy a reputation of unreliability in other countries." [54] But the peace which he felt Hitler would conclude now that he had everything he wanted, lay closer to his heart than any treaties with old Allies. As for his Majesty's Opposition, it was concerned only with having the two pilgrims go to Hitler with sincere offers of peace; it feared only that they might be harboring in the back of their minds some scheme based upon obsolete power politics.

The French were silent. They began to prepare a complaint to the League of Nations. The Italians were not silent. Mussolini ordered his ambassador to lodge a sharply worded protest with the Foreign Office. He mobilized two classes. This was to be the last offer of common action addressed by Rome to the democracies. It was destined to be ignored. Sir John and Eden were to return with the most painful impression of Hitler. But the elections—Labor—pacifism! No unpleasantness!

In the temple of pacifism in Geneva, the French formal complaint against the reconstruction of the German army and the breaking of the most important of all treaties came on the order of the day. The fanatics of collective security were cold and hostile. So the French wanted to trample upon Germany again? To the fanatics' great satisfaction, the League of Nations refused to be bothered with such trifles.

According to the League Constitution France's charge had to be studied first by a reporter who would then submit proposals to the Council. It was Spain's turn to act as reporter. But Spain refused to burn her fingers, and demanded that at least two other "neutral" Council members, Chile and Denmark, help her in drawing up the report. Denmark declared she was not bound to do this, and had no intention of doing it. It was no longer possible to secure a reporter in the League for a case involving Germany! The Council solved the problem by omitting the regular procedure and by passing a resolution condemning Germany's behavior. Another sheet of paper was added to the files.

Hitler listened and moved one step further. He had already announced the creation of a land army and an airforce. At the end of April, he proclaimed the initiation of a program of submarine construction. This aroused great bitterness in England. No one had expected it! For a few days even Labor was speechless. But the elections—pacifism! MacDonald and Baldwin and Sir John Simon decided that this was a case in which the principle of the limitations pact should be applied. Were Germany ready to pledge herself to keep the fleet, which she was by treaty forbidden to build, within reasonable limits?

Herr von Ribbentrop, who had recently been to Paris in the role of a former "front-line fighter," came to London as Hitler's special plenipotentiary. Yes, Ribbentrop explained, Hitler was ready to accept naval limitation. He was ready to limit the German fleet—"definitively and for all time to come"—to 35% of England's surface craft and 100% of England's submarines. But before he could negotiate this matter in detail, he declared, England must accept the principle. Otherwise he would leave at once —and the matter would be dropped forever. Thus the "negotiations" began with a German ultimatum.

The German fleet did not concern England alone; it concerned all the sea powers and all the signatories of Versailles. There were no less than seven valid pacts and agreements forbidding England to reach a separate accord with Germany on this question. The most recent of these agreements, concluded with France and Italy, was less than two months old. Sir John Simon—on the very day on which he left the Cabinet—asked the French and Italian governments whether they would agree to England's concluding a naval pact with Germany.

On June 15th, 1935, Rome replied that Mussolini refused to agree to any such thing, that this problem must be solved in common by all the parties concerned.

On June 17th Paris replied that Laval refused to agree and that the problem must be solved in common by all the parties concerned.

On June 18th, 1935, Sir Samuel Hoare signed the pact

which, in violation of the existing treaties, granted Hitler a larger fleet than France's or Italy's. It was the triumph of anarchy for the sake of peace. This time not Hitler but England broke treaties. A feeling of horror enveloped Europe. M. Laval found more willing ears than ever before when he perorated against England in political circles.

But Hoare and Baldwin came before the House of Commons and boasted of their achievement. This was an exemplary pacifist pact—wise, trustful, far-sighted and moderate on both sides. Only Mr. Churchill derided the new piece of paper. Otherwise, there was no disapproval. Even Labor found no pretext for pacifist criticism and suspicions. For four years to come, this harmful naval pact was constantly to serve as exhibit No. 1 in support of the thesis that really wise and reasonable pacts could be reached with Hitler. Its aura would shine undiminished until that day in April, 1939, when Hitler, having reached and outstripped the 100% quota on submarines, would throw it, too, into the scrap basket.

Yes, the danger zone was past. If anyone still wanted to obtain something from Hitler he would have to pay for it with streams of blood. One did not need to be a genius to know that the democracies were not ready for that. As long as their resolution to resist Hitler could have even the semblance of a decision freely arrived at, they would not be ready. Hitler's progress through the different stages of direct preparation for war was to be an easy promenade. He did not run any risks now.

The last stage was Hitler's transition from hastily improvised equality to overwhelming superiority. Of course, it would still have been possible to make his progress difficult. The democracies could, theoretically, rush into the same total mobilization, the same war economy, as Germany. But it was ridiculous to take this possibility seriously. Before they would begin even to envisage the inevitability of strenuous efforts and unpleasantness, Germany would have achieved her decisive advantage. Forward, march!

Part Four: Collapse

9: *Tragedy of Weakness*

THE WORLD now unveiled its mystery. As in an X-ray picture, the clothes, the skin and the flesh, the familiar, outward appearance vanished. The envelope of civilization grew increasingly transparent: laws, customs, contracts, ideologies, ideals, morality, property, progress—all began to disintegrate. The eternal primitive skeleton stood out more and more clearly: the skeleton of power. More and more events were determined by military power pure and simple.

Germany was totally mobilized. Her workers slaved nine and ten and more hours a day. Her factories were organized for war economy. Civilian consumption was reduced to a minimum. Her finances were socialized. To know what the result of all this would be, it was necessary only to read the record of the World War. Mr. Benes had calculated that by the spring of 1935, Germany would have 4,000 warplanes and that was only a beginning. What were the other countries doing?

They had not even begun to prepare. They lived under the most complacent, peaceful liberal regimes. France's air force consisted of 1,600 first line craft of obsolete design. The "three-year" plan submitted by the government in December, 1934, would not increase the air force, it would merely modernize two thirds of it: before 1937, 1010 obsolete machines were to be replaced by new ones. And even this modest program had to be imposed against strenuous opposition. M. Léon Blum denied that Germany had warlike intentions. He was against all armaments. He was for disarmament. The French Socialist and Communist parties voted against the military budget.

The French land army was even worse off. War Minister Pétain had only demanded the raising of the period of military service from one to two years. This was not a measure intended to strengthen the army, but merely to compensate for the fact that the next classes to be called up, who were born during the war years, were twice as small as they normally would have been. And even this measure of self-preservation was enforced only against the impassioned opposition of the Left. The French alliance with Russia signed in 1935 did not prevent France from declining in relative strength.

And England? England was an enigma. In November, 1934, Mr. Baldwin made declarations in the House of Commons which could only be described as grotesque. The R.A.F., he explained, disposed of 560 first line planes, while Germany had only 260. "Germany's real strength has not even reached 50% of that which we have in Europe alone." [1] Then he proceeded to develop a plan for the expansion of British aviators. Within one year, he said, England would have the phenomenal number of 760 planes, while Germany would increase her air fleet only to 520. Two years later, Mr. Baldwin himself made the most apt comment on a production of only 200 planes in one year by the greatest world empire, and on the reliability of its Intelligence Service which had estimated Germany's aviation gains in one year at the same figure. He said: "In my estimates I was mistaken. I was thoroughly mistaken on that point. I freely acknowledge it before the House: thoroughly mistaken, I repeat." [2] This was in 1934. In 1935, the government proposed to increase all types of weapons. Hell broke loose. Laborites and Liberals were unrestrained in their condemnation. "From the danger of war one cannot protect oneself by weapons," Mr. Attlee declared in the House of Commons, "one can achieve this only by moving forward into a new world of law and by disbanding the national armies. (Shouts: Tell that to Hitler!) Armaments cannot be fought by piling up armaments; that would be like getting Beelzebub to drive out the devil." [3]

The British rearmament program called for a 10% increase in expenditures on each of the three branches of the armed forces as compared to the previous year: 135 million pounds instead of 115 millions. This thimbleful was its reply to the billions spent by Germany. In April, Winston Churchill warned that England was at the mercy of any attack. Garvin spoke sadly of the unprecedented decay of English power.

Signor Mussolini realized that here at last was an opportunity to replace thirteen years of poses and gestures and parades by a real conquest. France was immobilized, eyes fixed on the German frontier, absolutely incapable of risking complications anywhere else in the world. England, behind its moat, perhaps felt safer with regard to Germany, but was immobilized by Japan. Two years before, Mussolini himself had foreseen the coming tragedy of Asia. "Today Japan invades and organizes China," he explained in justifying the Italian naval budget. "Tomorrow, driven forward by racial fanaticism, she will take up the fight against the White man." [4] Everyone knew that the Japanese who were building up their sea power while the other countries scrapped ships, were making ready, awaiting a favorable moment, and that if England, with her sadly reduced power, became involved elsewhere, she would have reason to tremble for her Asiatic possessions.

In these circumstances, it was most unlikely that France and England would voluntarily expose themselves to a threat from Italy. Neither morally, nor materially could they prevent her from conquering Abyssinia. Mussolini began to concentrate troops on the Abyssinian frontier. He did it noisily, trumpeting his intention to invade the African kingdom once his preparations were complete.

The French were apathetic. Would the League of Nations fanatics really try to set the dead machinery in motion? For seventeen years, they had been protecting Germany's resurgence as a military power. Recently everyone had seen how they behaved when Hitler proclaimed the reintroduction of conscription. Somewhat bitterly, the French hoped that no one would now try to play the League game again. At any rate, they could not be partners in it. After Hitler's proclamation they had been forced to transfer two thirds of the troops stationed on the Italian border to the German border. They had no freedom of action.

The British government, too, was resolved to avoid an armed conflict with Italy at any cost. But Mr. Baldwin had to cope with Labor and the League enthusiasts. They were clamoring at full blast. They tried to prove by hook or by crook that England must not arm. If you use the League, they clamored, you won't need armaments! The League is our Robot, they contended, it does things for us without any effort on our part. Let the League apply sanctions whenever necessary—economic sanctions are all that is required. And to show that economic sanctions were sufficient and that armaments were absolutely unnecessary, they demanded sanctions against Italy; this in 1935, in a world that had been turned upside down, with a discredited League, the members of which were far weaker than the non-members. The demand grew more and more general. Mr. Baldwin did not know where to turn. If he opposed sanctions, he could not avoid a crushing electoral defeat; if he supported sanctions, he ran the risk of war. As a result, Baldwin's Cabinet made strenuous efforts to prevent the question from being taken up by the League.

Sir Samuel Hoare thought up a plan for settling the whole matter outside Geneva: Haile Selassie was to yield part of his territory; the English were to compensate him with a small piece of Somaliland. The French, too, were to contribute something. Mr. Eden went to Rome and adjured Mussolini to accept the arrangement, promising that if he accepted it England, France and Italy would compel the Lion of Judah to accept it, too.

Mussolini refused. He wanted all of Abyssinia, and not in the form of a gift, but as a glorious conquest which he needed for prestige. There was a turbulent scene between him and Eden. The would-be conqueror stood his ground: he knew that his opponents were helpless.

Meanwhile, his divisions on the Abyssinian border grew more numerous, and Haile Selassie's petitions to the League more urgent. The propaganda of the Laborites and League visionaries became more and more violent. During the long years when England was able to make free decisions, they had persistently favored Germany's violations of the treaties and opposed sanctions and in-

˙tervention. Now that England no longer had freedom of action they demanded sanctions against Italy. They did not realize that peace was irretrievably lost, that the period of atonement for the sins committed during the last seventeen years had begun.

As in chess the whole game was lost because of early moves. But the pacifists refused to see that. They denied that sanctions against Italy were in any way related to military matters. They maintained that "economic sanctions" should replace guns, that a few commercial barriers would suffice to bring Italy to her knees.

Actually the effectiveness of the economic sanctions which the League might impose was questionable. Japan, Germany, Brazil and the United States were not members and were not bound to apply sanctions. When the League voted them, Argentina, Austria, Hungary and Switzerland, all League members, refused to apply them, and these countries could supply Italy with the few imports she needed.

Aside from this, who could guarantee that economic sanctions would remain purely economic, that Mussolini would not resort to arms if he were seriously bothered by them? And behind the possibility of a war with Italy there lurked the risk of two other more dangerous wars.

The visionaries refused to admit this risk. They refused to see that economic sanctions had to be backed up by military strength. A "peace ballot" organized and sponsored by all sorts of progressives and perfectionists in trousers, skirts or cassocks was sweeping England. This "ballot" demanded simultaneously that the League crush the wicked aggressors and forbid the possession of arms to its own members. An amazing combination. The "peace ballot" obtained 11 million votes, more than half of the English electorate.

Mr. Baldwin faced a difficult situation. The results of seventeen years of pacifism now bedeviled his country. There was practically no English army and no English air force to speak of. The battleships that had survived the scrapping were obsolete. Japan and Italy had quietly built a large number of cruisers; together they now had more than twice as many cruisers as England. An inventory disclosed that there were not enough munitions in the arsenals to supply the British navy for even one large engagement. Then came the *coup de grâce*: at the end of August, 1935, while Italy was moving closer to warlike action, America adopted her neutrality law, that monument of foolhardy isolationism and pacifism. Without the stream of munitions from America, the Allies would have lost the World War by 1915 or 1916; now this source was stopped. It was obvious that England could not accept the risk of war before building up her strength. But it was equally obvious that Mr. Baldwin would lose the elections if he allowed Italy to proceed without setting the League in motion.

In this predicament he resorted to a manoeuvre. He decided to get the League to act, but in a manner which would not really hurt Mussolini. As Churchill later explained, at the very beginning of the Ethiopian affair Mussolini had intimated that he would not object to sanctions which would merely impose restrictions on the Italian people, but that he would regard sanctions which restricted the freedom of action of his armies as hostile acts. Mr. Baldwin drew the proper conclusions. In order to preserve his party from an electoral defeat and England from war he gave the English voters the appearance, and Mussolini the substance.

This was an undignified expedient. It had been used before in English history and would be used again, but always with demoralizing effect. According to the British historian Mandell Creighton, ever since 1500 England had got herself into difficult positions and exposed herself to the charge of double-dealing because of her inability to back up her policies by military force. "If my lips were not sealed," Baldwin was to groan later. But this could not repair the damage done. Churchill later condemned such manoeuvres, remarking that when a country is determined not to wage war nor to do anything that might provoke its enemies, it should keep in the background. It must be granted that at least in the opening stages of this affair, Mr. Baldwin succeeded perfectly in camouflaging his designs. Churchill later wrote that he did not grasp the meaning of the economic sanctions for many months.

The French were dismayed. They wanted to avoid the appearance of sabotaging the imminent League action. M. Laval wrote a public note to London asking to what extent England intended to oppose future violations of the Covenant "in Europe, too" [5] by sanctions. "In Europe, too" meant: if Germany were the violator. After sixteen days, Baldwin and Sir Samuel replied with a long note whose substance was that one could not meet all situations in the same manner. "There are various degrees of guilt and aggression." The Covenant must be applied "with elasticity." It must not be forgotten that "the world is not static." [6] No such long note was really needed to say: "No."

But oddly enough, the most ardent supporters of col-

lective security in the case of Ethiopia were far from willing to defend it "in Europe, too." The conservative Morning Post indulged in mockery: "Our Liberal and Socialist
friends apparently imagine that we can choose and pick
out what is convenient for us." [7] In fact, that was what
they imagined, without realizing it. Since Versailles, before and after Mussolini, they had always been uncom-
promising toward Italy, a power of a minor importance.
Since Versailles, before and after Hitler's advent, they
had always blindly supported Germany, the really important enemy. They actually wanted to choose and pick
out what was convenient for them.

But the time for debate was past. On October 3rd,
1935, the little dictator, greedy for glory, gave his troops
the order to march. Britain vigorously demanded a vote
of sanctions from the League. Laval declared: "Our
duties are inscribed in the Covenant. France will not side-
step them." This meant: we will do exactly what is provided for by the letter of the Covenant, and not a whit
more. A "sanction committee" began to function.

It is noteworthy, although it was barely noted, that the
British proposals to the committee did not even go as far
as the letter of the Covenant. The Covenant prescribed
that all trade with the aggressor be suspended at once,
and even that all maritime, railway and postal communi-
cations with him be cut off. The Committee did not even
discuss the closing of the Suez Canal, which was the
surest method of frustrating the entire campaign. Instead,
only "progressive" sanctions were voted, that is, gradually sterner sanctions. This was in October; the elections
to the House of Commons were to be held on November
15th. How far would these "progressive" sanctions go in
the intervening six weeks?

On the seventh day of the war, the sending of arms and munitions to Italy was forbidden. But she did not need any arms or munitions. On the twelfth day, she was refused credits which no country would have granted her anyway. On the seventeenth day, certain raw materials were banned: the black list contained aluminum with which she was abundantly supplied, but did not contain coal, iron, oil and cotton which she needed. The Baldwin Cabinet appeared as the St. George of the crusade advocated by the voters in the "Peace Ballot." Labor saw with consternation that its thunder had been stolen.

On the 29th day of war, that Sanctions Committee met to discuss the ban on oil deliveries to Italy. This was the first sanction which, despite the existing gaps, might have had a paralyzing effect upon Italy. Mr. Eden declared himself vigorously for the oil sanctions—but on one condition: as they might provoke the Italian fleet to warlike action, and as the British alone would not be able to cope with the situation, the French fleet must first be mobilized. Laval replied that the Covenant did not impose upon upon its signatories the obligation to mobilize and fight, and that France in this case chose not to fight, because for France, war with Italy meant not only sea engagements, but also land warfare, and with the German army on her flank she could not run the risk of war with Italy. Mr. Eden regretted this very much; if France took that position, he said, oil sanctions were impossible. He expressed his hope that Paris would reconsider its stand. And there the matter rested.

Then, on the 43rd day of the war, the elections were at last held in England. They were a triumph for the Baldwin government. Basking in the glory of its leader-

ship in the peace crusade, it won almost two thirds of
the House. It was one of the greatest electoral victories
in the history of the Conservative Party, all the greater
because only shortly before, an equally great victory for
Labor seemed certain. Mr. Baldwin gained much deserved admiration.

After the election, it was no longer necessary for the
government to pose as a champion of the League of Nations. It hastened to throw off its obligation to apply the
sanctions. On the 65th day of the war, the world was
suddenly confronted with the Hoare-Laval Plan which
gave Mussolini two thirds of Ethiopia and placed the
rest under a sort of protectorate.

A cry of indignation arose in England from the devotees of the League of Nations. The Conservatives were
horrified by the crudity of this move only three weeks
after the elections. Mr. Baldwin beat a retreat: Sir Samuel Hoare resigned within 48 hours. The Prime Minister
assured Parliament that the Hoare-Laval Plan was "dead,
irretrievably dead."

But he took no further action and made no effort to
extend the sanctions. How could he? The French were
sabotaging them. It was all Laval's fault, for he had refused to mobilize the French fleet. Mr. Baldwin discreetly
shifted the blame on France which in fact was pursuing
exactly the same policy as England. And what he did discreetly, others did brutally. While Mussolini gained his
facile triumphs in Ethiopia, Labor and its sympathizers
took up their favorite old theme: They indulged in a
real "campaign of slander against France." [8] Their absurd
propaganda in favor of the theory that no effort and no
real weapons were necessary to stop an aggressor, that

the mythical League of Nations robot could accomplish this unpleasant task, ended in a barrage of abuse of England's ally.

Laval was only a mediocre politician. But in this case he was justified in thinking that he had been unfairly treated. The English and his own political opponents in France had no right to make him a scapegoat. He had behaved as any other French Premier would have behaved in the same circumstances. But in France, too, elections were at hand, the elections of May, 1936. The old "Cartel of the Left" had been extended to include the Communists and had developed into the Popular Front. The agitation of the Popular Front against Laval took up the English slogans, and mercilessly attacked him for a policy which any Frenchman in his place would have pursued and which was later pursued by the Popular Front government. Laval was overthrown. He left office with his heart full of hatred and resentment at having been maliciously dealt with, cheated, "done in," outwitted by people cleverer than himself. Some day he would teach the Left a lesson! He would show those English a thing or two.

Despite all the disappointments that France's last great men had suffered at England's hands they had never forgotten that ultimately England and France would have to stand together. And they had always adjured their countrymen not to forget this essential fact. Clemenceau's voice from the grave warned the French never to let themselves be drawn into real hostility toward the less intelligent English: "The Englishman is not intelligent," General Mordacq quotes him as saying, "he does not grasp things quickly. He realizes his danger only in the moment of extreme peril. History eternally repeats itself.

We have not finished with Germany. . . . Any understanding with her is impossible, and England, whether
she likes it or not, will be compelled to march with us at
the moment of danger in order to defend herself. Despite
the misunderstandings and the dissensions that may separate us now, England will be forced to come to France's
side exactly as in 1914, at the moment of real danger. We
must guard ourselves from rejoicing over anything that
weakens England, for it weakens us, too, on the day of
peril." [9] But Laval was the opposite of a great man. Wisdom and patriotism were beyond his range. He left office
with a brooding anglophobia in his heart, with the obsession that one day he must repay his opponents on the
other side of the Channel with interest.

In the meantime, one year had passed since Hitler's
proclamation concerning conscription. Another year of
war production and war recruiting in Germany. Another
year of liberal nonchalance in the democracies. German
"equality" had already become superiority. Governments
and general staffs were full of fear. Italy and Japan continued their invasions and campaigns of plundering in
Ethiopia and China. Cannon, firing or threatening, ruled
the world. Herr Hitler was not in a hurry: his superiority
had not yet reached the point where he could act without
running any risks. But he, too, wanted to march some-
where. On March 7th, 1936, his army marched into the
Rhineland.

There was no enemy to oppose him, only a sign saying "Forbidden." German troops and fortifications were
not allowed within a zone fifty kilometers wide west of
the Rhine, do you remember? Hitler tore down the sign
and put an end to the No-Man's-Land character of the
province. This was an act of war, defined as such eleven

years ago. It was defined as such in the Locarno agreement, remember?—that celebrated model of a binding "voluntary" contract. Germany had recognized in this pact that any violation of the demilitarized Rhineland zone would be equivalent to a declaration of war, and England had pledged herself to come to France's assistance in this case. The League of Nations had put its seal upon this agreement. Hitler himself had pledged himself to observe it at least three times—in a note to France on March 13th, 1934, in a note to England on April 16th, 1934, and in a speech before the Reichstag on May 22nd, 1935. His march into the Rhineland was a deliberate act of war.

It was more than that: it was obviously, unmistakably a prelude to other acts of war. This had been realized since the days of the peace conference. A passage in Tardieu's memorandum of February, 1919, explains that the demilitarization of the Rhineland "is also an indispensable protection for the new States which the Allies have called into being to the east and south of Germany. Let us suppose that Germany, controlling the Rhine, should decide to attack the Republic of Poland, or the Republic of Czechoslovakia. Established defensively on the Rhine, she would hold in check, for how long nobody knows, the Western nations coming to the rescue of the young Republics, and the latter would be crushed before they would receive aid." [10] Decidedly, in 1919 the French foresaw everything!

Hitler's remilitarization of the Rhine caused general apprehension. Would this mean war? What was going to happen? One thing was sure: this time, the event had taken place "in Europe," not in Africa. The tanks and guns that rumbled into the Rhineland over the torn-up pieces of the Locarno agreement struck the ears of the peace experts with an entirely different sound than the tanks and guns that had rumbled into Ethiopia over the torn pieces of the Covenant. Here was doubtless a breach of the pledged word. Nor could the method be approved. But after all the Rhineland was German territory, was it not? Had it not been an ignominious mistake to prevent the Germans from doing whatever they pleased in their own country? Was it not true that the entire demilitarization, although approved by the League, was one of those insults to German honor which had caused so much trouble? And had not Hitler said in a speech made while his troops were on the march that the Rhineland was his last concern in Europe, positively his very last? Was he not now explicitly offering twenty-five years of peace and a whole mass of pacts filled with the most authentic Labor and Peace-Ballot verbiage? One thing was necessary above all now: to prevent the French from venting their rage on Germany.

As to the French, their faces were livid and their knees shook. On paper, they were entitled to do anything they pleased. They had the right, without saying a word, without wasting a minute, to mobilize and march; to demand English mobilization and military assistance; to demand all the sanctions the League could impose. They had everything they required on paper but they lacked everything they needed in their arsenals and barracks. And they also lacked will. Everyone lacked will, the Ministers and the men-in-the-street, the Rightists and the Leftists. To act or not to act? In this game, no move could any longer be good. After a few confused, pointless and stammering speeches, the chiefs of the French government went to London. Did they want to drag England into war

with the lasso of an eleven-year-old signature? The pacifist press assailed them with as much hatred as if they
were Genghis Khans. The Liverpool clergy resolved to
omit the traditional prayer for their own government, because, as their spokesman, a Minister named Davy, explained, it was about to yield to France's "wish for revenge" and commit the "monstrous injustice" [11] of a
punitive action against Germany. The St. Vitus dance of
Francophobia and Germanophilia which had seized the
Leftists and humanitarians in England since the conclusion of the Versailles peace reached its climax.

The hysteria of the Liverpool churchmen was, however, groundless. The two democratic governments had
not the slightest intention of replying to the German act
of war by other acts of war. The Locarno agreement, that
miracle which had allowed M. Briand to insure peace by
evacuating the Rhineland—the glorious Locarno agreement proved empty when there arose the very situation
for which it had been planned.

Two Premiers and two Foreign Ministers sat toegther.
They did not discuss methods of checking Germany and
putting into effect the clauses of the Locarno agreement.
They discussed the masks and disguises with which they
could conceal their failure to put these clauses into effect. They could not find any good ones. The tension
petered out into pointless chatter.

The faith and hope without which mankind cannot live
were now supplied by someone else.

In France an election campaign was going on, the campaign of the Popular Front, something that did not yet
exist anywhere in the world, except in Spain. It was an
alliance ranging from Adam Smith to Karl Marx, from the
exponents of liberalism to those of the dictatorship of the

proletariat. Along the streets, there marched arm in arm
Daladier, a member of the lower middle class and the
leader of the Radical Socialists; Léon Blum, who came
from the upper middle class and was the leader of the Socialists; Thorez, a worker, the leader of the Communists;
they all sang the Marseillaise and the Internationale.
"Une France libre, forte et heureuse." The Popular Front
obtained a two-thirds majority. On the eve of his assumption of office as Premier, Léon Blum defined his future
policy in a long speech, in which the ugly world outside
was given the space of fifteen lines. "We want to bring
back faith and hope. And we want to electrify this faith
around two ideas: mutual assistance and general disarmament." [12]

2.

Germany continued to increase its initial advantage in
preparedness with all the speed possible in an age of mass
production. In the summer of 1936, the Honorable Winston Churchill asked Chancellor of the Exchequer Neville
Chamberlain whether he knew that in 1935 Germany had
spent 800 million pounds sterling for military purposes,
and whether he did not think that she would spend at
least the same amount in 1936.

Mr. Churchill's figures were rather on the conservative
side; Germany's expenditure was nearer 1,000 million
pounds. But 200 millions more or less really mattered little. Neville Chamberlain replied that according to the
information on hand the British government saw no reason for assuming that the figures quoted by Churchill
were exaggerated, whether for 1935 or 1936.

What were England's expenditures for military purposes? 135 million pounds for 1935; 180 millions were scheduled for 1936, and 257 millions for 1937. France spent 120 millions in 1935; 150 millions were to be spent in 1936, and 180 millions in 1937. To obtain a graphic view of the military situation in Europe, it suffices to combine these figures and compare them to the German. For 1935, we have 255 millions spent by the Western democracies against 800 millions spent by Germany; for 1936, the respective figures are 350 and 900; and for 1937, 437 and 1000. Thus, year after year, German superiority grew by leaps and bounds.

The governments were aware of this; they knew that the game of power was lost for the democracies, lost to Germany alone, and doubly lost if Japan and Italy were added to Germany. And it was more and more obvious that they would have to be added. The three powers had not concluded a definite alliance, but in 1936 Berlin and Rome announced a vague agreement which received the name of the "Axis." A few weeks later, Berlin and Tokyo announced the conclusion of a vague "anti-Comintern pact." This was enough to impress upon France and England that they would have to cope not only with Hitler.

The world understood. The X-ray picture was studied. The shift in military power revolutionized the entire situation. The small states which always reflected the conflicts between the big ones, tried to act accordingly. All along the line, each ran for his life. The King of the Belgians announced the end of his alliance with France: he had hit upon the brilliant idea of playing an isolationist game. In Rumania pro-French Foreign Minister Titulescu left the Cabinet, for the Rumanian King, too, wanted to be an isolationist. In Yugoslavia, Prince Paul began to make overtures to Germany. In Poland, Foreign Minister Beck assumed a pro-German attitude.

The time for diplomacy was really over, Mars dominated the scene. All that remained of the previous political structure was France's alliance with Czechoslovakia and with huge distant Russia. The pressure of events drove Britain's conservative government closer to France. "Our frontiers are on the Rhine," said Mr. Baldwin. The group of anti-German powers was, however, crassly inferior in military might to the Axis. Their influence, their freedom of action, decreased day by day. They could no longer attack Hitler, for he was too strong; nor could they try to check his preparations for attack. The initiative was completely in Hitler's hands. There was only one hope for his opponents: to regenerate their military might by an unprecedented effort, to regenerate it sufficiently to withstand at least his first onslaught on land and in the air, and thereby gain time. To arm with feverish energy, to go all out for armaments, to mobilize all their resources, to work twenty-four hours a day and seven days a week.

This effort was not made; democracy failed to overcome that weakness which is the other side of its strength. Democracy, that instrument for creating civilized amenities, proved unequal to the task of deliberately creating hardships. In England, the resistance of the Leftists to any kind of rearming continued. They clung tenaciously to their peace and appeasement illusions. When War Minister Duff Cooper made a speech in Paris emphasizing Franco-British friendship, Labor attacked him in both Houses of Parliament. The unfortunate character of this speech, Henderson Junior said, was sufficiently demonstrated by the serious criticism of it expressed in the German press. Mr. Attlee moralized: "Such strong emphasis on friendship with one country induces other countries to wonder why they are not addressed with similar friendship." [13] The Conservative government had a hard time defending Duff Cooper and defending its armaments program. Aside from the Opposition, its own frame of mind prevented it from going too far. "Baldwin appealed to the country to rearm with the utmost speed, but at the same time he insisted that the rearmament must not be too extensive," [14] wrote Churchill in 1936. The rearmament effort was to remain within the framework of normal financing, without causing any disruption of business as usual, consumption as usual, wages as usual and working hours as usual.

In France, the Left theoretically clung to the appeasement idea, although in practice it understood the necessity of resisting Hitler. The opposition against rearming died. The Communists had ceased to oppose rearmament since May 16th, 1935, when Stalin told Laval that he completely approved of France's policy of national defense. From that day on, the French Communists, hitherto furiously anti-militaristic and anti-patriotic, began so strongly to emphasize patriotism and military preparedness that the cause of national defense was harmed thereby. The Socialists abandoned their hostile attitude to the army in 1936.

But what a tragedy! What a contradiction! The Popular Front had come to power as a movement intended to create a better life by improving the conditions of the common people. One of its slogans was the thirty-six hour week, *la semaine à deux dimanches*. On the other side of the Rhine, a highly industrialized country of over 70 million inhabitants was forging offensive weapons, straining every nerve and lowering all its living standards. On the French side of the Rhine, a far less industrialized country of 40 million inhabitants believed that the time had come for relaxing its efforts and improving its living standards. Thus in France there was no prospect of improving, let alone reversing, the relation of strength between the democracies and the Axis.

In addition, an atmosphere of civil war began to develop in France. There cannot be a spirit of class struggle on one side of the barricades alone. Strikes swept the country, sparing no factory, office or shop. Whatever may have been the merits of this pseudo-revolution, it occurred at a horribly unfortunate moment. The social conquests it achieved were doomed in advance to be wiped out by the approaching danger of war. It was untimely because it helped to prevent France from concentrating on her most important task; rearming; and because it split the country at a time when unity was more indispensable than ever.

The country was indeed split. Suddenly, the Right assumed toward Germany the attitude that the Left had had for the previous seventeen years. Until 1936, the policy of the Left had been appeasement of Germany to the point of blindness. When the Right propagated distrust of Germany, the Left branded their propaganda as an instrument of partisan politics. Now, during the last act of the drama, the roles were reversed. The Right began to accuse the Left of pursuing a partisan policy draped in patriotic phrases. It could be no accident, the Rightists argued, that the same people who advocated revolution were "warmongers" against Germany. The

Communists were accused of playing Moscow's game, of trying to unleash war in order to promote the world revolution.

Such arguments were at best the result of confused thinking. Whatever Moscow's intentions might have been, Hitler was Hitler, and his intentions with regard to France were not changed thereby. But reason has little influence on a mood of civil war. A new form of the old appeasement attitude began to take hold of even the moderate Rightists: we must not let our class enemy plunge us into dangerous adventures against Germany, we must find a *modus vivendi* with her. Down with the poisoners of the political atmosphere! The extremist Rightists assumed an openly treacherous attitude: the enemy of my enemy is my friend; Hitler is better than Blum; Germany is our ally against our class enemy. Out of the morass of impotence into which France had sunk, and from the seeds of the quasi-civil war tearing her apart, grew the flower of treason.

To the veiled civil war raging in France was added the open civil war in Spain. The Blum government was naturally inclined to help the Spanish Frente Popular against General Franco. But two days after the outbreak of the Spanish conflict, an Italian military plane made a forced landing on French territory. It turned out that the plane was destined for Franco. Thus behind Franco emerged Italy, and behind Italy were Germany and Japan: it was the Ethiopian situation all over again. Once again, it seemed impossible to run the risk of war, once again weakness and compromise dominated the scene.

The English government was unwilling to fight for the continued existence of a Socialist-Communist government in a foreign land. Baldwin refused to take any interest in the Spanish struggle; aside from this fact, he was militarily too weak to risk any warlike involvements. He felt that interventions would bring no political advantage to England. Baldwin's attitude made Blum even more timorous but he refused to admit to his electors and to the world that he had been condemned to inactivity. He imitated the British expedient in the Ethiopian affair and invented the "non-intervention pact," whereby all governments were to pledge themselves to let Spain settle her own problems.

All the governments concerned agreed. The Italian and German governments broke their pledges on the very first day; and as a result the non-intervention pact made things worse. England and France could have maintained that Spain did not concern them but the constant violation of a pact which they had initiated was a matter that did concern them. Their impotence was revealed clearly and shamefully. Moreover the Russians, too, intervened, although to a lesser extent than Germany and Italy, because of technical difficulties. The obvious purpose of their intervention was to induce France to intervene as well and this was a hopeless undertaking from the very beginning. The Russians only succeeded in adding fuel to the Rightists' propaganda that the Soviets were behind everything and that they wanted to unleash a war at all costs. The French appeasers gained new recruits, and the traitors new incentives. The Spanish affair plunged the democracies into a thick morass of lies, dishonor, disillusionment and sinister propaganda.

Germany's superiority in armaments continued to increase. By 1937, democratic impotence reached a new low. Now even the Labor Party began to see the truth that only arms could overcome arms. In September, 1937, the Laborite "National Council" adopted a resolution which stated that "in the present state of the world, a government must be strongly armed in order to defend the homeland." [15] It was of no avail; it was many years too late.

One distant hope, one single hope, shone on the dark military horizon. At last aircraft production in England began to show signs of progress. Factories and training schools expanded. If everything went well, there was hope of producing 1,750 first line planes during 1937, and 2,800 by the spring of 1940. In a few years' time, England might be able to catch up in the air, at least enough to defend her own shores.

Unfortunately the negligence of the French in this branch of armaments was disquieting. The French did not spend even one third of what the British did on aviation. After three years of vain labors they finally put forward their "Plan No. 1" which provided for 1,010 craft destined not to strengthen, but to modernize their air force. Then they began to work on "Plan No. 2" which provided for an air fleet of 1,500 first-line machines by the spring of 1940. How many of these machines would be ready in 1938 and 1939? From the air came the greatest threat and it was in the air that France was as good as non-existent. Thus were the two democracies immobilized.

In Asia, the Japanese juggernaut began to move for the third time, this time attacking China proper: Peking, Tientsin and Nanking, and, for the second time, Shanghai, which in 1932 had been saved by the prestige of the Great Powers. The question as to whether the robot named the League of Nations could do anything was not even raised. The Powers interested in China, including the United States, met in Brussels, but no decision was taken. There was no action, not even a proposal of action. The triple alliance of the armed powers, plundering, each for itself, and threatening the world together, had the unarmed powers by the throat.

Only to squeeze out another few years of peace! This passionate desire made no hope, no dream, no argument, seem too absurd. Rightists and Leftists crowded around Hitler. At his court in Berlin or Berchtesgaden, there appeared the Labor leader Lansbury, the Labor Lords Allen and Arnold, the great Liberal Lloyd George, and above all, his ex-secretary, Lord Lothian. From the Right came their Lordships Londonderry and Clive and McGowan and Mount Temple and Riverdale and Brocket. All of them returned full of hope. Hitler had good reason for keeping the hope of peace alive while he piled up overwhelming armaments. He helped them build their castles in Spain. He let them talk and he talked, too.

They talked about colonies for Germany—a proper subject for devotees of "national honor." They talked about equalizing the "haves" and the "have-nots," a subject dear to the friends of the proletariat. They talked about the just distribution of raw materials, a favorite theme for those who felt that all wars were determined by economic factors. They talked about giving Germany a free hand to fight Bolshevism. This was the idea of those who clearly discerned the crusading streak in Hitler's character. There was talk about everything and everyone talked as though the Nazi Reich were a state set on certain well-defined, limited advantages with which it would be satisfied. And Downing Street seemed willing to listen to almost any suggestion. Neville Chamberlain took over the government. Only posterity will know what he fully believed, what he only half believed and what he did not believe at all. Many documents will have to be published before it can be said with certainty that he was as stupid as he often appeared to be. The naked truth is that England had no other choice than to try to win a few years' time. Mr. Chamberlain talked and let others talk; he built castles in Spain and let others build them.

1937 went by. Germany's superiority kept increasing. In Russia, marshals and generals were executed as traitors, and tens of thousands of officials of all ranks were purged. In France, dissension continued. Appeasers and traitors were active.

Came 1938 and the game was up. In February, Hitler threw out the last few "moderates" who had been sitting in his antechambers as *décor*. The preparatory period was over and the pirate ship ran up the black flag.

German divisions massed on the Austrian frontier. Hitler's headquarters were in Berchtesgaden. Chivalrous von Papen dragged Chancellor Schuschnigg to the Fuehrer who ordered him to sign eleven conditions at once. These implied the handing over of Austria to its native Nazis. If possible Hitler preferred a "legal" annexation. Helpless Schuschnigg parleyed for a whole day. Finally, he was permitted to sign only three conditions on the spot; it was agreed that he would give his answer on the other eight from Vienna. Then he returned home.

From that day on every government knew what was in store for Austria. If the League of Nations and collective security had any reality, they had to assert themselves now in order to save Austria—and more than Austria. "Austrian independence is supremely important," Sir Austen Chamberlain, Neville's brother, had written. "If Austria goes, Czechoslovakia will be indefensible, and all the Balkans will be subjected to a new irresistible influence. The old German dream of a subjected Central Europe extending to the Mediterranean and the Black Sea will become a reality." [16] Only a few years before, in 1932, Europe had been plunged into a serious crisis as a result of Bruening's Anschluss project.

But it was too late. Even those governments and parties that saw all this had to resign themselves to the inevitable. And there were others who even approved. As it happened, the unfortunate Austrian Chancellor failed to comply with the rest of Hitler's ultimatum. He prepared a plebiscite on the question of Austrian independence invoking the right to "self-determination." Hitler saw that "legal" annexation would not work, and ordered his army to march. On March 12th, 1938, General von Bock entered Austria.

No one budged. Europe was silent and paralyzed.

The British military budget for 1938 amounted to 350 million pounds, most of it for the fleet. Aside from the smallness of the sum, the deceptive character of budget figures was well-known. It was a long way from appropriations of money to their transformation into actual weapons. Dispelling recent optimism over British aviation, the government was forced to admit that the 1,750 planes which were to be ready by 1937 would not actually be in service before 1939. There was a bottleneck which Churchill called a "mystery"; [17] for some time production declined instead of increasing, and factories had to work at half their capacity because something or other had gone wrong.

But compared to France the British situation was ideal. The Popular Front had burst asunder. Daladier's party was back in the saddle. The cries of alarm over the state

of French aviation multiplied. The government was at
last forced to investigate. It was discovered that the
French air force was rotten at its very core. The aircraft
industry was producing junk. During 1937 it had managed to produce 38 planes a month, and toward the
beginning of 1938 increased production to a full 41 a
month. It was still on a 1918 basis; the total value of its
machine tools was 42 million francs, one million dollars.
Only now did France begin to study the problem of tool-
ing it with modern machines, and only in June, 1938,
were these machines contracted for. The most optimistic
estimates foresaw a production of 100 planes a month toward the beginning of 1939, and 200 planes by the middle of that year. For a long time France could not build
in one year as many planes as could be shot down in one
week.

And Hitler granted the world no breathing spell. On
the day of his annexation of Austria he opened his campaign against Czechoslovakia, demanding the Sudetenland which contained some of his beloved German
fellow-nationals and the Czech fortifications. Once again
the world shuddered at the sound of his imprecations and
the threatening tramp of his troops. The Czechs knew
that their existence was at stake. They had an army and
were ready to fight. No one even mentioned the League
of Nations: it was now admittedly dead. The Czechs appealed to their allies: to Russia, France, and indirectly,
through France, to England. Whether the Czechs would
submit or not depended upon the attitude of their allies.
Help us and risk war, Benes urged them. Do not help
them and secure peace, said Hitler.

Once again the democracies were at the crossroads. It
was by now a familiar situation, but this time Hitler,

backed by the two other gangsters and Colonel Beck's
Poles, was even more overwhelmingly superior than before. Daladier raised his eyes with horror from the text
of the Franco-Czech alliance to the French skies, empty
of planes, to his arsenals, empty of anti-tank artillery. Mr.
Chamberlain considered the situation of his French ally
and his own barracks empty of troops and his air fields on
which planes were only beginning to gather at a snail-
like pace. Once again in this ghastly chess game no good
move was possible. War meant catastrophe. Dodging war
meant another catastrophe. Which was worse? Which
course was more ruinous?

Opinion was divided. There was the criterion of honor
and morality. From the moral point of view the situation
was clear as far as France, Czechoslovakia's ally, and
England, France's ally, were concerned. According to this
criterion, war had to be accepted. And as usual there
were many arguments and illusions in support of this
thesis. Perhaps Hitler would be deterred if he were confronted with a will to resist to the utmost. Perhaps the
democracies were not as weak as they seemed. Perhaps
Czechoslovakia could withstand the onslaught. Perhaps
Russia, though she had no common frontier with Germany, could and would send speedy help. Perhaps an
earlier war was better than a late one.

But there was also the realistic criterion. Czechoslovakia was lost, even if war were accepted on her behalf.
There was no chance that she could withstand the German nutcracker, that she could be given direct assistance. Her fate would be sealed on the fourth or eighth
day of the war, and the war would then be a war without Czechoslovakia. If this was the case, what was lost if
war was avoided? The same group, France-England-Rus-

sia, that would have to fight without Czechoslovakia now, could also fight without her later. There was no indication, no warning, no likelihood, that one member of this group would fall out. From a strictly realistic point of view it seemed worthwhile to lose Czechoslovakia— which was lost anyhow—in order to gain time. This thesis, too, was supported by arguments and illusions. Perhaps it was true that Hitler wanted only to bring his Sudeten German brothers into the German Reich; at least one could hope so. Perhaps it was even true that the Sudetenland was his last claim, and that, having obtained it, he would be satisfied. Perhaps it was even desirable not to give the Bolsheviks an opportunity to advance with their armies. Perhaps it was desirable that the French lose their eastern alliances which could no longer be backed up with real strength. Thus the real reason for not acting, the terrible all-pervading weakness of the democracies, was rationalized.

Mr. Chamberlain decided to abandon Czechoslovakia, which was lost anyway. A gain of two years or even of one year might mean the difference between life and death, the difference between an R.A.F. capable of defending the English skies at the beginning of the conflict or an impotent R.A.F. Mr. Chamberlain stubbornly stuck to his line, and no doubt the overwhelming majority of the people, both in England and France, were on his side. Aside from the Communists, only small circles in each country were ready for war. The leaders of the Left were depressed and evasive. Their followers were for Chamberlain's policy. The Right had made up its mind, and the French clique of civil war maniacs and traitors displayed such exultation that even Charles Maurras, the old high priest of Royalism, the most extreme of the anti-Republicans, anti-democrats and anti-Semites, cried out indignantly: "There are certain conservatives in France, who fill us with disgust. Why? Because of their stupidity. What kind of stupidity? Hitlerism. These French 'conservatives' crawl on their bellies before Hitler. These former nationalists cringe before him. A few zealots wallow in dirt, in their own dirt, with endless Heils. The wealthier they are, the more they own, the more important it is to make them understand that if Hitler invaded us he would skin them much more thoroughly than Blum, Thorez and Stalin combined. This 'conservative' error is suicidal. We must appeal to our friends not to let themselves be befogged. We must tell them: be on your guard! What is now at stake is not anti-democracy or anti-Semitism: France above all!" [18]

Came Munich. Seven-eighths of the French and English were jubilant. The party of honor and morality veiled its face. Once again, as a consequence of their lamentable military weakness, the democracies had landed in a morass of demoralization. "I am divided between a feeling of shame and cowardly relief," was M. Léon Blum's comment on Munich, which adequately sums up the situation. There can be no doubt that Daladier and Chamberlain, too, were divided when they had to make the decisive move. They knew that they had a choice only between bad and worse. Apart from the shameful moral spectacle presented it may be questioned whether the choice they made was really worse than the other alternative. Would the world have fared better if the war had begun in 1938 instead of 1939? In retrospect, now that the emotions aroused by the Czech crisis have died down, it is clear that the effect of the sins committed during the two previous decades was overwhelming even then. If all the reasons for which the victory of the First World War begot the blackest hours of the Second were to be listed Munich would occupy an inconspicuous place.

The ink of the Munich agreement had scarcely dried when Ribbentrop declared that "slowly, but irresistibly, the old world is sinking. Nothing can now stop Germany on her path." [19] And Goebbels declared: "It does not often happen that the earth is redivided. Once it is apparent that the hour is ripe and that the goddess of history is dragging her mantle over mankind, responsible men must have the courage to grasp the edge of this mantle and cling to it. I am convinced that today we are passing through just such a historic moment." [20] The Italian Chamber of Deputies, under the majestic gaze of the Duce, staged a fifteen minute demonstration shouting: "Tunisia! Corsica! Savoia!" In Asia, the Japanese landed in south China.

1939.

Mussolini fell upon Albania and devoured her. Hitler fell upon the rest of Czechoslovakia and devoured her. The fiction that he was interested only in his German brethren, that it was possible to make an agreement with him, was forever dispelled. On March 17th, 1939, in his speech at Birmingham, Chamberlain announced the end of the appeasement policy toward Germany. From now on force would oppose force. London assumed a new tone.

But then, suddenly, Moscow, too, assumed a new tone. After all the accusations of democratic unwillingness to risk war, suddenly there came the vague accusation that the democracies were warmongering. After all the accusations that Hitler was being manoeuvred into a war against the Soviets, there came the sudden accusation that the democracies wanted to manoeuvre the Soviets into a war against Hitler. "We will not pull other people's chestnuts out of the fire!"[21] exclaimed Stalin on March 10th, 1939, at the XVIIth Congress of the Russian Communist Party. "Our people may rest assured that we will not be drawn into the adventures of the capitalist powers,"[22] said Voroshilov, on May 1st, 1939.

The week following his entry into Prague, Hitler suddenly bared his teeth against Poland. For five years Foreign Minister Beck had been a valet and accomplice of the Nazis. He had fallen upon Czechoslovakia at the same time as Hitler. Now, in spite of the vaunted Polish-German friendship, Hitler began to exert the same terror against Warsaw that he had formerly exerted against Prague. Following a German ultimatum concerning the corridor and Danzig, Poland mobilized part of her army, and asked for assistance. This time, England's resolution to stop Hitler was evident. She hastily concluded a military alliance with Poland, then with Rumania and Greece, Italy's new neighbor. She hastily introduced conscription (April 26th, 1939). It was clear that this time she meant business, that if Hitler let loose his armies against Poland there would be war.

And at the exact moment when this was made clear, Maxim Litvinov, Commissar for Foreign Affairs, was dismissed. His successor made a speech which, far from mentioning "indivisible peace," declared that Hitler's intentions were "clearly directed only against the chief democratic powers in Europe."[23] Moreover, England and France were both accused of "warmongering" and preparing new capitulations. The vice-Commissar for Foreign Affairs refused to accept a conference with the French and English foreign Ministers. And War Commissar Voroshilov rejected an invitation to attend the British war manoeuvres (on June 3rd, 1939). A ceaseless propaganda around the slogan "don't pull other people's chestnuts out of the fire," swept through the Russian press. The special envoy sent from London to Moscow to conclude an Anglo-Russian alliance and offer a common guarantee to the small states on Russia's western borders made no headway. The Franco-British military commission sent to Moscow made no headway, either.

Italy and Germany announced that the Axis had become a firm alliance. The Polish crisis grew increasingly acute. On August 24th the world was stunned by the news that Stalin and Hitler had concluded a pact of neutrality and friendship; Stalin, too, had had the brilliant idea of retiring into isolation, the same brilliant idea that the King of the Belgians, the King of Rumania, the Prince Regent of Yugoslavia and Colonel Beck of Poland had had before him. And Russian isolationism had a little Rapallo twist to it. Russia's strongest international asset was her propaganda potential which during the long period when the Rapallo agreement was in force, had always worked in favor of Germany. This interrupted tradition was now resumed. Russia's isolationism was only material isolationism; her international propaganda favored Germany at the expense of her enemies.

Stalin's motives may be debatable; the question will always remain an important one. But Russian isolationism was a fact. England and France, with a Poland doomed to rapid defeat, stood alone in the world. They stood alone on land and in the air facing an immensely superior Germany. The war could begin now. . . . It did begin. The cycle of two accursed decades was closed.

10: *Darkness and Light*

T HEY SAT in Bordeaux, endlessly calculating how many miles closer the Germans had come. Their war had been just like their peace. After the outbreak of war, the two democracies had remained under the same blight as before: their only purpose, now as before, could be to win a few years' time in order to regenerate their military might. War had actually become the "continuation of politics by other means." The democracies' only possible grand strategy was to postpone the decisive battles as much as possible. The battles might be fought in 1941, 1942, 1943. The democracies hoped and prayed for that postponement.

Hitler did not wait. He fell upon the democracy which was most accessible. The worst anticipations of the French in 1919 came true. They had warned of their inevitable weakness in a new war. Even the promised alliance with the two Anglo-Saxon Great Powers had failed to allay their fears. They had wrangled and begged for the establishment of an advance bastion between France and Germany, manned by the troops of all the three Western democracies: a collective Maginot Line. This alone, they had repeatedly warned, would guarantee "that French territory will not be overrun in a few days."

Now French territory was overrun in a few days. The French leaders sat in Bordeaux, amidst indescribable chaos, trying to choose between surrender and continuation of the struggle from Africa. The civilian government collapsed and handed power over to an old marshal. Even during the last war, it was notorious that Pétain, under the mask of majestic serenity, was a defeatist of the worst kind. Poincaré, Clemenceau and Foch had stopped their ears not to hear the unbearable pessimistic utterances in which the Marshal indulged at every crisis. He had intended to give up Verdun as untenable; the civilians had forced him to hold it, and to be victorious. He had wanted to give up Amiens and the Channel coast; he had had to be forced to hold them. Now again this man, so prone to succumb to defeat, failed to see a glimmer of hope anywhere. France was overrun. England would inevitably be overrun in a few weeks. Everything was over.

Laval went farther. Displaying a feverish energy he tried to convince everyone that Hitler would be merciful, that he really had nothing against France, that his real objectives were England, the Left, democracy and Bolshevism. He argued that if France surrendered now, Hitler would not treat her as a defeated enemy, that if France did what she should have done long before, if she broke with England, crushed democracy and exterminated the Communists, he would accept her as a belated, but welcome convert. A man of many intrigues, he had never cut his connections with Berlin, and he exploited this fact to give his statements a semblance of authority. Pierre Laval felt the hour of revenge coming closer. Indefatigably he directed the manoeuvres of his followers. The idea of a retreat to Africa was abandoned. Pétain capitulated.

Thus a destiny was accomplished in which all the evil of two accursed decades was focussed. The French war, rout and collapse symbolize the guilt piled up by the whole democratic world during twenty years of folly.

This guilt consisted not only in France's inadequate armaments. Even with the arms she had, although her defeat was still inevitable, she could have waged a more manly, more dignified, more courageous fight. Even with her European territory overrun and her army crushed, she could have continued the war on sea and in the colonies.

The French mind and the French soul had become brittle in all classes of society, in all ranks, in the army and among civilians. France's inglorious fight and submission were brought about by her soul's disease. The Right and the Left, France herself and France's allies of 1918, had contributed to the disease. No French faction had the right to point at another and say: this one is guilty. No country, no matter how righteous, could accuse crushed France. All of them, in the course of twenty years, had contributed their share. A world, an epoch, ended with the collapse of France.

The character of the Frenchmen who took over the stage in the last act of the tragedy was seen only too clearly. The appeasers of the Right had agitated from the very first day of the war. With the help of all the adopted pacifist slogans, they carried on a whispering propaganda denouncing the war as unnecessary and criminal. In good faith out of stupidity, or in bad faith as traitors, they had done their part to weaken France's will to fight. When in the end the German Panzer divisions advanced, the law that those emerge in time of defeat who most resemble the conqueror asserted itself. The Lavals and de Brinons completely dominated the last scenes of the last act.

But that was the death agony, not the disease which had brought the whole organism down to this level of impotence. The guilt goes further back, and it was ubiquitous.

A large part of the guilt is borne by those Frenchmen who had inculcated into their people the idea that all nations are equal, that they are all good and brotherly; that all wars are undertakings by capitalists, munitions makers and "imperialists"; that every war is waged only against the humble people; that all armies are weapons of class oppression, that all soldiers are only cannon fodder and all generals "drinkers of blood." The Communists had interrupted their destructive propaganda for four years but after the Stalin-Hitler pact they resumed it with renewed violence. Half of the Socialist leaders, more than half, had tried during the last three years to free themselves from the traditional mythology. But how could growths embedded for decades and decades be uprooted within three years? The soldiers lay in casemates and trenches, under a barrage of shells and bombs, and thought: What has all this got to do with me? Why die for the capitalists?

A large part of the guilt was borne by the other nations and governments who decided to believe that mankind had suddenly become different from what it had always been; who had prevented France from achieving security after four years of hell; who had deprived her of every fruit of her victory; who suspected and abused her and always took the side of Germany. The French of all classes grew weary and embittered: what was the purpose of victory, they thought, if we are not permitted to gather its fruits? Why suffer and bleed and die, if in the end we are abandoned and forced to go through the same hell twenty years later?

A large part of the guilt was borne by a whole generation, in France and outside of France, which was corrupted by nihilism and perfectionism and complacency. The real world and its values had, for them, fallen into oblivion. The most important thing of all, a secure minimum standard of freedom and law, of human dignity and morality, was either taken for granted or regarded as a swindle. All efforts were focussed on material progress. It was assumed that mankind could devote itself entirely to improving the standards previously attained, whereas in fact it must always be devoted to preserving them by dint of struggle and sacrifices. It was forgotten that there can be no rights without duties. People lived in an unreal world, from which the eternal forces of evil had been dreamed and chattered away, and which imaginary good fairies had filled with charity, harmony and comfort. People got into the habit of demanding less from themselves, of counting extravagantly upon others. It was a world which frivolously dismissed 5,000 years of history and enthroned all sorts of optimistic hypotheses. The French had been living in the softness of an emasculated age; they went into battle in the same spirit and plunged into catastrophe.

With France, a whole age of complacency collapsed. The first phase of the war ended in grim disaster.

A second entirely different phase will be born of the first, a war waged in a different spirit and with different forces. But for a long time, which cannot as yet be measured, the war will drag along the heritage of the first phase. The loss of the French army was not the only result of that first phase. The collapse of France also immobilized the British army and confined it to the defense of the British Isles. But the worst consequence of the French defeat, which became gradually clear, was the one of which the French had so insistently warned in 1919: the irreplacable nature of France as a purely geographic entity. Tardieu's memorandum had explained this quite clearly: "Should there not remain enough French ports for the overseas armies to debark their troops and war supplies, should there not remain enough French territory for them to concentrate and operate from their bases, the overseas democracies would be debarred from waging a continental war against any power seeking to dominate the continent. They would be deprived of their nearest and most natural battleground. Nothing could be left to them but naval and economic warfare."

The second phase of the war began with a grandiose resurgence. The crash of the French collapse awakened England from her trance. The Channel, that miraculous strip of water which had so often saved England, once again granted her the most precious of all gifts: time to rally morally and materially. A new England was born from the misery of her loneliest, blackest hours. The good old England re-emerged. She had the good fortune to find a leader whose right to leadership had been tested in many years of political activity. For twenty years Winston Churchill had defied the temptation of popularity, refusing to be taken in by the hocus-pocus of the accursed decades. In an erring world, he had not erred on any essential issue. He had been almost alone in his own country, and now his country sought his guidance. England, awakening and rallying in darkest night, at the very edge of the abyss, found her Clemenceau. In tears and toil and blood and sweat she began to forge her resurrection.

And this miracle was followed by another. In a world, in which everything, everyone, one government after another, one country after another, had fled from solidarity to isolationism, a country and a government appeared which moved forward from isolationism toward solidarity. Mr. Roosevelt refused to be a mere spectator of England's fall. He gathered whatever there was at hand to help a sister democracy survive. A country which had been in a trance as much as any other and which will have to suffer the consequences, began to free itself from the spell, and to understand. It began to scrap Utopias and to prepare itself step by step for realistic action.

And Stalin's isolationism collapsed, as had Minister Beck's, King Leopold's, King Carol's and Prince Paul's. Hitler refused to tolerate it. War gripped Russia. And a new miracle was seen: an army which, instead of melting away like butter in a frying pan, waged battle. The Russian army fought in 1941 and 1942 as it had fought in 1812 or in 1914–1917. It fought even while it retreated and suffered reverses.

And Japan struck. There was the morning of Pearl Harbor, and war came to America. The last great power, the greatest of all, took leave of the spirit of peace. The fate of mankind now rested on America's shoulders and on the military might growing in her training camps and war factories.

A new war was born. Its course cannot be clearly discerned. The state of the world on the day of victory cannot be foreseen; and the details of the order which will have to be created are uncertain. But rarely has mankind been better prepared for a tremendous task, than it is for the next peace settlement. The same problem had to be solved before, and was dealt with unsuccessfully. The story of this failure is still in our memories. In chemistry small-scale tests can be made and their results used. History knows no laboratory tests. Its experiments are always full-scale and everything is at stake. The experiment of 1919 and the following two decades had the most crushing consequences; nevertheless, it was an experiment. For all the misery it produced, the world at least has the advantage of being able to study it. Almost all the problems of the future were problems of the past; almost all the projects and hypotheses put forward to solve them have been tested during the last twenty years. All plans that are not based on a thorough study of these twenty years are dilletantish or Utopian.

We must profit to the utmost from the terrible fact that we are experiencing the same thing for the second time. Let us learn everything we can from the verdict branded with a red-hot iron on the tablet of history. Even then many questions will remain open; but many mistakes will be avoided. Even then there will still be room for dreams and poetry; but the language of bitter experience will be concrete, clear, and earthy.

Dispelled forever is the dream of 1918, that once Germany, this powerful, energetic and highly gifted nation is freed from its bad rulers, it will be saved and become like the other nations. It will not. Not because of any unalterable racial characteristics, but because its spirit and instincts have been molded by an age-long education and tradition. It is these which have produced its predatory and self-destructive extremism; and if one lost World War did not suffice to cure the Germans, a second lost war will not, in all human probability, suffice either. If the operation was unsuccessful after the relatively mild Hohenzollern infection, it will be all the more unsuccessful after the virulent Hitler infection. The products of education and tradition can be changed only by new education and new traditions. Unfortunately there is little hope that the

German people will reform itself by its own forces under its own control; at best, this process would take generations. The voice of twenty years warns us that for a long time to come we cannot risk leaving Germany to her own devices.

An extremist nation like the German cannot be made harmless for the world and itself by relative half-hearted disarmament. There is no hope of really and effectively demilitarizing Germany as long as she is left with nuclei in which her militaristic traditions can be continued and rebuilt at the first opportunity. Before Germany can be called demilitarized, generations will have to pass of which no one has ever held a gun in his hand, or crouched behind a machine gun, or served a cannon or a tank or an airplane, or had anything to do with the manufacture of weapons or the handling of troops. Only then will it be possible to hope that the military tradition which is the curse of the Germans as well as of their neighbors has been interrupted. There must be no room for any ideas of "equality" or "equal rights" on this point. The voice of twenty years warns us that the idea of German equality must not have the slightest bearing upon military questions.

Never again must we succumb to the myth that power and armaments and compulsion are of themselves sinful and evil as such. They can be the opposite as well. All order, all civilization, all law and dignity, rest on the existence of weapons and power. They have achieved their highest triumph if they are so effective that they can remain almost invisible; and if they are never put to use that very possibility requires that they exist. Without them, the law of the jungle and anarchy prevail within each nation and among nations. The "moral" value of power and weapons and compulsions is determined exclusively by the purpose they serve. It is a great misfortune when the defenders of peace, justice and freedom are infected with formalism and relativism and begin to doubt their own motives. Everything is lost when indecision undermines and paralyzes these defenders. This indecision was one of the tragedies of the accursed decades. The voice of twenty years warns us to defend peace and justice and freedom with pride and assurance; to accumulate weapons; to build up superiority; and to cultivate and use these instruments of freedom with wisdom and resolution.

Never again must we believe that in the work of securing peace, can power and compulsion be replaced by any economic or social magic. Social and economic developments made great strides during the last twenty years, but they contributed nothing to the preservation of the peace. The connection between economic progress and war or peace is a mythical one. Germany went to war in 1914, when she was one of the richest "have" countries. In 1939, she went to war when she was allegedly a "have not."

The preservation of peace consists in securing our house from external attacks. Social progress consists in improving its internal organization. There is no relation between the two tasks. We should perform the second as we see fit, but we must never fall into the delusion that thereby the first is also performed. Once peace is concluded, it can be used for social progress; but this simply means that the same opportunity is being used for furthering two tasks, which, nevertheless, remain unrelated. Internal social progress does not insure mankind against new wars. The voice of twenty years warns us that tanks and guns can crush a land of milk and honey as easily as a land of stones and barren soil. No magic of prosperity and social justice is capable of checking the hungry lust for power.

Never again can we believe that any new magic can achieve what we ourselves must achieve by hard work. Mankind is not capable of sudden rebirths. The Egyptians and Jews and Greeks and Romans were not a whit more stupid than we are; their problems were in no essential respect different from ours; their desires and yearnings and dreams were the same as ours. There are good reasons for the fact that the millennium has never materialized. Mankind and human communities change their essential nature in the course of thousands of years as little as the wolf and the pack of wolves or the sheep and the herd of sheep, change theirs. No, the task has always been the same. Against the eternally lurking jungle, weapons and compulsion are always the only defense and nothing liberates us from the duty of doing the utmost for ourselves. New attempts may be made to create a sort of League of Nations. In truth, the prospects of ever creating a reliable league of sovereign states are as good as non-existent. No human brain has ever been able to show how the collective will of mankind can be made compatible with the continued existence of individual sovereign states wielding individual sovereign power. But even the existence of such a league must never distract us from developing our own power and will to the maximum. Even such a league in point of fact lives only on the will, power and strength of the great powers belonging to it. All the other powers, the middle and the small ones, impressive as their abstract sum may be, are only satellites which gravitate around the great powers. And if the great powers have a common will, everything is well. If not, there is no collectivity, and once again we are alone; with our nearest friends we are thrown back on our resources. We must always be prepared for that eventuality. The voice of twenty years warns us that in the business of enforcing peace and order there is no substitute for our own will and our own power.

And never again believe that the unpleasantness, sacrifices and responsibilities that all this implies are too heavy and too great to be borne. They are heavy and they are serious. It is a burden to police the world, or at least its most dangerous quarters. It demands work and energy to see to it that no weapons are accumulated in dangerous hands. It demands toil and effort to prevent the establishment of dictatorships, those definitely intolerable neighbors for democracies. It is neither easy nor inexpensive.

But it is a thousand times easier and less expensive than any of its alternatives. And it is incomparably more pleasant than the consequences of hesitation and belief in Utopian experiments. And it is practical. The voice of twenty years tells us not to be afraid. There is nothing under the sun that must not be paid for with toil and labor.

Notes

Chapter 1

1. Woodrow Wilson, Address in Baltimore, Apr. 6, 1918.
2. *Papers relating to the Foreign Affairs of the U.S.A.* 1918, Supplement 1, p. 355.
3. Ibid.
4. Ibid. Supplement 1, Vol. I, p. 349.
5. Seymour: *The Intimate Papers of Col. House,* Vol. IV, p. 75.
6. Note to Germany, Oct. 23, 1918.
7. Note to Germany, Oct. 14, 1918.
8. Seymour: *The Intimate Papers of Col. House,* Vol. IV, p. 77.
9. Ibid., p. 78.
10. Lloyd George: *War Memoirs,* Vol. VI, p. 260.
11. Ray Stannard Baker: *Woodrow Wilson, Life and Letters,* Vol. VIII, p. 466.
12. William E. Dodd: *Woodrow Wilson and His Work,* p. 354.
13. Ray Stannard Baker: *Woodrow Wilson, Life and Letters,* Vol. VII, p. 572.
14. Pershing: *My Experiences in the World War,* Vol. I, p. 390.
15. Ray Stannard Baker, op. cit., Vol. VIII, p. 96.
16. Pershing, op. cit., Vol. II, p. 174.
17. Note to Germany, Oct. 23, 1918.
18. Ray Stannard Baker: *Woodrow Wilson, Life and Letters,* Vol. VIII, p. 500.
19. Seymour: *The Intimate Papers of Col. House,* Vol. IV, p. 93.
20. Raymond Recoouly: *My Conversations with Marshal Foch,* p. 246.
21. Seymour: *The Intimate Papers of Col. House,* Vol. IV, p. 145.
22. Pershing: *My Experiences in the World War,* Vol. II, p. 165.

23. Ray Stannard Baker: *Woodrow Wilson, Life and Letters,* Vol. VIII, p. 536.
24. General Mordacq: *L'Armistice du 11 November 1918,* pp. 164–166.
25. Ray Stannard Baker: *Woodrow Wilson, Life and Letters,* Vol. VIII, p. 523.
26. Address of February 11, 1918.
27. Seymour: *The Intimate Papers of Col. House,* Vol. IV, p. 243.
28. *Amtliche Urkunden zur Vorgeschichte des Waffenstillstands 1918, Herausgegeben vom Auswertigen Amt,* Berlin. No. 76a.
29. Seymour: *The Intimate Papers of Col. House,* Vol. IV, p. 65.
30. Ray Stannard Baker: *Woodrow Wilson, Life and Letters,* Vol. VII, p. 235.
31. Ibid., Vol. VII, p. 180.
32. Ray Stannard Baker: *Woodrow Wilson, Life and Letters,* Vol. VIII, p. 235.
33. Ibid., Vol. VII, p. 561.
34. Ibid., Vol. VII, p. 180.
35. Ibid., p. 500.
36. *Foreign Relations of the U.S.A.,* 1918, Suppl. 1, Vol. I, p. 424.
37. Ray Stannard Baker: *Woodrow Wilson, Life and Letters,* Vol. VII, p. 180.
38. *Foreign Relations of the U.S.A.,* 1918, Suppl. 1, Vol. I, p. 424.
39. Seymour: *The Intimate Papers of Col. House,* Vol. IV, pp. 162, 163.
40. Address of Sept. 27, 1918, "Five particulars."
41. Address of July 4, 1918, "Four ends."
42. Seymour: *The Intimate Papers of Col. House,* Vol. IV, p. 193.
43. Ibid., p. 165.
44. Ibid.
45. Ibid.
46. Ibid.
47. *Foreign Relations of the U.S.A.,* 1918, Suppl. 1, Vol. I, pp. 425, 426.
48. Ibid., p. 424.
49. Seymour: *The Intimate Papers of Col. House,* Vol. IV, p. 174.

50. Ray Stannard Baker: *Woodrow Wilson, Life and Letters,* Vol. VIII, p. 554.
51. Seymour: *The Intimate Papers of Col. House,* Vol. IV, p. 143.

Chapter 2

1. *Schulthess' Europäischer Geschichtskalender,* 1918, Vol. I, 305.
2. *Preliminary History of the Armistice,* No. 12.
3. *Schulthess' Europäischer Geschichtskalender,* 1918, Vol. I, p. 338.
4. Scheidemann: *The Making of New Germany,* Vol. II, p. 214.
5. Prince Max of Baden: *Memoirs,* Vol. II, p. 241.
6. Ibid.
7. Lutze: *Fall of the German Empire,* Vol. II, p. 543.
8. *Eine Ehrenrettung des deutschen Volkes. Der Dolchstoss-Prozess in München, Oktober-November 1925. Zeugen und Sachverständigen-Aussagen,* p. 217.
9. Prince Max of Baden: *Memoirs,* Vol. II, pp. 312–13.
10. Scheidemann: *The Making of New Germany,* Vol. II, p. 214.
11. William E. Dodd: *Woodrow Wilson and His Work,* p. 232.
12. *Vorwärts,* Oct. 31, 1918.
13. *Schulthess' Europäischer Geschichtskalender,* 1918, Vol. I, p. 342.
14. Prince Max of Baden, *Memoirs,* Vol. II, p. 362.
15. *Schulthess' Europäischer Geschichtskalender,* 1918, Vol. I, p. 338.
16. Gabriel Terrail (Mermeix): *Le Combat des Trois,* p. 212.
17. Seymour: *The Intimate Papers of Colonel House,* Vol. IV, p. 396.
18. Wickham Steed: *Is It Peace?, The Fortnightly,* Jan. 6, 1935.
19. Tardieu: *The Truth about the Treaty,* p. 96.
20. Clemenceau: *Grandeur and Misery of Victory,* p. 121.
21. Ibid., p. 100.
22. Ibid., p. 199.
23. Ibid.
24. Ibid.
25. Clemenceau: *Grandeur and Misery of Victory,* p. 105.

26. Jean Martet: *Le Tigre*, p. 284.
27. Jean Martet: *Georges Clemenceau*, p. 275.
28. J. M. Keynes: *The Economic Consequences of the Peace*, p. 29.
29. Ibid., p. 32.
30. Ibid., p. 33.
31. Ibid., p. 35.
32. Martet: *Le Tigre*, p. 72.
33. Martet: *Georges Clemenceau*, p. 20.
34. Clemenceau: *Grandeur and Misery of Victory*, p. 106.
35. Ibid., p. 154.
36. Martet: *Le Tigre*, p. 74.
37. Tardieu: *The Truth about the Treaty*, p. 96.
40. Ray Stannard Baker: *Woodrow Wilson, Life and Letters*, Vol. vii, p. 176.
41. Ibid., p. 203.
42. Ibid., p. 255.
43. Ray Stannard Baker: *Woodrow Wilson, Life and Letters*, Vol. viii, p. 38.
44. Ibid., p. 277.
45. Seymour: op.cit. iv, pp. 48–50.
46. H. W. V. Temperley: *History of the Peace Conference*, i, p. 174.
47. Ray Stannard Baker: *Woodrow Wilson, Life and Letters*, Vol. viii, p. 74.
48. Lloyd George: *Memoirs of the Peace Conference*, i, p. 359.
49. Ibid., p. 359.
50. Robert Lansing: *The Peace Negotiations*, p. 43.
51. George B. Noble: *Politics and Opinions in Paris*, p. 113.
52. David Hunter Miller: *Drafting of the Covenant*, i, p. 217.
53. J. M. Keynes: *The Economic Consequences of the Peace*, p. 33.
54. David Hunter Miller: op.cit. ii, p. 242.
55. Ray Stannard Baker: op.cit. viii, p. 43.
56. David Hunter Miller: op.cit. ii, p. 293.
57. Ibid., p. 295.
58. Ray Stannard Baker: op.cit. viii, p. 43.
59. Ibid., viii, p. 399.
60. Ray Stannard Baker: op.cit. viii, p. 235.
61. Hearing of September 12, 1919.
62. Clemenceau: *Grandeur and Misery of Victory*, p. 199.
63. David Hunter Miller: op.cit. ii, p. 359.
64. Ibid.

65. Seymour: op.cit. iv, p. 396.
66. Ibid.

Chapter 3

1. H. W. V. Temperley: *A History of the Peace Conference of Paris,* Vol. i, pp. 429–430.
2. Lloyd George: *Memoirs of the Peace Conference,* Vol. i, p. 77.
3. André Tardieu: *The Truth About the Treaty,* p. 166.
4. Ray Stannard Baker: *Woodrow Wilson and World Settlement,* Vol. iii, pp. 234, 235.
5. André Tardieu: *The Truth About the Treaty,* p. 166.
6. Lloyd George: op.cit., p. 308.
7. Ibid., p. 260.
8. Seymour: *The Intimate Papers of Col. House,* iv, p. 360.
9. André Tardieu, op.cit., p. 174.
10. Seymour: op.cit., p. 191.
11. Ibid.
12. Paul Birdsall: *Versailles Twenty Years After,* p. 204.
13. Ibid., p. 207.
14. Seymour: op.cit., pp. 280, 281.
15. Ibid.
16. Ibid.
17. Lloyd George, op.cit., p. 285.
18. *Congressional Record,* Senate, Aug. 23, 1918.
19. William E. Dodd: *Woodrow Wilson and His Work,* p. 294.
20. *Congressional Record,* Senate, Dec. 21, 1918.
21. Ibid.
22. Ibid.
23. Ibid.
24. Winston Churchill: *The Aftermath,* p. 193.
25. Ibid.
26. Ibid.
27. Ray Stannard Baker: *Woodrow Wilson, Life and Letters,* Vol. vii, p. 235.
28. Robert Lansing: *The Big Four,* pp. 114–116.
29. Ray Stannard Baker: *Woodrow Wilson and World Settlement,* Vol. iii, pp. 291–295.
30. Robert Lansing: op.cit., pp. 114–116.

31. *Schulthess' Europäischer Geschichtskalender*, Vol. 1918, December 4.
32. Ibid.
33. Tardieu: op.cit., p. 208.
34. Tardieu's Memorandum to the Peace Conference, Feb. 9, 1919, as quoted in his book, *The Truth About the Treaty*, p. 149.
35. Ibid.
36. Ray Stannard Baker: *Woodrow Wilson and World Settlement*, Vol. ii, p. 11.
37. Tardieu: op.cit., p. 181.
38. Ibid., p. 185.
39. Treaty of Versailles, Art. 429.
40. Ibid., Part viii, Annex ii, Art. 18.
41. Ibid., Art. 213.
42. Tardieu: op.cit., pp. 206, 207.
43. Gabriel Terrail (Mermeix): *Le Combat des Trois*, p. 230.
44. Tardieu: op.cit., p. 433.
45. Isaiah, Chapter ii.
46. Jean Martet: *Georges Clemenceau*, p. 20.

Chapter 4

1. *Eine Ehrenrettung des deutschen Volkes*. Des Dolchstoss-Prozess in München, Oktober-November 1925, Zeugen und Sachverständingen-Aussagen, p. 244.
2. Treaty of Versailles, Art. 227.
3. Ibid., Art. 228.
4. Lloyd George: *Memoirs of the Peace Conference*, Vol. i, p. 55.
5. Ibid., p. 57.
6. Temperley: *A History of the Peace Conference of Paris*, Vol. iii, p. 306.
7. Deputy Kahl, German Constitutional Assembly, Session of June 22, 1919.
8. Temperley: op.cit., p. 306.
9. *Preussische Kreuzzeitung*, May 11, 1919.
10. German newspapers of June 24, 1919.
11. Ibid., Jan. 7, 1920.
12. Stosch: *Die Kriegsbeschuldigtenfrage*, p. 60.
13. Note of November 19, 1919.

14. Claude Mullins: *The Leipzig Trials, Preface of Sir Ernest Pollock*, p. 10.
15. Ibid., p. 17.

Chapter 5

1. Margarete Ludendorff: *Als ich Ludendorff's Frau war.*, p. 271.
2. Trebitsch-Lincoln: *Autobiography of an Adventurer*, p. 158.
3. Ibid., p. 159.
4. *National Review*, London, April, 1920, p. 155.
5. Lüttwitz: *Im Kampf gegen die November-Revolution*, p. 121.
6. Lord Riddell: *Intimate Diary*, p. 196.
7. Ibid., p. 188.
8. Bergmann: *Der Weg der Reparation*, p. 155.
9. House of Commons, May 25, 1922.
10. Lord d'Abernon, Vol. i, p. 269.
11. Ibid.
12. *Le Temps*, March 28, 1922.
13. Ibid.
14. Bergmann, op.cit., p. 163.
15. Edward Grigg: *The Greatest Experiment in History*, p. 131.
16. April 21, 1922.
17. House of Commons, May 25, 1922.
18. Saxon Mills: *The Genoa Conference, Preface by Lloyd George.*
19. Ibid.
20. House of Commons, Feb. 16, 1923.
21. *Livre Jaune*, p. 31.
22. Ibid., p. 32.
23. *Livre Jaune*, ii, p. 50.
24. House of Lords, February 13, 1923.
25. Chamber of Deputies, January 11, 1923.
26. Speech in Bar-le-Duc, April 23, 1923.
27. June 14, 1923.
28. Stresemann: *Memoirs, Letter to the Crown Prince*, July 23, 1923.
29. Note of August 11, 1923.

30. R. Poincaré: *Récit Historique,* p. 226.
31. *Vorwärts,* Berlin, May 22, 1924.

Chapter 6

1. Lord d'Abernon: *The Diary of an Ambassador,* Febr. 9, 1925.
2. Ibid., Jan. 21, 1925.
3. Petrie: *Life and Letters of Austen Chamberlain,* Vol. II, p. 256.
4. House of Commons, March 24, 1924.
5. Stresemann: *Vermächtnis,* Vol. II, p. 91.
6. Wolf von Dewall: *Der Kampf um den Frieden,* p. 122.
7. Stresemann: op.cit., p. 553.
8. Ibid., p. 70.
9. Petrie: op.cit., p. 255.
11. Ibid., pp. 250–260.
12. House of Commons, March 24, 1925.
13. Session of Oct. 16, 1925.
14. Stresemann: op.cit., p. 1941.
15. Ibid.
16. Ibid., p. 196.
17. Briand, Dec. 1, 1925.
18. House of Commons, Nov. 19, 1925.
19. Speech of November 11, 1925.
20. Stresemann: op.cit., p. 553.
21. Stresemann: *Vermächtnis,* Vol. II, p. 553.
22. Ibid.
23. German memorandum of September 23, 1924.
24. Annex F to Locarno agreements, October 16, 1925.
25. Lord d'Abernon: *Diary of an Ambassador,* Vol. III, p. 240.
26. Ibid.
27. Reichstag Session of March 23, 1926.
28. *London Times,* Nov. 4, 1933.
29. Petrie: *Life and Letters of Austen Chamberlain,* Vol. II, p. 228.
30. Stresemann: op.cit., p. 553.
31. Briand, *Message to America,* April 6, 1927.
32. Ibid.
33. Bryn-Jones: *Frank B. Kellogg,* p. 231.
34. Ibid., p. 232.

35. Pact of Paris, Aug. 27, 1928.
36. Bryn-Jones: op.cit., p. 239.
37. Reichstag Session of Feb. 1, 1929.
38. Leon Archimbaud: *La Conference de Washington*, p. 121.
39. Council of Foreign Relations, Feb. 17, 1922.
40. Lancelot Lawton: *The Evasion of Washington*, Fortnightly Review, 1922.
41. F. Buell: *The Washington Conference*.
42. Conference in the Royal Colonial Institute, May 9, 1922: United Empire, 1922, p. 371.
43. Terrail: *Le Combat des Trois*, p. 230.
44. Stresemann: *Memoirs, Letter to the Crown Prince*, July 23, 1923.

Chapter 7

2. *Schulthess' Europäischer Geschichtskalender*, Vol. 1929, Dec. 6.
3. Ibid.
4. Reichstag Session, Feb. 11, 1940.
5. Schulthess: op.cit., p. 126.
6. Ibid.
7. Ibid.
8. Ibid., Aug. 31.
9. Ibid., Vol. 1930, Dec. 3.
10. Ibid., Dec. 7.
11. Ibid.
12. Ibid., March 30.
13. Ibid. Aug. 16.
14. Ibid.
15. Ibid., Feb. 11.
16. Ibid., Oct. 16.
17. Ibid.
18. Ibid., Aug. 10.
19. Briand, Chambre des Deputés, session of March 3, 1931.
20. Briand, French Senate, session of March 28, 1931.
21. Schulthess: Vol. 1931, March 23.
22. Arnold J. Toynbee: *Survey of International Affairs*, Vol. 1931, p. 306.
23. Briand, French Senate, Session of May 28, 1931.
24. Henry L. Stimson: *The Far Eastern Crisis*, p. 82.

25. Ibid., p. 42.
26. Ibid., p. 20.
27. Ibid., p. 71.
28. Schulthess: Vol. 1931, Sept. 1924.
29. Ibid.
30. Henry L. Stimson: op.cit., p. 56.
31. Ibid.
32. Ibid., p. 153.
33. Ibid., p. 77.
34. *Le Temps,* Oct. 27, 1931.
35. Ibid.
36. House of Commons, May 13, 1932.
37. *Manchester Guardian,* Aug. 3, 1942.
38. Arnold J. Toynbee: op.cit., Vol. 1932, p. 541.
39. Ibid.
40. Lytton—Report, p. 127. . .

Chapter 8

1. Ernst Roehm: *Die Geschichte eines Hochverräters,* p. 361.
2. Ibid.
3. Ibid., p. 366.
4. Adolf Hitler: *Mein Kampf,* German Edition, p. 754.
5. Ibid., p. 438.
6. Ibid., p. 315.
7. Ibid., p. 438.
8. Ewald Banse: *Germany Prepares for War,* p. 15.
9. Dr. Schweyer, quoted by Konrad Heiden, *Das Neue Tage-buch,* Paris, Vol. 1933, October 16.
10. Ibid.
11. *Schulthess' Europäischer Geschichtskalender,* Vol. 1930, Oct. 18.
12. Leopold Schwarzschild: *End to Illusion,* pp. 226–231.
13. House of Commons, March 23, 1933.
14. Speech at Scarborough, *Manchester Guardian,* May 17, 1933.
15. House of Commons, Nov. 14, 1933.
16. Ibid.
17. *Le Temps,* April 8, 1933.
18. Speech at Scarborough, *Manchester Guardian,* May 17, 1933.

19. House of Commons, March 23, 1933.
20. House of Commons, May 23, 1933.
21. Speech of Nov. 9, 1933.
22. House of Commons, May 26, 1933.
23. House of Commons, July 5, 1933.
24. House of Commons, May 26, 1933.
25. House of Commons, Oct. 24, 1933.
26. Schulthess: Vol. 1933, Oct. 14.
27. House of Commons, Nov. 13, 1933.
28. House of Commons, Nov. 10, 1933.
29. Chambre de Deputés, Nov. 10, 1933.
30. *London Times,* Dec. 15, 1933.
31. British Memorandum of Jan. 29, 1934.
32. *Mein Kampf,* German Edition, p. 757.
33. *Das Neue Tagebuch,* 1934, p. 243.
34. Stalin, xvii. Congress of the Communist Party, Feb. 1934.
    Quoted by J. A. Taracouzio: *War and Peace in Soviet Diplomacy,* pp. 181–182.
35. July 3, 1934.
36. July 28, 1934.
37. *Observer,* London, July 29, 1934.
38. July 27, 1934.
39. *Das Neue Tagebuch,* 1934, ii, p. 774.
40. Ibid., p. 751.
41. *Le Petit Journal,* Aug. 1, 1934.
42. *Das Neue Tagebuch,* 1933, p. 135.
43. *Daily Mail,* Nov. 12, 1934.
44. *Das Neue Tagebuch,* 1934, ii, p. 1135.
45. *Volkstimme* and others, June 1, 1935.
46. *Daily Herald,* London, January 31, 1935.
47. Speech in Königsberg, quoted in *Das Neue Tagebuch,* 1934, ii, p. 1169.
49. *The Economist,* March 9, 1935.
50. *Daily Herald,* March 6, 1935.
51. Ibid., March 7, 1935.
52. *Daily Chronicle,* March 7, 1935.
53. *British Communiqué* of Feb. 3, 1935.
54. House of Commons, March 21, 1935.

Chapter 9

1. House of Commons, Nov. 28, 1934.
2. House of Commons, June 29, 1936.
3. House of Commons, March 11, 1935.
4. *Das Neue Tagebuch*, 1934, I, p. 27.
5. French note of Sept. 10, 1935.
6. English note of Sept. 26, 1935.
7. *Morning Post*, Sept. 14, 1935.
8. House of Commons, Churchill, April 7, 1936.
9. General Mordacq: *Clemenceau au Soir de sa Vie*, I, p. 138.
10. André Tardieu: *The Truth About the Treaty*.
11. *Das Neue Tagebuch*, 1936, I, p. 293.
12. *Le Populaire*, May 11, 1936.
13. House of Commons, June 29, 1936.
14. *Das Neue Tagebuch*, 1936, II, p. 684.
15. *Daily Herald*, Sept. 4 and 11, 1937.
16. *Das Neue Tagebuch*, 1938, II, p. 1064.
17. *Daily Telegraph*, April 28, 1938.
18. *Action Française*, March 25, 1938.
19. Speech, Nov. 17, 1938.
20. Speech, Nov. 20, 1938.
21. XVIII Congress of R.C.P., March 10, 1939.
22. Speech, May 1, 1939.
23. Supreme Soviet Council, May 31, 1939.

Index

instructions for armistice negotiators, 24; admits loss of the
war, 41; cheered in Berlin, 161;
with Hitler, proclaims "march
on Berlin," 224, 225; 49, 145,
158, 162–65, 168, 178, 218

Luettwitz, Gen. Walther von, German army chief, makes proclamation to the troops, 152; dismissed, 164; withdraws from
Kapp government, 170; 159,
160, 163, 168, 169, 177

"Luetzow Free Corps," 143

Luftwaffe, built behind the screen
of the "flying police corps," 339;
expenditures on, 352

Luther, Hans, German Chancellor,
232, 234, 235, 238, 243, 245;
new president of the Reichsbank, 296

Lytton, Victor Alexander George
Robert, Lord, 313

Lytton Committee Report, 317,
318

MacDonald, James Ramsay, defeated for re-election, 107; de-
clares any pact better than no
pact, 346; with Baldwin, pub-
lishes White Book on Sir John
Simon's mission to Hitler, 362,
363; 215, 249, 269, 299, 306,
309, 315, 332, 334, 337, 339,
342, 345, 367

Malcolm, Gen. Sir Neill, member
of the Interallied Military Control Commission, 160, 167, 182

Maltzan, Ago, Baron von, permanent secretary of the German
Foreign Office, 191–93

"Manchester Guardian," on the
Rapallo pact, 194; on Germany's
demand for rearmament, 310

Manchukuo, *see following*

Manchuria, seized by Japanese,
299, 313; transformed into Manchukuo, 314; recognition by
League refused, 318

Mandel, Georges, Clemenceau's
former secretary, 343

"March on Berlin" from a Munich
beer hall, 224, 225

March on Rome, 312

Marek, Viennese engineer, hacks
off leg to obtain insurance, sentenced to prison, 197; 223

Markgraf, German warship, crew
strikes, 48

Marks, their grotesque devaluation,
198, 218, 221, 224

Marne, miracle of the, 123, 348

Martet, Jean, letter from Clemenceau, 138

Marx, Karl, mentioned, 386

Marx, Wilhelm, twice Chancellor
of Germany, 117

Matteotti, Giacomo, Italian Socialist, assassinated, 239

Maurras, Charles, French Royalist,
400

Max, Prince of Baden, Chancellor
of Germany, announces abdication of the Kaiser, and renunciation of rights by Crown Prince,
49; takes his leave as Chancellor,
59; 11, 39, 43, 45, 50, 51

McGowan, Harry Duncan, Baron,
395

Mein Kampf, Hitler's book quoted
on his attitude toward France,
346

Memoirs of Lloyd George, 100

Midi, Paris newspaper, 361

Militaer Wochenblatt, German
military organ, 361

Military Control Commission, *see*
Interallied Military Control
Commission

Military power of Germany, methods of its destruction to be considered, 95, 96

Millerand, Alexandre, French
statesman, 176, 177

Ministry of Reconstruction in German Cabinet headed by Walter
Rathenau, 185, 186

Mirabeau, Honoré Gabriel Ri-
quetti, French revolutionary, his
definition of the Reich, 61

Mitchell, Col. William, opposed
naval pact, 274